THE WORLD OF

Whitetail Hunting

SINCE 1895

FIELD & STREAM

THE SOUL OF THE AMERICAN OUTDOORS

CREATIVE PUBLISHING international

MINNETONKA, MINNESOTA

Field & Stream
The World of Whitetail Hunting

Introduction by Mike Toth, Senior Editor, FIELD & STREAM

CREATIVE
PUBLISHING
international

President: Iain Macfarlane
Group Director, Book Development: Zoe Graul
Director, Creative Development: Lisa Rosenthal
Executive Managing Editor: Elaine Perry

Executive Editor, Outdoor Group: Don Oster
Project Leader and Article Editor: David R. Maas
Managing Editor: Denise Bornhausen
Associate Creative Director: Brad Springer
Photo Researcher: Angie Spann
Copy Editor: Janice Cauley
Mac Production: Joe Fahey
Desktop Publishing Specialist: Eileen Bovard
Publishing Production Manager: Kim Gerber
Cover Photo: Mark Raycroft

Special thanks to: Jason E. Klein, President, FIELD & STREAM; Duncan Barnes,
Slaton White, Mike Toth, and the staff of FIELD & STREAM magazine

Contributing Photographers: Jim Berlstein, Mike Biggs, Bob Brister, Dembinsky Photo
Associates, Jeff Gnass, Donald M. Jones, Mark Kayser, Bill Kinney, Lee Kline, Lon E.
Lauber, Bill Lea, Steve Maas, Wayne McLoughlin, Ian McMurchy, Mark Raycroft,
Jerome B. Robinson, Len Rue, Jr., David J. Sams/Texas Inprint, Danny R. Snyder, Ron
Spomer

Contributing Illustrators: Dennis Budgen, Bart Forbes, Kim Fraley, Luke Frazier, Frank
Fretz, David A. Johnson, Chris Kuehn, Chris Magadini, John Rice, Shannon Stirnweis,
John Thompson, Craig White, Richard A. Williams

Printed on American Paper by: R. R. Donnelley & Sons Co.
02 01 00 99 98 / 5 4 3 2 1

Library of Congress Cataloging–in–Publication Data

Field & Stream : the world of whitetail hunting/from the editors of
  Field & Stream and Creative Publishing international, Inc.
      p. cm.
    ISBN 0–86573–083–0 (hardcover) . – – ISBN 0–86573–084–9 (pbk.)
    1. White-tailed deer hunting.   I. Creative Publishing international.
  II. Field & Stream.
  SK301.F536 1998
  799 2'7652– –dc21   98– 19054

FIELD & STREAM is a Registered Trademark of Times Mirror Magazines, Inc.,
used under license by Creative Publishing international, Inc.

Table of Contents

THE DEER HUNTING TRADITION 6

WHITETAIL INSIGHTS 48

THE CHALLENGE OF THE HUNT 98

Introduction

EVERY FALL, A FEW WEEKS BEFORE THE beginning of deer season, I take my backpack out of the closet and empty its contents onto the floor. Although I've made other preparations by then, such as zeroing my rifle and scouting out my hunting territory, I like to save this pleasant chore for a chilly and quiet late afternoon, when the creak of tree branches and the rustle of spent leaves blowing across the yard seem to make the wind bite through my jacket a little harder than usual. It's a kind of microcosm of the deer woods, and it sets the mood for what I'm about to do.

So I go inside and upend the backpack and sort through my stuff. A topographic map and a compass. A half box of ammunition. A small flashlight. A torn copy of the game laws. Gloves, waterproof matches, and a first-aid kit. A buck-grunt tube and a bottle of cover scent. Some orange ribbon to mark a trail and some string to tie a tag onto a deer. A crumpled candy-bar wrapper and a folded-up good-luck note from my wife and children. As I pick and sort through it all, the previous deer season and all the seasons before it start replaying in my mind—the planning and preparation, the people I hunted with, the strategies planned and replanned, the deer I took and the deer I missed, and the lessons about the sport that I learned and learned again. They are memories, experiences, and emotions that I treasure, and that I build upon every year.

In a sense, the book you are holding contains the collective memories, experiences, and emotions of dozens of whitetail hunters. It's as if every one of the authors of the stories in this book emptied his or her backpack onto the floor, picked up one object—an empty cartridge, say, or a knife, or a hand-drawn map—and started talking to you about it. Magazine editors refer to a written version of such a narrative as a "story" or "article" or "piece," but each one is really a distillation of some of the experiences of each of those hunters.

Interestingly, the hunters who wrote the following stories have varying backgrounds—yet share many traits.

Some of them are tremendously experienced at the sport. They hunt deer all fall, in many different regions, and have done so for many years. There are only a few such hunters in existence. Their stories outline specific deer-hunting techniques and strategies, and reflect a level of expertise that can be arrived at only by devoting the better part of their lifetimes to chasing whitetails.

Other authors are experienced deer hunters as well as seasoned reporters (observers, actually) who have studied one specific aspect of whitetail hunting—a certain place, a particular pursuit, or even another hunter— and have put together revealing, all-encompassing stories.

A few other authors are neither whitetail experts nor professional writers. They are simply deer hunters who have experienced a wonderful, fascinating, or momentous event in the field, and have written a compelling story about it—so compelling that it met the strict and rigorous standards set by the editorial staff of FIELD & STREAM magazine.

And that is where all of the following stories were originally published. FIELD & STREAM, which has been in existence since 1895 and is the largest, most widely read outdoor magazine in the world, has always searched for, assigned, and published the finest hunting and fishing stories available. The editors have constantly striven to provide a variety of voices, opinions, and points of view, realizing that the diversity of interests in and approaches to hunting and fishing must be reflected when producing a magazine for such a wide audience.

The incredible growth of the popularity of whitetail hunting in the past three decades resulted in a corresponding increase in the audience demand for deer hunting articles. When whitetail populations began rapidly increasing in the 1970s, many states began offering longer seasons, more generous bag limits, and more opportunities to hunt (such as in bow and blackpowder-rifle seasons) just to keep populations at a manageable level. These new conditions in turn created more whitetail hunters, who wanted —and still want—to know as much as possible about the animals, hunting methods, and other hunters like them.

FIELD & STREAM responded by publishing a wide variety of whitetail-related articles. And you are about to read the absolute best of them.

The articles have been organized into three distinct sections. The first section, called "The Deer Hunting Tradition," is a compilation of moving and fascinating tales about whitetail hunting. Such narratives—or "me and Joe" pieces, as they are sometimes called—are the classic type of deer hunting articles. Each author tells you a story about a hunt—and not necessarily a successful one. But each story in this section is so well told that the reader can feel as if he or she were right in the woods with the author.

The second section, "Whitetail Insights," contains articles that deal with the specific traits of the whitetail: physiology, behavior, biological requirements, habitat preferences, and all the other facets of the animal. Basically, we find out why the whitetail does what it does—and what makes it such a difficult and yet captivating big-game species to hunt.

"The Challenge of the Hunt," the third and final section, contains articles that outline all the techniques and strategies that have been developed over the years for hunting whitetails. They range from the very simple to the quite complex, but they all work—sometimes. Read closely and you'll find that there's no guaranteed method for taking a deer every time you go out.

And we should be thankful for that. Whitetail hunting will always be a great mystery, with no definitive solution. Even the best deer hunters in the world will agree. And that promise-filled uncertainty is what compels us to return to the woods late every year, when the wind blows cold and the leaves begin to scatter.

Mike Toth, Senior Editor, FIELD & STREAM

The Deer Hunting

Deer hunters tell the best tales.

This quality isn't innate, of course, but seems to occur naturally. It's as if the bite of a cold wind, the dancing shadows of bare branches, the unnerving stillness of the fall woods, and the muffled crunch-pause-crunch of a hidden whitetail slowly walking through fallen leaves endows us with an uncanny ability to accurately and colorfully relate the story of the hunt.

There's just one catch—the audience has to consist of another deer hunter (if not more than one), because only another deer hunter will understand and appreciate such a tale. And the stories never get tired or outdated. Some even improve with age.

Telling tales—successful and otherwise—is the essence of the deer hunting tradition. In honor of that, this book opens with a collection of the finest whitetail-hunting narratives published in FIELD & STREAM magazine. All the stories are different and thus reflect the wide range of terrain and temperature encountered, and application and methodology used, by whitetail hunters in North America. But even if you hunt for deer in just one area at the same time of year with a never-varying approach, you'll feel a kinship with these stories because you're a deer hunter and, in a way, a part of them.

SINCE 1895

FIELD & STREAM

THE SOUL OF THE AMERICAN OUTDOORS

Tradition

By Todd Tanner

Hunting the NAMELESS

A VALLEY CAN BE MORE THAN A PLACE TO HUNT DEER; IT CAN BE A SANCTUARY.

THERE'S A VALLEY IN WESTERN Montana that doesn't have a name. Or, more accurately, it has a name that my fingers, for reasons of their own, can't seem to spell on a keyboard. If you're an outdoorsman, you probably understand my affliction. Someone might ask you the location of a secret fishing hole, or your favorite grouse cover, and you suddenly find that your tongue's grown thick in your mouth, and your words come out sounding like a leaky balloon being flushed down a toilet—slurred consonants and broken syllables all wrapped up around each other.

This valley—let's call it the Nameless—is long, 40 miles or more, and narrow. Pine and fir and larch cover the mountains that stretch up on either side, and a nameless river winds its way across the valley's floor. The sides of the mountains are scarred with clearcuts, and sometimes it seems like the ghosts of all those felled trees are caught in the mist that comes off the river in the morning.

The valley also holds another type of ghost—the kind that keeps big-game hunters awake at night. The Nameless has more than its share of legend-bucks and spirit-bulls, those half-real, half-ethereal beasts glimpsed back in the deepest cedar shadows. You say to yourself, *No, it couldn't have been that big. It must have been my imagination.* Still, your heart knows the truth of what your mind can't accept.

I don't live in the valley year-round, and I'm not sure I'd want to. If I stay around one place too long, I usually start taking it for granted. The valley is too special for that. Instead, I come back every year and take root for a while, and I'm renewed.

MY TIME IN the Nameless is the fall. I show up in October, as the first skim ice is forming on the little back eddies of the river, and I stay until winter has the valley locked up, usually sometime in December.

One of my favorite places to hunt deer here is in a cluster of small, ten-year-old clearcuts carved from a huge stand of lodgepole at the end of a gated logging road. It's a 5-mile walk in, but it's worth it. The combination of cover from the lodgepoles and browse in the clearcuts draws deer from all over the area.

Two years ago, I was still-hunting along the edge of those clearcuts when I saw a movement back in the trees. I paused for a moment, and a doe came into sight, glancing over her shoulder every few seconds. After twenty nervous yards she stood still, testing the wind and eyeing her backtrail. At that exact moment two fine four by fours appeared behind her, obviously following her scent but showing no inclination to move closer. I couldn't understand their behavior—neither seemed dominant, and they both shared the tentative look of a young boy tiptoeing past the neighborhood bully's house.

All of a sudden the doe took off running, and a massive buck materialized out of the shadows behind her, matching her step for step. He dwarfed the two 4 by 4s, and I was praying that he'd give me an opportunity for a shot. Unfortunately, he never slowed or came into any kind of opening, and my memory of his huge rack bobbing through the trees is all I have left of our encounter. In a few moments both he and the doe were gone into the dim recesses of the forest, and I was left standing there with those two lovelorn whitetails. To this day, I'm not sure who was more disappointed at the way things worked out.

As I get older, I find that I'm not quite so quick to let the arrow fly or pull the trigger—even on a dandy buck. It could be that I've started to learn from my mistakes, of which there've been plenty, or maybe I've just reached the point where I don't have much to prove. Either way, I've found that there's as much pleasure in the shot I don't take as in the one that puts my quarry down.

I spent the tail end of this past season hunting a place at the north end of the valley where the forest has an ideal mix of old, mature trees and new growth. With the number of does and the quality of food and cover here, I knew there had to be a dandy old buck hanging around. And sure enough, I put in the legwork and found a real bruiser.

I saw the buck five different times over the course of the next week. He was one of those whitetails who was always a bit out of range, or moving too fast, or behind a tree. At one point, he followed a hot doe right to the edge of a tiny clearing that would have given me an unobstructed shot from 30 yards away. I could see him pacing back and forth behind several thick pine trees, intent on the doe but not wanting to abandon his cover. Finally he stepped right to the edge of the clearing. . . and vanished. I waited for 20 minutes, then snuck over to the last spot I'd seen him. I don't know where he went, or how he left without offering me a glimpse, but he was gone.

⊷ ⊰⬦⊱ ⊶

THE LAST MORNING I hunted for that buck was overcast and still. I was sitting on a log, almost nodding off, when I glimpsed a hint of movement 200 yards away on a fairly open hillside. When I pulled up my binoculars I saw

it was the big fellow I was after, but he was moving right along and didn't offer a shot.

I jumped up and took off through the woods, thinking that I could loop around and come up right behind him. Half a mile later, I stopped to glass above me, certain that the buck would be working along the ridge in front of me. I'd only had my binoculars up for a second, though, when I heard a grunt directly behind me. I turned around and there was the buck, 30 yards away. It didn't take him long to figure out his mistake, though, and he scooted off about 40 yards before he turned to see what kind of creature he'd mistaken for a pretty young doe.

I counted four long, heavy tines on one side of his rack, and five on the other. His neck was swollen, and there was steam jetting from his nose. I settled the crosshairs on his heart, flipped off the safety, and then said to myself, *This has been a great hunt. Man, I love this valley.* Then I watched him trot up the ridge into the trees.

Maybe next year I'll try him with the longbow.

HE WAS A MAJESTIC
WHITETAIL THAT
DISAPPEARED DURING
HUNTING SEASON.
AND FOR A WHILE,
HE GAVE A SLEEPY,
SMALL TOWN A
SENSE OF PURPOSE.

By Paul Quinnett

The Tyler GHOST

SAM CALLED R.B. THEN R.B. called me. "They just saw him again." "Where?"

"Down by the Church. Just standing there. Sam says he has so many points now he can barely hold up his head."

"Just two more weeks to hunting season," I said, imagining setting the crosshairs on a buck so big people used the word "majestic" to describe him.

"Yeah," said R.B., his voice dropping off into pessimism. "That's when he turns back into the ghost."

"Maybe not this year," I said.

"Dreamer."

OVER THE YEARS most everyone in the little town of Tyler had seen the big buck. Standing in a wheatfield, crossing the road out to Hog Canyon Lake, or running through the timber with a doe, even in deer country he made a lasting impression on those who caught him up close in their headlights.

For the first few years he was simply called "the big buck." "Saw the big buck again last night," someone would say. If you were a local, you knew which big buck had been spotted. Sometimes when the buck was spotted, the phones rang. Mr. Brown would call Sam, Sam would call his neighbor, and then Sam would call his brother, R.B., my neighbor and hunting companion, who would call me. The only thing that sparked more communication along the rural routes in those parts was a brush fire.

It was Sam, who lived on a small acreage outside of Tyler, who finally named the buck. Sam names everything. "The Church" is a stand of aspen on the end of his meadow; "Herbie" is his John Deere tractor; and, after he'd personally seen him, Sam named the big buck "The Ghost." The Tyler Ghost.

Little towns need something to lift them up. Something special. The town of Tyler had once been a thriving little city with its own train and fire station, blacksmith shop, jail, and general store, and like lots of Western towns, it had hoped to make it big when the Burlington-Northern Railroad laid tracks out across the wilds of eastern Washington State. But then came fast cars, eighteen-wheelers, and modern times, and eventually the general store and the last gas pump closed. People moved out and deer moved in. And now there was a buck called the Tyler Ghost.

The scabland sinks, fields, sage, timber, and broken lava canyons that make up the countryside around Tyler provide perfect deer territory. A wise old buck could live out his days and never hear the *whiz* of a bullet or the *whirr* of an arrow over his back. If he so chose, a whitetail would never have to get closer than a real country mile to the predator that hops on two feet and smells bad. But unlike some great whitetail bucks that make secrets of themselves, the Tyler Ghost was seen all the time. Except during hunting season.

"We'll spread out along the tracks from the Church to Brown's fence," some strategist in our party would say. "Keep close so he doesn't sneak between us. We'll drive through the aspens and across the marsh. If he's in that thick stuff, we'll push him out and the blockers should get a shot."

This particular drive took about six hunters and 45 minutes. Even though it never worked, it was a great plan—sort of like Caesar's invasion of Gaul, absent the victory. Design and execution were simple. But since none of us would admit to being dumber than a buck deer, each opening morning the plan was dusted off and tried again—with the same result.

Magical explanations sprang up. "Disappeared into a patch of ground fog." "Slipped down a badger hole." "Caught the 4 A.M. train while we were still having coffee." No excuse for failure seemed too improbable, or too bizarre.

Still-hunters, we knew, had no chance at all. Stand-hunters, after taking their first chill, would soon remember last year's hopeless vigil and begin to still-hunt—a tactic proven so useless one Ghost hunter remarked, "I know I'll never sneak up on him, but at least the scenery changes."

A handful of us hunted him hard. Well, pretty hard. The truth was that as the years passed, we began to lose hope of ever seeing the Ghost. We'd slipped through his woods. We'd stalked his canyons. We'd glassed his thickets and aspen groves and the low sage ridges where he ran. We'd laid so many plans for his demise that we'd begun to name them: Plan A, Plan B, Plan C. And then we began to misplace the plans. But after all that, we never got so much as a glimpse of him during the season. Not once.

Eventually Sam stopped hunting the Ghost. He never said why. "You guys get him," Sam said the last year R.B. and I showed up for the opening-day drive. "I saw him across the road last week over by that little draw. He could be laying up in the marsh. Or over by the tracks. But who knows…" Then Sam grinned.

R.B. and I figured to give the Ghost one final morning; one morning for a buck neither of us had ever seen. By then we knew that if we were ever to take the Ghost, he'd have to give himself to us. But of course he didn't. R.B. was back at Sam's house drinking coffee by midmorning. I arrived a little later, dragging a wagon full of hopelessness behind me.

"Giving up, boys?" Sam smiled, sipping his coffee.

R.B. and I nodded.

"Just as well," said Sam. "I mean, if he was just an ordinary deer somebody would have shot him by now. Right?"

"Right," said R.B.

"Then why don't you guys give up?" asked Sam. I looked at R.B. R.B. looked at me. Without saying a word, each of us knew we would never come back to hunt the Tyler Ghost.

THE CALL CAME early on a December evening of the same year.

"They got him," R.B. said.

"Got who?" I asked.

"The Ghost. Sam just called."

"But it isn't hunting season," I said. "Who got him?"

There was a long pause on R.B.'s end. "A red Datsun pickup."

"A what? A red Datsun?"

"Sam said that if we hurried, we could drive out and see the Ghost before the fish and game guys get there to pick him up."

I thought a moment. I remembered all the frosty mornings and drives and ambushes and still-hunts and good times. "No," I said, softly. "I don't want to see him. Do you?"

R.B. paused. "Nope… but if you haven't had your dinner, I'll buy you a drink. There's a deer I want to toast."

"I'm on my way."

By Cheryl Kerr

Season of the DEER

THERE'S MUCH TO BE LEARNED ABOUT HUNTING AND RELATIONSHIPS FROM A MORNING IN A BLIND.

FAMILY BONDS GROW STIFF with disuse, like the stubborn working of my old rifle that must be oiled and coaxed at the start of hunting each fall.

Deer season is a time for oiling things, both guns and family ties. The ritual of providing, of coming together in a special place and shared tradition, brings us a sense of belonging, a remembrance of each other. The relationships, tight on arrival, loosen and ease until they click like an old and well-used rifle. And we settle back into a familiar rhythm, different from that of our usual lives.

I feel that change of cadence this morning on the old ranch as I walk where the moonlit road winds to the left and is eclipsed by night-black trees. When I married Michael, long years ago, I began to learn its turns. Although I think of this place as home, this is John's, Michael's grandfather's place, and I am still learning my way.

I am a solitary hunter, whether my sport is with camera or gun. This morning it is a photo I'm after, of a buck I've glimpsed but never had a clear shot at, whether aiming with rifle or lens.

The road looks different in the moonlight. The chalky limestone catches and holds the night sheen, a satiny ribbon between the dark woods on either side, echoed by the white cliffs beyond the trees.

I stop my thoughts and pause to orient myself. I've passed three openings, by my count, and should be near the deer blind John described. I think I see it on the shale rise ahead. I squint, and shadows separate into the light and dark of boards and a crooked door. The night crowds me as a lone cloud hides the moon, and I head thankfully for the shelter.

Not used much, I decide, as I settle on its rough bench, and ease my pack to the ground.

Above me a cliff rises, its base choked with brush and tangled trees. My view from the blind is just right, a long shallow valley angling slightly downhill. I feel a stir of excitement; the restlessness that hunting brings. But deer are hard to read, at least the kind I'm after, and I may have a long wait.

A sound catches my ear. I turn and search the cliff, but see just rock in the moonlight. Looking back down the road, I sense a faint movement.

A figure comes from the darkness and turns my way, and I realize it is John. His breath is labored as he works his way up, and I rise, unsure of offering help. But he makes it on his own, leaning once on the rifle he carries.

He stops on seeing me, unexpected, in this place.

"Morning," I say, more nod than word, to not disturb the quiet.

"You got the wrong opening," he tells me." Yours is one more up the road."

I start to lift my gear, and he waves me back down.

"No, no, stay. The deer'll be moving soon."

"This looked right; it looked old," I say, to explain my being here.

"It is."

I settle back and we eye each other. For some, hunting is camaraderie, but I've always liked the solitude.

The deer blind presses in, and I sigh; aware of being in the wrong place, an intruder. But as I return to my vigil, contentment bubbles back, like the creek among the trees.

Dawn is still long minutes away, and my thoughts go back to when I married John's grandson; when I'd asked what I should call him.

"John'll do," he said, and it has, throughout our long years together.

John doesn't say much to anyone, and as he sits silently, I think about how little I know him; how seldom I've needed his name.

Sometimes, within a family, it's easy to get lost.

＋──❦──＋

BUT NOW THE day is graying in, and I must pay attention and put my thoughts aside. In this slide of night to day there is a moment of absolute stillness—no wind, no sound of creeks or rustle of grass, as if everything takes a pause to await the morning light.

I ready my camera. If my shot comes, it will be in the next moments.

As the cedars turn from night black to green, a branch moves, high, way off the ground, and I feel a thrill of sureness. I know it's not the wind; there is none. And I, too, hold my breath.

The branch becomes an antler and my buck steps into view with deliberate calm. He is bigger than any I've ever seen. My heart pounds in my ears as I try to think him toward me. As if in answer, he comes my way, then stops, filling my lens with weight and antler. And the dignity of age.

My shutter whispers once, drinking in the light for the shot I want, then closes with a sigh. I ease my breath out,

> "For some, hunting is camaraderie, but I've always liked the solitude."

careful not to jiggle. At my faint sound the deer is gone, and for a moment I wonder if I saw him. But the film counter is one up, and beside me John is nodding.

I relax, my camera heavy on my thigh. The instinct in me that comes with my best efforts eases. Somehow I know I won't see another such shot this morning.

I reach for my thermos and raise it toward John. He nods and the strong coffee smell steams in the cold morning as I offer him a cup.

"That your shot?" he asks. He doesn't whisper; talk usually means the hunting is done, though he hasn't moved. Puzzled, I follow his lead, and answer aloud.

"Yes."

"Just one?"

"That's all I'm after today. You didn't shoot?" I ask.

"Yours looked good. I'll come again tomorrow," he replies, gazing toward the cliff. I lapse into silence again, and wonder what he thinks of my coming and sitting, just to take a picture. But his next words surprise me.

"Used to be Indians up there." He raises his coffee cup toward the cliff.

I turn, and can almost imagine figures crouched among the brush and sunlight-caught rock.

"Look." He scuffs a worn boot at the shale and an arrowhead turns up, as if on demand. I take it and run my thumb along the chipped and chiselled edge. I have always felt in step with this old and well-used ranch, but now I am awed. I feel connected to time itself.

I cradle the flint in my palm and think of all who've sat here, just like John and me, watching the sunrise.

My gaze goes to the cliff again, and for moment I'm an Indian girl, beginning my day as the sun rises.

"Gone rabbiting?" John's voice is dry, and gentle.

"I guess so," I grin, caught with my thoughts showing.

"You can almost see 'em sometimes."

His tone holds no question and I turn, surprised that he's followed the wanderings of my mind.

I choose my words carefully. "The Indians I can imagine, but..."

"But not an old man sitting around thinking that?"

"Well, not you." I am frank, the best way to be with John.

"I like the quiet, too," he says, and then I know what brought him to the blind this morning.

"Sometimes hunting can be a camouflage," I say. "A way to think things out."

"It's a way to have any thoughts you want," John says.

He sits back and I recognize the tilt of his head. I wonder if he knows how often Michael stops and looks, just like that. Now I know where it comes from, this looking.

"Here," he holds the flint out to me, "for a thought piece. It makes it real, doesn't it? Shows how their life was here. Hard."

He's mirrored my thoughts once more into words; and I understand that they are his as well.

"There are," he says after he finishes his coffee, "a lot of things to hunt for."

Almost as an afterthought, he adds, "Next time is for meat." I notice that the sun is now full up. Time to go.

I slide the arrowhead into my pocket, way down out of sight, and John nods. "Some things are for keeping."

"I enjoyed today," I tell him.

His eyes hold mine. "And I."

I latch the door, and as I turn to leave he says, "I believe this place could be for two hunters."

"I'd like that." I speak past a sudden lump in my throat: in the years I've known him, he's always hunted alone.

He nods, and it's a deal. Done, no more to say.

I hesitate, then offer my hand. And he takes it, easing to his feet. I feel the groove in his thumb. It could be from working, or maybe from a habit of arrowheads, stroked for many a year.

Overhead, a fluted sound echoes on the wind. I don't choose to know if it is bird or Indian. The flint seems heavy in my pocket, a reminder of today.

I keep his hand in mine. And we go home, together.

By Gene Hill

WANDERINGS

HUNTING SHOULD INCLUDE A SENSE OF ADVENTURE THAT GOES FURTHER THAN MERELY AIMING A RIFLE.

DEER HUNTING FROM A stand is the sport of wanderers. The experienced hunter knows beyond question that any buck he sees will be about 30 yards from where he is on stand, trying to stay awake and not freeze to death. Yet, never, not once, have I been completely satisfied that my stand was in the ideal spot. For some mysterious reason the whole landscape seems to change as soon as you settle in. Trees slide over and block your view of the dip in the ridge where a buck is most likely to appear. The rock in front of your stand slowly elevates itself to hide the little valley below you, and the log you so carefully chose for comfort sprouts a stub, or else begins a high-frequency creaking.

Moving from stand to stand in search of perfection has one common result—it causes deer to pass close by the last place you were. I doubt if deer hunters are more restless than normal people; maybe it's the carrying of a rifle or shotgun or bow that reawakens the latent pioneer spirit to move on. Whatever it is, I have no doubt that this restlessness has done more to increase the deer herd than any planned conservation effort I've ever heard of.

The reason deer have a reputation for being so wily is because only the unlucky or dumb ones blunder in front of a hunter who is sitting still for a moment before he moves on to the next place. All a deer has to do to live out his allotted years is stand relatively still during the hunting season and let the sports rotate aimlessly and noisily around him, in what an outsider might think was some sort of strange ceremonial dance.

The random thinking that goes into selecting a wilderness deer stand is something most hunters can't explain; the reasons for trying to "improve" on a traditional closer-to-home crossing where generations of hunters have gotten their deer are more obvious. But the migratory instinct that overwhelms us all in deer season even carries over into the more or less permanent blinds in Texas. I have found myself in a state approaching sinful comfort in such a stand. Nestled deep in a soft swivel chair with iced soft drinks close at hand, I stare out at the established runway where I've taken deer in the past. But am I content and satisfied? Of course not. I'm looking with considerable envy at the top of another stand exactly like mine on a neighboring ridge where I'm convinced any number of ten-pointers are this very minute scratching their backs on the guy wires.

It is a given that the wanderer hunting in unfamiliar territory will not be where the guide expects to find him at dusk. This problem is unavoidable. The guide tells you that yesterday two big bucks were seen crossing by the beaver pond. He points out the exact spruce tree to lean your back on and goes off, telling you that as soon as he hears you shoot, he'll turn up.

The minute the guide leaves, your mind starts wandering. The closer you get to the guide's chosen spruce, the more irresistible another one appears. Surely, the guide meant *that* tree! A tiny feeling of superiority comes over you as you realize how strong your instinctive animal sense is compared to the guide's. Why, it's totally obvious that spruce B is *the* place to be because spruce A is downwind, or the crossing allows you a better view of the meadow, or whatever.

Leaning against spruce B, it is immediately apparent that spruce C has the kind of promise that only a total greenhorn could resist. After a while, it's a simple slide to spruce D which is a little higher, and offers a better view and a log that will make a perfect rifle rest.

It takes about two hours to arrive at spruce T and it's ridiculous why you didn't see all its advantages right off. You settle in and begin to compose a lecture for the guide on how to choose a deer stand. It can be best delivered, you decide, while you're both admiring the number of points and the heft of beam. This lovely daydream helps to while away the time.

You will probably be awakened in the near-dark by the honking horn of a pickup and the flashing of headlights. The first thing the guide will ask is "where's your deer?" Of course, he knows exactly what has happened, but he just wants to find out if your story is any better than the one he heard the last time the exact same thing happened. I usually end up telling him that I saw this deer but he was over there (indicated by a broad indefinite sweep of my arm), and after my stalk he just seemed to fade away but I thought I'd wait, etc., etc. If the guide has a mean streak, which your behavior may bring out, he's going to take you over and show you fresh tracks exactly where he said they'd be. If he has a very mean streak, he'll ask you to show him the tracks of the deer *you* saw to see if it's the same one.

But the wanderer, although not always successful, has a great sense of satisfaction when things do go right and the big buck does indeed drift by spruce X instead of where it was supposed to pass. The true delight of hunting is the element of surprise, the "you never know" factor. Hunting, unlike real life, shouldn't have a structured beginning, middle, and end. Part of what we're hunting is a sense of accomplishment in ourselves that goes further than merely pointing a rifle. We get *drawn* to a spot for reasons we can't explain, except that it appeals to our sense of adventure.

And who knows when we might get lucky and be able to relate to the boys back at camp a story that starts out like this: "…I figured that old buck might do something a little different, so I made a careful sneak…"

There should be a surprise ending, of course. Good stories, like good deer stands, should wander a bit and include a touch or two of surprise.

By Jerome B. Robinson

On the Track
OF THE KING

THE ANIMAL WAS LIKE A FANTASY—THERE, BUT ALWAYS OUT OF REACH. IN THE END, THOUGH, IT LED THE HUNTER TO A VERY REAL REWARD.

*I*FIRST SAW HIM THE YEAR I built my log cabin up in the big woods along the New Hampshire/Quebec border. I had gone down to the river for a plunge after work and was sitting on the bank letting the early October breeze dry me when I looked upstream and there he was—a massive buck with a memorable high and heavy lyre-shaped rack that stuck out past his ears. He was wading the riffle when he spotted me. For a moment our eyes met; then he was gone.

I remember noting that he had already rubbed the velvet from his antlers; they shone slightly in the red and golden light reflected in the water from the maples that were turning color on the ridge across from camp. I remember

knowing the instant I saw him that he was the biggest buck I had ever seen. Even in that country, where many of the big ones weigh more than 300 pounds on the hoof, he was the King.

NEXT MORNING I went upstream to where he had crossed and studied the track where he had stepped in the hard clay at the water's edge. At the heel, his footprint was exactly as broad as my fist; the cloven hooves were longer than my middle finger. His dewclaws speared the ground a full 3 inches behind his heel. I let the look of the track sink in and memorized its distinctive impression.

I didn't know it then, but that track was to become my talisman. Over the next ten years it has led me to places I might never have visited. I have searched for that particular track on each November snow, following it whenever I could to wherever it led—through cedar swamps on the backsides of mountains, to hardwood ridges with long views into Canada, and once to a spectacular waterfall in the most remote headwaters of a river I fish for trout.

Following the track has taught me the hidden places where groups of deer yard up in winter and where they can be expected to begin gathering after the first deep snow. It has shown me ancient migration routes that deer follow from miles away to reach special yarding areas. The big track has taught me where there are mountaintop thickets in which a deer can stand and let a man walk by at very close range and not be seen, and taken me to countless places where deer go to feed on beechnuts, paw for fern roots, nibble mushrooms, rub their antlers, make their ground scrapes, and do their rutting. By following the track of the King I have learned the country where I hunt.

Once when I had followed the deer's track north all morning along the ridge that follows the Canadian border, it crossed the pug marks of another solitary hunter whose presence in the country I had heard reports of but had always been skeptical about until this moment. Deep cat tracks as large as my palm were clearly sculpted in the wet snow. Bobcats are common here and occasionally a larger-footed lynx passes through, but these tracks were too big to have been made by either of these felines. They had to have been made by a mountain lion.

It is difficult to explain how I know that the track that I have been following year after year has been made by the same deer and not by some other big one. I can only tell you that I do know. I know it just as you know your own track when you see it in the snow, even though other hunters wear similar boots and leave similar signs.

Often my buck travels over identical routes to the exact places he has taken me to before. He uses the same scrapes year after year and returns to beds I remember him using before. And when I'm trailing him and he knows it, he has foiled me with the same tricks that have gotten rid of me on earlier occasions. But mostly I know his track because it strikes a mystical chord in some rarely visited attic of my hunter's soul that stridently proclaims, "That's him!"

And, just often enough to prove there's no mistake, I have seen the King making the tracks himself.

I have only shot at him twice. The first time was the same year I had seen him standing in the stream.

I was halfway up on the ridge across from camp on a frosty popcorn morning when the frozen leaves made walking quietly impossible. I had paused to lean against a tree and watch when I heard him up above me.

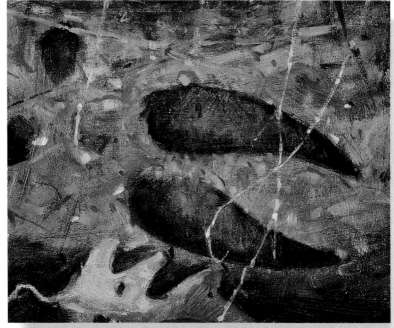

"I didn't know it then, but that track was to become my talisman. . . ."

There was no mistaking the sounds. He would take a few quick steps, then stop. A few more quick ones, then stop again. I turned slowly and brought my rifle around to where it would jump to my shoulder smoothly. Suddenly the buck was coming.

He was running now, taking the broken ground in long bounds that ended in mighty crashes coming downhill right at me. When he broke into view there was no mistaking him for another deer. The high and heavy lyre-shaped rack, the massive gray-brown body with legs as thick as those of a Jersey heifer were recognizable features of the buck I knew.

My rifle rose to my shoulder as he came tearing past about 40 yards away. When I fired, the scope was filled with hair, and the back edge of his shoulder was showing. I lowered the gun, sure that I had hit him right behind the shoulder and that he was running away dead on his feet.

After he had disappeared and I had followed him for several hundred yards without finding either blood or his piled-up carcass, I returned to the spot from which I'd fired and recreated the scene. I left my hat where I had stood and walked straight out to where the deer had been, then turned around to face the spot I'd shot from. Then I saw the bright fracture on the side of a maple sapling 10 feet away. My bullet had pierced the tree instead of the deer.

The next year the deer made another major mistake and I had him dead to rights, but he bamboozled me again.

I was driving my pickup over the mountain we call Buck Hill when I saw him bedded out in the middle of a clearcut. Right out in the open, plain as day, his big lyre-shaped rack was sticking up and shining in the sun, his neck as thick as a tree trunk. I gawked, but kept on truckin' without changing the engine's rpms until I got over a rise of ground and out of sight.

Then I put the brake on and left the engine running so there would be no vibratory change to arouse his cautions. I slipped my rifle off the rack. As I crept into the woods, I slipped a single round into the chamber, closed the bolt without a sound, and moved quietly through a spruce thicket to the edge of the clearcut.

He was still there, not a hundred yards away, lying down with only his head and neck showing. There was no wind. The sun was in his eyes. I eased to the side of a solid tree and leaned against it as I raised my rifle. He saw no motion and remained perfectly still. In fact, it seemed to me, he was too still.

I studied him through the scope. His antlers were surely like those I remembered, but something about him seemed too perfect. His eyes were shining in the sunlight, and his black nose glared as if it were coated with varnish. His burnished brown neck looked groomed; his white throat patch, bleached. He held one ear out straight and the other slightly dipped. I'd seen this pose on taxidermy mounts a hundred times.

Fake! my brain shouted. *Fake!*

A warden's counterfeit deer way out here in the woods? It didn't make sense. What could I be doing wrong? I was well off the road, and anyway, the road was only a temporary seasonal logging track. How could this be a trap? My brain reeled with doubts and paranoia, but my finger stayed off the trigger as I continued to study the big deer's immobile head.

I don't know why I'm not allowed to shoot here, but that is definitely a mounted deer head propped up out there, and I'm not falling into the trap, I told myself, lowering the rifle, but still studying the deer.

Then, far off in the valley, a logging truck shifted down for a hill. At the sound, the big deer turned his head.

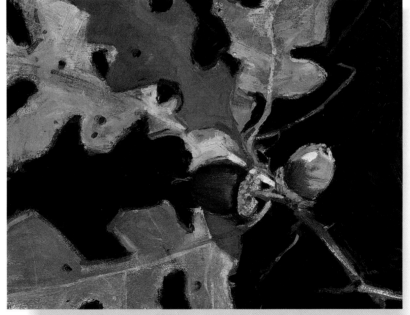

"By following the track of the king I have learned the country where I hunt."

You paranoid fool, that's your deer! my inner voice chuckled.

I reraised the rifle, retook my lean, and brought the crosshairs up onto the too-bleached throat patch on the too-groomed neck, but by then I was shaking. When I squeezed off the shot I felt the flinch and knew as the bullet left the barrel that it was going high.

The buck and a doe that had been lying unseen behind him now jumped to their feet, but hearing the shot's echo, they turned and faced the hardwood forest behind them. The two stood staring with their backs to me. I dipped into my pocket for another shell and hurriedly tried to reload, but in my haste, failed to pull the bolt back all the way. The spent cartridge remained inside. I crammed the new one in and slammed the bolt shut again, solidly jamming both brass cartridges in the breech.

My eyes remained on the huge buck while my hands fidgeted to free the jam and get a live shell in place. Hearing my jittery rattling sounds, the King now turned and faced me. Just then the doe turned and started bounding away, and a moment later the King switched his tail and left, too, leaving me to cuss myself and stamp on my hat.

Later that same year I got another chance. I had picked up his tracks on a wet blizzardy morning and followed them into a copse of thick spruce just above the river. I was moving silently in the snow, traveling into the wind just as he was, knowing by the freshness of the tracks that he was only minutes ahead. I was moving in suspended animation, ready to see him at any moment.

Suddenly he was there, not 30 yards away, looking right at me. I have a mental picture of him at that moment; he was covered with wet snow, his breath steaming around him, his big lyre-shaped rack wet and brown and stuck with crusted snow. I raised my rifle as his head began to turn away, shouldered it as his hind legs compressed, and brought the scope to bear just as he began his leap—but then the picture went blank. I lost sight of him and never fired. Snow had plugged my scope.

Judging by his immense size and the thickness of his antlers, the King must have been at least five or six years old back then, which means he is more than fourteen now. As the years pass he has become increasingly crafty, and when I see him at all these days, it is only at long range.

Several times he has lost me by running straight to the top of the ridge across from camp into a big patch of hardwood saplings growing in very close profusion. You can't move in that patch without bumping against saplings and making them shake and rattle in their top branches, and the growth is so thick that you can't see more than a few yards at eye level.

His tracks show that when he goes in there he immediately beds down. If I begin to get close to him, he stands up and flits through the saplings for 40 or 50 yards, then beds again. He'll do this for hours, never leaving the patch, just moving around me and instantly bedding down.

I figured out what he was up to once when the snow was deep. Wherever he had bedded in the deep snow, I found the long impression of his throat where he had extended his neck and rested his chin. When I got down in the snow myself and put my chin at snow-level, the whole thing became clear. Bedded, with his head held low, he could see my feet moving among the base of the saplings long before he could have seen my body had he been standing.

I know the exact locations of dozens of ground scrapes the King uses every year, each one overhung by a branch that he nuzzles and licks and marks with his scent. But he patrols his scrapes only at night and never goes near them in daylight.

For years now he has been moving mostly at night, leaving tracks that are hours old when I find them in the morning. By daylight he is up on the ridgetop or over on the backside of one of the mountains that stretch away toward Canada. And yet, several times each week he still crosses at the riffle just above my camp and I can pick up his trail in the morning within rifle-range of my doorstep.

He has never been the kind of deer that goes bounding around in the woods when he knows he is being followed. Instead, he moves only a short distance and then stops in thick cover, watching, listening, taking the scents from the air.

Six times in the ten years I have tracked him, the King has thrown me off his trail for one more year by leading me to another buck which I have shot instead. I don't mean that I mistook the other deer for the King. No, each time it's happened I simply came upon another pretty good buck and decided it was good enough for that year.

At first I thought it was just coincidence, but then I started wondering if I would have encountered the deer I'd shot if the King had not led me to them. To shoot a deer in the woods you and the deer must come to the same place at the same time. The only reason I was in position to make these kills was that the King had put me there. I now believe the King has learned to save himself by sacrificing his lieutenants.

Each year I think I know his habits well enough to predict where he is likeliest to go when followed. I suppose that's the way to get him—put someone else on his track while I try to predict what he'll do and attempt to intercept him. But at heart I am a solitary hunter and am not drawn to group efforts.

I didn't hunt him much last season. I can't explain why. I told myself I was waiting for the snow that never came, but I know that wasn't the whole reason.

On the last night of deer season I had a dream. I had followed the King way out toward Canada to a little set of knobby spruce-topped hills where he had often given me the slip. Suddenly he rose up out of his bed and stood before me. I could feel my thumb nudge the safety off as the rifle came up. I saw the crosshairs settle behind his shoulder and felt my finger begin to tighten on the trigger. Then I hesitated for one last look at him.

I awoke startled.

Outside it was snowing hard, but deer season was over.

I sometimes think I know just where he would have been bedded under the thickening blanket of snow that morning, but I can't be sure.

By Wayne McLoughlin

The Improved WHITETAIL

DEER HUNTING CAN BE A TOUGH, HUMBLING EXPERIENCE. WHAT IF BUCKS COULD BE ALTERED TO MAKE IT EASIER FOR US?

OVER THE YEARS I've sat around a lot of campfires listening to exasperated hunters' dissertations on deer. Haggard and luckless at the end of a long day, they lament about different bucks they heard but couldn't see; bucks that exploded from the brush at their elbow, leaving them alone in a vast silence, dazed and shaking, with their rifles no closer to their shoulders than before. Wistfully, they've gone on about those bucks that got away: ten-pointers fast enough to qualify for pole position at the Indy 500; big, wary old bucks that could hear a rifle rusting in a rainstorm and spook at least 2 miles away if a hunter's eyes even dilate.

Indeed, deer hunting can be a tough, humbling experience. Is there some way we could change that? Equipment can't get much better, but what about the deer?

For starters, everyone wants a nice buck, so what if the average whitetail were a twenty-pointer (typical), weighing in at 1,700 pounds dressed, and had hooves like a Clydesdale? That would help slow the bucks down a bit and tracking them would sure be easier! At that size, their stealth quotient would be about the same as a rhino dragging Venetian blinds through a rock quarry.

Also, deer don't come in the easiest color to spot. Chartreuse would be much better, and it would simplify things in the woods—hunters are bright orange; deer, bright green.

What about a deer's spectacular eyesight and incredible hearing? It might be better if their ears were smaller and their eyes were about as good as a fruit bat's. Maybe their nose should be so ineffective that they couldn't detect a swimming pool full of ammonia at 10 feet.

Think about it!

After all those changes, whitetails would certainly be a lot different. . . but then so would hunting.

True, you might get a rack that you could do chin-ups from and tenderloin steaks the size of hubcaps, but where's the challenge, the thrill, the pride of accomplishment, or the exhilaration of the hunt? Where could you get a carpet for your trophy room that didn't clash?

When I really think about it, I like deer just the way they are—unimproved.

By G. Sitton

SONORA
Again

THE COUES DEER MAY BRING YOU BACK, OR THE DOVE HUNTING, OR THE UNSPOILED COUNTRY…OR ALL OF THEM. IT DOESN'T MATTER; IF YOU GO ONCE, YOU'LL RETURN.

As A BOY GROWING UP IN small Western towns, I could take a gun and wander far enough in a morning to find a boy's full portion of wonder and reward. Later on, the world got bigger and I hunted in some far places, where the people and the game were literally fabulous.

Now, my fiftieth birthday is past, and it seems the journeys that please me most are those leading to a middle ground of sorts, where the strange and the familiar combine. Having seen something of the altogether alien, and recalling the special pleasures of the commonplace, I want most to hunt where they are found together, balanced and (perhaps) resolved. The state of Sonora, in northern Mexico, is such a place.

As this is written, October is almost finished. In two more weeks, I will go south again, across a line that is both imaginary and real, to hunt in Sonora. My rifle is exactly zeroed. The ammunition is as close to perfect as I can make it. The necessary visa and the very official Mexican gun permit, with its properly serious photograph, are on the shelf by the front door. I am ready and the need to be hunting in big country is strong.

So, come the appointed morning, I will leave my home in Tucson, drive to the airport, and make the brief flight to Hermosillo. Ramon Fernando Campillo Garcia, the outfitter who has become my friend and is called Laffy, will be waiting in the baggage area. He will welcome me, escort me through customs, and we will begin the five-hour drive through the blasted rock of the Rio Sonora Canyon to Rancho de la Cienega, the base for our Coues deer hunt.

Along the way, we will pass through a town called Baviacora, where long ago a beautiful stone church was built. We may stop to eat the plain, honest food of rural Sonora. By the time we leave the pavement at Banamichi, the sun will be down, and the dirt road into the mountains will be dark. Finally, the ranch house will appear, its lights a hard white greeting in the night.

Renee will be busy in the kitchen, tending his perpetual source of refried beans. Chapo, the cook's helper and handyman, will give me a cup of dense coffee, and I will go out in the yard to look at the small chapel that stands beside the house. I will be in a foreign land, and I will be home.

I first met Laffy and his brother Roberto, who also answers to Bobby, on a dove gunning trip in the late winter of 1990. My frequent hunting partner, David Miller, had suggested that they might help put an end to my ten-year search for a respectable Coues deer. Yes, I spent fifteen or sixteen weeks and ten seasons in the mountains of southern Arizona without so much as thumbing the safety on a rifle. There were plenty of junior deer to be taken, but the two bucks I saw briefly and wanted desperately might as well have been smoke. The lovely little whitetails had my number, not to mention my zip code, bank balance, and blood type.

So we went to Sonora for doves. The Campillos put us up in a beachside condo at Kino Bay, some 60 miles west of

Hermosillo on the Gulf of California. We were too early for the fine fishing for the sails, tuna, and dorado that come into those waters in the spring and early summer, but the dove shooting was hot.

The farmers around Hermosillo grow lots of wheat, corn, sorghum, and sesame seeds. These crops come in at different times during the five-month season, and the shooting sites are rotated to follow the harvests. In the latter part of February, corn was the featured item on the dove diet. We shot over cornfields.

The birds were frequent—mourning doves, mostly, but whitewings and the handsome, dusky rose-and-slate-blue pigeons called *patagon* were plentiful, too. There are no doubt more famous venues for doves and pigeons in South America, but how many birds can one shooter frighten?

The regulations allow fifty rounds to be brought in per gun per hunter. I had two guns and 100 shells from Winchester in the States; after that, the noise came from black-hulled loads made in Mexico by a Remington subsidiary.

I ran out of red shells while working a hitch out of my swing the first morning. By the time I got serious about actually hitting something, the black empties were ankle-deep. At $10 a box, ammunition is about the only pricey item an American hunter is likely to find in Sonora. According to my rationalization, when you find yourself standing under a crowded sky with a shotgun in your hands, thoughts of money are petty, unworthy, and the chief cause of flinching.

My shagger, a typically polite lad with a typically acute Mexican sense of the silly and Elton John sunglasses, made a great show of collecting the rare, fate-stricken doves that fell our way. Two or three times, I caught him closely examining the birds. He was probably looking for born-to-lose tattoos. When it became obvious that refraining from laughter might stunt his growth or otherwise injure the youngster, I quit shooting. It had been a splendid morning.

The balance of the trip was more of the same, except for the fact that my shooting improved slightly. In my case, practice makes mediocre. The food was memorable, the company was congenial, and a Coues deer hunt was booked for the following December.

Hunters accustomed to the usual whitetail and mule deer habitats will find the world turned upside-down in

Sonora. The Coues subspecies of the whitetail is mountain game, occupying steep and rugged terrain at elevations of 3,500 to 7,000 feet, depending on annual rainfall and available forage. Its range is limited to the dry lands of southeastern Arizona, southwestern New Mexico, and adjoining parts of northern Mexico. In such surroundings, the standard methods of still-hunting, squatting on stand, and driving are no good. Glassing and stalking are the order of the day. Good binoculars and stout boots are essential. Likewise, the trusty lever-action .30/30 is hopelessly out of place. Proper is the accurate, far-reaching bolt gun or single shot with a telescopic sight that might be taken to Wyoming for pronghorns. The average shot on Coues deer will measure more than 200 yards; conscience alone limits maximum range in these sprawling places.

Physically, the Coues deer is a whitetail in miniature. The live weight of a mature buck is often less than 100 pounds, sometimes much less. Grey-brown in color, they match their surroundings to the point of near invisibility. In his prime, a good buck may carry antlers with only eight points, including brow tines. If the spread is 14 inches or more, he is definitely a keeper.

Despite his lack of heroic stature, the Coues deer is among North America's rarest and most highly prized game animals. The distribution of the species is quite limited, the carrying capacity of the habitat is not great, and north of the border, hunting pressure is considerable. The deer's high and rugged home places heavy physical demands on the hunter. Typically long ranges call for skilled shooting. And the animal is, after all, very much a whitetail—hyper alert, clever, and entirely certain of his ground. He is admittedly less expensive than the wild sheep, and permits are not so scarce; otherwise, he is far tougher to come by.

With these cheerless facts in mind, I went to Rancho de la Cienega the first time. Well before noon on the third day, I had my buck, a solid nine-point example of Coues deer maturity.

How, you may ask, was my protracted quest so easily completed? The answer is straightforward: relative to the norm north of the line, there were crowds and hordes and herds of deer. The first morning out, before the sun was fully up, I saw two bucks that would have brought tears to my eyes in Arizona. By evening, I had passed on more than

a score of respectable animals. And that is why I am going to hunt with Laffy Campillo again.

While the sweet taste of success lingered, a try for mule deer was scheduled at the end of 1992. Sonora's mule deer occupy the lower ground, the gently rolling desert floor, where palo verde, mesquite, and giant cacti prosper in defiance of meager rainfall. The few ridges and eroded mountains that afford vantage are of small use; old bucks know to avoid them. The canyons and rimrock frequented by mule deer hunters farther north are absent. The local hunting techniques have evolved accordingly.

Since the brush makes spotting game at any distance largely impossible, and the bucks of desirable size are distributed in miserly numbers over huge expanses of trackless land, special abilities are required. Instead of glassing and stalking or lurking around the high features, tracking is the only productive method.

No description of the Sonoran trackers' work can do justice to their skills. Having seen them in action, I am still nowhere close to sure how they manage it. In brief, the day begins with a meandering hike through the desert. From time to time, a track is crossed. When, by some subtle reckoning beyond my comprehension, it appears that the track belongs to an exceptional buck (rather than an ordinary one), and the sign is new enough to merit optimism, the guide follows it. If all goes well, the track will lead to the deer.

The distinction between the hoofprints of a merely mature mule deer buck and a *macho* is fine enough. Knowing whether it was made within a matter of hours or the day before yesterday is boggling, because the ground can be both stony and as dry as bleached bones.

The hunter is not idle or disengaged while the tracker puts on his magic act. Absolute concentration on the brush ahead and to the sides is essential. If and when the buck is finally found standing or lying in his tracks, after what may be a span of several hours, important things happen all at once. The entire hunt collapses into perhaps three or four seconds. The buck is seen, most often at 100 yards or less, the decision to shoot or not is made, and a bullet is sent, if at all, in an instant.

That is generally the way it went on the first morning of my stay at El Rancho Datil, south of Coborca, last December. Except the buck Gustavo Valdez was tracking crossed over a low ridge, and we jumped him from the brush on the far side. He paused as mule deer are supposed to do at 200 yards or so, and I had time to count twelve or thirteen points on thick beams. Then, I estimated his spread to be about 32 inches. Then, with no ready rest, I stood there and missed.

We followed that deer until early afternoon. In the end, we were within 50 yards. We heard him blow and stamp as he left his bed, and we never saw him again. Not until I had taken a good but lesser buck. The heart-breaker showed again as we were hunting javelina to fill out the week. He stood on an open slope and let me admire him for 15 minutes. It was one of those sights you remember. The memory will have to do until I can return to Bobby Campillo's mule deer camp.

So much for the hunting I have done in Sonora. Luck and health permitting, I mean to go for some of the untried opportunities in the years ahead. There are wild turkeys to be had around Obregon, the Gould's subspecies that we do not have in the States. Friends of mine have done well down there on gobblers the size of compact cars. The ducks that congregate around that city call for attention as well. It should be added that javelina are routinely taken as a bonus on the deer hunts; in most areas, they are so plentiful that hunting them is a casual proposition. Right now, quail hunting is problematical: abundant birds, but no outfitters with dogs to make it worthwhile. This will almost inevitably change before too long.

Travel is supposed to be broadening. This may or may not be true. I have met some narrow, boorish types with dogeared passports. But traveling and hunting in Mexico is about the best way I know to break stereotypes and wear out preconceptions. Forget the grainy, black-and-white images of armed brigands. Ignore horrific tales of squalid jails. An American can find big trouble in Mexico, but stupidity, recklessness, and/or criminal behavior are almost always required. I reckon the odds of falling victim to random harm are infinitely better in Cleveland, Miami, or Los Angeles.

In Sonora, the people respond warmly to common courtesy. With a pocket dictionary and a smile, I have gotten on with them nicely, though my Spanish is little better than pidgin.

The food and water are no cause for terror, either. Sonoran cooking does not depend on heavy spices. The guides in camp are much amused by my fondness for peppers; many of them eat no chilis at all. As for the water, the pure, bottled varieties are readily available everywhere.

For me, it all comes down to good hunting in a setting both familiar and exotic. To my mind, there is no place to rival Sonora. Going there is a comfortable adventure. Whether you ask me now or after the next hunt is finished, I am going there again.

Selecting An Outfitter

Mexican law requires all nonresident hunters to retain the services of a licensed outfitter. As is true in the U.S., selecting an outfitter calls for a certain amount of caution and investigation. Here are some suggestions for minimizing the risk of a bad experience.

1. Check references. Ask for at least half a dozen names from the previous season. Write or phone, and inquire about everything, not just the hunting. Ground transportation, food, lodging, sanitation support services, trophy preparation, and other matters can make or break a hunt.

2. Dealing through a reputable booking agent on this side of the line is recommended. Of course, there is only so much an agent can do, but a good one will cut through the language barrier, expedite paper flow, and protect his own business interests by protecting yours.

3. If the booking agent and/or oufitter won't assist in acquiring the necessary permits and licenses, find another booking agent and/or outfitter.

4. If the oufitter doesn't routinely meet his clients at the port of entry closest to his base of operations, see #3.

As for prices, the best outfitters' fees are roughly comparable to those charged in the U.S. for the better hunts for the same species. In my experience, however, the value received in terms of game populations and trophy quality is substantially higher.

By Jack Kulpa

BURNING BRIGHT

AN ABANDONED TREE
STAND BUILT BY A MAN
WHO IS NOW A GHOST
REMINDS US OF LIFE'S
IMPERMANENCE.

THERE'S AN OLD TREE STAND in the woods where I usually hunt. Whenever I pass it I feel compelled to stop. The rough-sawn boards of its frame are as gray as an old gun barrel. The rotted planks that form its deck are as loose as bad teeth.

I have no idea who built the stand. It was already long abandoned and useless when I found it in this remote corner of Wisconsin, twenty years ago. Since then the white pine that supports it has been struck with blister rust. The tree is tottering and dead—it will not last the winter—and when it falls it will take with it my only link to a life lived long ago and now forgotten.

Although I don't know who built the stand, I do know something about the man. It's obvious the fellow knew his stuff. He built his stand at the top of a ravine, 8 feet off the ground. An isolated patch of oaks—rare in this boreal forest—grows on both sides of the chasm, and even now the long grass under those trees is crosshatched with the trails of deer seeking acorns. At the bottom of the chasm is a spring—I have seen deer drink at the pool from August to freezeup. West of the stand is an old field that was once seeded with alfalfa; at its edge lie encroaching aspens. Over the years I have taken deer early in the morning at the edge of the field and late in the day among the oaks near the spring—all of which were dropped within 100 yards of the old stand.

A wooden ladder used to lean against the stand. Pieces of it now lie in the duff's dry needles. A rusty coil of barbed wire hangs from a stub below the stand. Nearby, in the field, is an old brown hayrake, the sort that was hitched to horses.

No one has farmed this land for over fifty years; yet the barbed wire and the hayrake have a sense of immediacy, as though the farmer who left them here intends to return at any moment. I listen for the sound of footsteps, the lowing of cattle, or the distant calls of children. There is only the sound of the dead pine and its forgotten stand, creaking in the wind.

People tell me there was a farm on this spot until the 1940s, the last one in the township. By then the pioneers who settled here early in this century had given up on farms that yielded only stumps and rocks. Loggers used the abandoned fields to keep horses until skidders and gasoline became cheaper than making hay. When I first hunted here in the 1970s all the land within a week's walk had been logged over, every sawmill was gone, and only ten people lived in the entire township. Now, twenty years later, no one lives here at all. In less than eighty years—the length of a life-time—the land has gone from wilderness to a logging community, and back to wilderness again.

So much for the constancy of men.

ON THIS AUTUMN afternoon, A week before deer season, I'm sitting on a log below the stand, cleaning a pair of partridge in the spring at the bottom of the chasm. Like deer, ruffed grouse seek out oaks whenever acorns are plentiful. Both birds flushed from beside the spring before rocketing uphill, and for the first time in a long time I made a double with my tiny twin-barrel Stevens. This day I'll remember for years to come.

I slip the birds into my game vest and walk uphill toward the abandoned stand, wondering what memories it gave to the man that built it. I imagine him on that stand on an icy November morning, clad in his wool mackinaw and Malone pants, cursing at the cold and snow, the price of deer tags and cartridges, and the whitetail that was there and gone before he knew it.

I wonder how many sandwiches he ate while perched on that stand? How many cigarettes did he smoke; how many times did he forget his matches? It's easy for me to imagine him stamping his feet, trying to pump blood through toes as numb as ice cubes. How often did he force himself to stay put rather than move?

I wonder if the man had children. If so, did those youngsters take their first deer from this stand? It's a secret I will never unravel. Only the ravine's old oaks remember if these woods rang with shouts of joy and laughter.

Most of all, I wonder what became of the people who hunted from this stand? The youngest of them would be silver-haired by now, as gray as the weathered pine boards on which they spent the happiest hours of their youth. Do they still hunt, or ever think of this place? The silence of this haunted land is my answer.

Like the crumbling colonnades of a lost world, the abandoned tree stand makes me painfully aware of life's swift impermanence. Deer still bed in the alfalfa and drink at the chasm's spring, but the man who built this stand is a ghost. I, who felt a kinship with the past, suddenly feel the terrible press of time. I, who spent a leisurely afternoon hunting birds, have become the one pursued.

In the gathering dusk an owl calls. I quicken my pace to be out of the woods before dark. But on a distant ridge the setting sun totters like a trembling red globe, igniting the sky with the blazing fire of its afterglow. I stop to savor the moment, thrilled by the fiery sunset, and no longer anxious about cheating time. To be sure, more than daylight burns as I watch. But while it lasts the light it casts is lovely.

By Bob Brister

"EL TEN"

THE BIGGEST DEER CANNOT BE TAKEN BY SKILL AND LUCK ALONE. ALSO REQUIRED IS THE UNREASONING REFUSAL TO QUIT.

THE BLUFF WITH THE JUMBLE of broken boulders below the rim seemed a practical place for an ambush. Also for rattlesnakes. In pitch darkness an hour before daylight, there was plenty of time to think about both. A seriously big buck had crossed the *sendero* at the base of this bluff, maybe within rifle range. I couldn't tell for sure because I'd seen him from half a mile away, glassing with 10x50 binoculars. But even in the mirage of distance the sweep of his antlers was awesome as he walked away, swaggering like an elk, antlers projecting well past his withers on both sides.

With my backpack wedged between the boulders as a backrest and my rifle laid out on the flat rock in front, I braced my elbows and strained the binoculars, scanning the vague paleness of the bufflegrass opening surrounded by the blackness of South Texas brush.

Dawn grayed, and the clearing was empty. So much for trying to outsmart one big buck in 4,600 acres of South Texas brush.

But I had to get his pattern. Old bucks are like old men—set their ways. If they live long enough, they learn the safe ways to go. For this buck, the creekbed at the base of the bluff had to be the equivalent of a fire escape. It was the only cover that went completely across the opening. Almost a mile to the east, at the far end of the *sendero,* was an oat patch where a large herd of does fed early and late, and a lot of younger bucks were hanging around them. The peak of the rut comes around mid-December in the South Texas brush country near the Mexican border, and I'd planned my hunt to coincide with that period when even the smartest bucks are temporarily vulnerable. But not too vulnerable. There was an elevated blind overlooking that oat patch with all the does, but the buck with the wide antlers had never been seen from that blind. He probably knew all about blinds.

His logical way to reach the oat patch was to cross the open *sendero* at the other end via the creekbed, exactly where I'd seen him. From there he could hold to the brush, and pick off promising does going to or coming from the open oat field. I figured he would cross about dawn, and there would be only a second to get the scope on him where a washed-out ranch road crossed the brushy creek.

Something moved in precisely that spot. The scope was on it instantly, and out stepped a big coyote, stalking. Then he jumped high in the air and pounced down stiff-legged, but whatever it was got away; his jaws came up empty.

My kind of coyote, looking sort of scruffy, and with no luck at all.

The coyote lay down in the open *sendero*, catching the first warming rays of sun, napping. I had a mighty urge to do the same. This was supposed to be a vacation, the hunt I'd waited for all year, with no deadlines, nobody to please or displease, no pictures that just *had* to be made. I could hunt my way—alone and mostly on foot—with a camera, spotting scope, food, and water in the backpack. If I wanted to stop and watch or photograph wildlife, I could. If I wanted to sleep late, I would.

GREAT PLAN. EXCEPT that one look at the wide-horned buck had turned it into a survival test.

The coyote got up and stretched, exactly as my Lab retriever does after he's had a nap. Then he sat down at the edge of the brush and howled, cocked his ears, and listened intently for an answer. It came from somewhere far across the brush. But then he heard the camera's shutter and was gone.

I eased out of the boulders and stalked behind the ridge and into the brush for about a mile to the edge of the oat patch, wondering if the big buck had used some other route to doeville. The ladies were still out feeding on green oats, and the young bucks were still bugging them, but the old man was nowhere to be seen. I figured he was back in the brush, waiting on the does. He would not miss out on all this action.

A covey of blue quail was dusting in a ray of early sun, a beautiful picture, but before the camera cleared the backpack a hawk soared low over the ridge and the blues scooted into a bush and froze there, invisible. Even the hawk didn't see them, or if he did he knew better than to try to fly through a thornbush.

We hunters weren't doing worth a damn.

It was noon when nature threw some barometric switch. A bank of clouds from the north put a fresh chill to the wind, and suddenly bucks were working like worms in and out of the brush, heads down, trailing. Does came darting into the opening, ears laid back and zigzagging, the

bucks behind them. Somehow, every buck in the territory got the message that the does were coming into heat around this *sendero* with the green oat patch at the end.

FROM NOON UNTIL dark I witnessed a spectacle that I may never see again—perhaps a dozen does coming into estrus at once and producing more love triangles than three months of *Dynasty* and *Dallas* combined. Bucks would pop out of the brush, prance around as if to show their style, then lope back inside. Next they'd emerge in hot pursuit of a doe who'd apparently been watching the display back in the brush.

There was one lone mesquite in the opening near the oat patch, and it was busy as a small-town soda fountain on Sunday afternoon. A fine young eight-point buck busily pawed the ground beneath an overhanging limb, urinated on the circular depression in the dirt, then bit off bark from the limb above and carefully rubbed it with the pre-orbital gland in front of his eye. It took him maybe 20 minutes to get all that done, and 5 minutes after he'd gone another eight-pointer came along and went through the identical process, urinating on the same scrape as if to cancel the other guy's message.

It was like a condensed course in whitetail behavior, confirming old suspicions that one scrape doesn't necessarily mark off the territory of just one buck, nor that a fight is assured if he chases a doe into another buck's territory.

Several times I watched two bucks chasing the same doe, and if it didn't work they sometimes just stopped and began feeding together. In all that scraping and chasing I saw no bucks fight, but I did see a couple of dandy doe battles in the oat patch. They'd stand up on their hind legs and slug it out with their front hooves and I could hear the blows from 200 yards away.

Despite all that's written about how bucks are supposed to behave, they do as they damned well please, which mostly consists of staying close to the doe they're after. And no form of rattling, calling, grunting, or conjuring can be depended upon to pull 'em away from the real thing. I think that rattling horns work best when a buck is temporarily out of doe.

The ladies apparently have a lot to say about all this, and I believe they like big antlers. I watched two does trying to hide, lying down with only their ears above the bufflegrass, and a young eight-pointer spotted 'em, stuck his neck out low and came for them on the run. The does cut out on different routes, making more moves than Walter Payton. But when a beautifully high- and heavy-horned ten-pointer cut across from the brush, one of the does stopped. I watched the mating from a distance of less than 50 yards, and I can no longer blame does for running. Whatever else he may be, Bambi is not a gentle lover.

Maybe the old buck was watching, too, because suddenly he was there, like a magnificent statue, curved antlers making a menacing sweep of authority, literally shaking his head at a young buck that immediately decided he had business elsewhere.

Lordy, what a beautiful buck!

The scope trembled, settling on his shoulder, crosshairs confirming that it was slightly over 200 yards. He was strutting straight for a doe in front of me. Now the scope said 150. The trigger finger started to squeeze, but the mind raced.

What if he was just a young buck, a potential giant? My friend who owns this ranch, sporting-goods and ranching entrepreneur Bill Carter of Houston, had worked for years managing his Sombrerito Ranch for trophy whitetails, partly by making sure the best bucks were not harvested until they were old and had passed on their superior genes by breeding many does. Carter had trusted my judgment by letting me hunt alone, something that he very rarely permits. What if I let him down by killing the best young buck on the ranch?

Frantically I found the spotting scope in the pack and got it shakily focused at 36 power, trying to confirm the Roman nose and paunchy neck indicative of an old buck. And old he was! But he must have seen the glint of late-afternoon sun on glass because he whirled and was gone. I shouldered the pack and headed for the truck, sick at heart, yet excited in ways only a hunter can understand.

That night I drove into the nearest town, Laredo, on the Mexican border, and called my wife Sandy in Houston. I told her I was staying, indefinitely, and could the birthday party planned for her be put off? I told her this was one of the most beautiful bucks I'd ever seen; how he carried himself arrogantly as an elk. I told her to tell the Lab pup I'd be home soon as possible to take him duck hunting.

They say every man deserves one good woman and

one good dog, and I have both. But nobody says every man deserves one good deer.

In the next four days the old buck crossed the *sendero* five times, mostly like a ghost in the dewy mist of morning or at last gloom of dusk. Twice he had seemed within a long rifle shot of the gravel bluff at the west end, and once he was at the far eastern end more than half a mile away.

Always I'd been in the wrong place. And it dawned on me that somehow he was seeing my parked truck and staying far away from it. To see that vehicle, the way I'd been hiding it in the brush, meant he had to have elevation. And that meant he was using the bluff or the low, rolling hill of the *sendero* in front of it.

All my stalking, creeping, crawling, and scrape studying was finally paying off. His pattern was becoming clear. He lived in the impenetrable brush on the west side, but had a line of territorial scrapes to the east, nearer the oat patch and the does. The only reason he crossed the buffle-grass *sendero*, perhaps, was because of a high hump in the center of it from which he could see all the way to the oat patch, and because the opening is where does came for running room when chased by lesser bucks. Or maybe he just took a shortcut across when he had pressing female business on the north side.

Had there not been so many does coming in heat, I doubt he would have left the brush at all during daylight. But other bucks were moving in on his territory, and he had to make his rounds.

Maybe I needed to be doing the same thing back home. Days and nights were starting to run together, and fatigue was becoming a factor. Waiting until after dark to leave the buck's area and being back an hour before daylight left little time for eating or sleeping. But it had to be that way because during the peak of rut a dominant buck may come out of cover after a doe at any time. There was no going in for lunch or rest, just jerky and fruit, and black coffee from the thermos in the backpack.

It was important to enter and leave his territory under cover of darkness, because if he caught me homing in too close to his route, he would just stay in the brush and make his rounds at night. Old bucks have done me that way before.

My rattling horns were carried mostly as a last resort. Trying to rattle up a really smart buck in heavy cover is risky. He may circle in the brush and catch your scent, or see you first, or you may call up a smaller buck too close when the old boy is watching. When the young buck finally realizes his mistake and spooks off through the brush, he tells the old one all he needs to know.

Although some bucks around the Sombrerito Ranch house have become tame enough for photography, the rest of the 4,600 acres is hard-hunted with about thirty trophy bucks harvested each year. Old bucks don't need to witness much of that action to get the message. Hunting is done mostly by Carter's friends and by a few clients who pay hefty fees for carefully supervised, guided hunts where vehicles are used to cover territory, then stalking or horn rattling is employed. Which was one reason I was coming into the big buck's territory on foot. Old bucks know the sound of gravel crunching on tires a long way off.

The hunt was turning into a crusade, an old man and an old buck locked in an ancient scenario played by modern rules, one of which was that modern man tends to run out of time. So I had to risk getting into the middle of his crossing pattern. And I thought I knew where that was.

In the *sendero* in front of the rocky bluff was a low hill, merely a roll in the terrain, but it had to be the spot where that buck was stepping out of his creekbed to reconnoiter the opening on both sides. I'd seen him there.

So on the final morning, when the buck hadn't shown at the bluff by good daylight, I eased into the deep-cut bank of the dry creek, bent over, and when necessary crawled. The creek wound into deeper and thicker brush. At one steep bend, on hands and knees, I came face-to-snout with one of the world's uglier javelinas. Actually there were four javelinas, but the big sow in front was the problem. She was not about to turn back, and the creek banks were too steep for either of us to climb out. Brush pigs are not notoriously smart, and do not see well, particularly when trying to figure out something on its hands and knees wearing two-tone camouflage and a face mask. So she just spooked straight past, a wonderful "charging javelina" story had it happened to a more colorful writer.

> "He is like Bo Derek in the film Ten. 'El Ten' is a dream, amigo."

Javelinas are basically non-dangerous to people, but are hell on hunting dogs, and have ripped apart many a pointer hunting South Texas bobwhites. Also, a big sow going under one's nose can leave a trail of musky "perfume" sufficient to impress a skunk. The other javelinas turned back up the creek, making all manner of noise, and I immediately crawled up the bank to peep through the brush and see what deer they might spook out the other end.

Instead, there was this eye-level indigo snake just over the rim of the bank. Just as I raised my head, he raised his, causing us both to draw back somewhat. Indigos are harmless, but being face to face with something that's 8 feet long and eats rattlesnakes can be temporarily disconcerting. Having never photographed an indigo up close I made pictures to give Bill Carter and then crawled back up the creek to glass the brushline.

At first it was empty; then there was movement at the edge of the brush—antlers looking twice as wide as they actually were. It was him, all right, making his scrape route but going the wrong way. Damn his smart swagger! But he was beautiful, wide tines yellowed by early sun, just a little too far to chance a shot.

Then I saw a big eight-point buck trailing a doe along the brushline. I realized they would meet the big buck at the top of the rise, and the doe would immediately be in between competitors. That love triangle might buy me some time, particularly if the bucks fought.

I dropped back into the creek, crawled like crazy, then found a stretch I could cover by bending over low and running. Puffing from exertion I eased over the ridge, and a "tree" on the brushline moved.

Dammit! How did he get way over there? He'd seen me too. He raised his head high to make sure. For a split second we sized each other up at 500 yards, then, arrogantly, he turned and melted into the brush. Now he knew for sure I was after him, in the middle of his territory.

But there was still hope. Unless he was truly supernatural he would soon be in for female trouble. He'd confiscated the doe from the eight-pointer, and if she decided to come back across the *sendero* to her favorite oat patch for dinner, he just might follow her.

I crawled out to a big mesquite tree on the point of the brushline where I could see over the ridge in both directions. It was indeed his vantage point. The tree trunk had little bark left from antler rubs, a big scrape had been pawed beneath an overhanging limb broken from horn hooking, and droppings and big tracks were everywhere. So I climbed the tree to its first fork to see better.

After two hours of mesquite-thorn acupuncture, I saw a doe appear over the ridge. I hooked one arm around the tree and grabbed the fore-end of the rifle, locking myself to the limb for the shot. Antler tips bobbed behind her, multiple points, and I had the crosshairs on his neck when his nose cleared the ridge. But he was merely a heavy-horned, narrow-beamed ten-pointer. Not *the* ten pointer.

"He's beat you, fair and square," the body groaned and creaked, unclimbing that miserable mesquite. "You're whipped physically and mentally, and in the event you still have a wife back home, she is having a birthday dinner tonight you could just about make if you started driving right now..."

When I drove up to the bunkhouse to begin packing, ranch foreman Aranjelio Flores came over to see if I had seen the old *macho.*

"This buck is too smart," he consoled in Spanish, humoring my tendency to try to speak that language. "Runs like hell at first sight of my truck. You've seen him through the spotting scope. How many points?"

"Ten," I said sadly, "perfectly symmetrical, the perfect ten."

"Ah," he smiled, "like Bo Derek in the film *Ten,* you can see but not touch, Right, amigo? 'El Ten' is a dream."

"Dammit, no" I said. "If I had a tree stand within range of the bluff at one end and a long shot from the oat patch on other, he's got to pass somewhere there this afternoon. I know he will. He's too far from his main scrapes to spend the night on the other side. He's got a doe with him, and she'll go back to those oats."

"We gottee one tripod," he offered in his best English. "With two working, maybe thirty minutes to set up. You want to try?"

So we loaded the tripod blind into his truck, and I followed him in the Suburban and parked it at the end of the *sendero* where the old buck could see it, hoping he would think I was somewhere up there with it. If so, he'd hold close to his escape route along the creek within about 100 yards of my strategic mesquite.

We set up the tripod in the middle of that tree, machete-hacking limbs for shooting clearance to my left where I expected him to appear if he came. Then Aranjelio drove straight down the middle of the *sendero,* making a big show of mankind leaving the area while I hid motionless in the tripod blind in the tree.

For four hours, nothing happened except I thought a good deal about how much outdoor writer wives have to put up with, and how tough it would be to find another good one, particularly if she took the Lab puppy with her. Then about a quarter of five, Happy Hour started around the oat patch, much the same as any other singles bar—first the females showing up, then younger bucks sniffing around, and finally the heavy hitters arriving as the sun sank. Along with my spirits.

One dark-horned, gnarly-beamed eight-pointer escorted a doe almost under the mesquite, and to my right a thin-antlered ten-pointer, high and pretty of rack, came tiptoeing over the ridge. Either one would make a beautiful mount, and would have salvaged *some* excuse for having been down here in the brush a solid week, something for a wife to tell her friends the old man had been doing.

No way. Not with five minutes of light left to see El Ten.

In the gloom beside the brush line, antlers gleamed—heavy ones with multiple points. The rifle started up, then went down. That buck was hackled up like a dog ready to fight, and he was looking to my left.

Gravel crunched behind me. I turned, and there he was, El Ten, poised beside his creek like a wraith about to disappear, the last rays of light gleaming on the polished sweep of antlers, looking straight at me. Ever so slowly I tried to turn with the rifle. He caught my movement, and was running. The scope passed him as the 7mm magnum roared, and he was into the brush and gone.

But he made that special up-hop that means heartshot, and I yelled *Waa—hoo!* at the top of my lungs and didn't care if every deer in the world heard it.

Inside the brush about 15 yards, a curving antler projected high above the cactus. Walking up to him I felt that strange sensation of sadness, respect, and perhaps predatory satisfaction that some hunters and all hawks and coyotes satisfaction that some hunters and all hawks and coyotes know, but that few others nowadays, understand. Then I just had to reach down and touch those antlers that had seemed an impossible illusion.

They had already suffered some from shrinkage, as antlers invariably will between the shot and contact with the ground, but these were still about 27 inches wide. He'd broken off a brow tine fighting since I first saw him, no more a "perfect ten." But if Bo Derek covered the territory this old warhorse had, she might have a few blemishes, too.

That night when I called home, the lady was still there, getting excited about the buck as I described him, letting the pup listen in because he recognizes voices over phones. I told her the buck dressed out 155 pounds on ranch scales, that he was all antlers, downright skinny from chasing all those does. She said that's what happens to old bucks that chase too many young does.

I had to wait for morning for a bulldozer operator named Ish Crisp to make pictures for me with my wide angle lens that has such great focus-error margin and would make the antlers look almost as big as they were when the old buck was strutting around his *sendero*.

At Muy Grande Village in the nearby town of Freer, headquarters of the state's most prestigious annual big buck contest, a crowd gathered to peek inside the windows of the Suburban. Veteran hunter and guide Lionel Garza, who runs the Muy Grande contest, shook his head, then my hand, and claimed I might have had the year's best all-around buck in Texas (they score on a combination of antler points, circumference, spread, and body weight) but that the broken brow tine took him out of contention by making him score as a nine-pointer rather than a ten. Had that stump of a point been just 1 inch long he would have been a ten.

Easy come, easy go.

Taxidermist Carter Hood in Houston says the buck will make Safari Club International's record book, and maybe go pretty high in the Burkett record book, but with a brow tine missing and antler spread wider than mainbeam length, there's no way he'll make the Boone and Crockett Club book.

Which is just fine with me. He's No. 1 in my book, El Ten with all his points, exactly the way I want to remember him forever.

By Dan Sisson

GRANDPA
and the Kid

SOMETIMES, NO MATTER HOW CAREFULLY YOU PLAN, THINGS DON'T WORK OUT THE WAY THEY'RE SUPPOSED TO — ESPECIALLY ON THE FIRST DAY OF THE SEASON.

THE OPENING DAY OF deer season was less than a week away and all I could think about was when and where I was going hunting. The only thing I knew was that we were going somewhere. One day grandpa would talk about hunting blacktails along the coast; the next he'd ramble on about whitetails in the mountains of northeast Oregon. As usual, he kept me guessing, and the suspense was driving me crazy.

I knew he'd done his homework and read the game pamphlets, but I couldn't figure out what else he'd done. Aside from helping me sight in my new .270, the old man was acting like he'd forgotten there was anything called a deer season. Only twice in three weeks had I heard the words "opening day."

Now that's not like Grandpa. He's fond of saying, "The opening day of deer season possesses a magic all its own," and then talking about it for hours on end.

Well, opening day is pretty magical to me, too. It means autumn and the hunting season are in full swing and, for most everybody I know, that's what matters. Anybody who has sense is going deer hunting, so the whole world can wait and it won't hurt a bit.

Opening day's the only time of year I can take a week off school and not worry about cutting classes or getting into trouble with my teachers.

Getting ready for opening day is special too. It means setting up a deer camp and doing chores I'd never do at home—like cutting firewood or hauling water. It means I get to associate with Grandpa's friends as a near-equal and sit around the fire at night, listening to tales of past hunts and learning something from experienced hunters. It means talk about rifles and which calibers perform best under different conditions as well as what deer do under those same conditions. It means talking about scents and ways to attract bucks and what makes a good stand. And it means a discussion of hunting strategies and how a successful hunter has to adjust to rain, snow, and wind and try new tactics while still being patient. All this takes place in earnest a day or two before the shooting starts when you scout the country and pick a stand.

Opening day itself involves a series of exciting rituals that begin when it's still dark. You wake up in a tent when the pungent smell of boiling coffee hits your nostrils like smelling salts. The sounds of eggs cracking and bacon sizzling and pancake batter being mixed coax you out of a warm sleeping bag to the best breakfast you can imagine.

And then you start thinking about why you're in camp and anticipating that somewhere out there is a buck with your name on it. That anticipation carries you through the early morning darkness to your stand, and keeps your spirits high as you begin the long wait.

"Opening day itself involves a series of exciting rituals that begin when it's still dark."

There's a little bit of worry in that anticipation, too. You worry whether you bumped your scope against something in the dark and you'll be off a foot. And then, after a while, you worry if you've chosen the right stand and ought to move to a better one.

And while you're worrying about these things you start to think about how opening day is the best time to kill a buck, because from then on they get warier and the hunting gets harder until most hunters give up because the deer simply disappear.

Despite all the difficulties, though, in the end it's sweet success that you anticipate the most—especially the moment when you bring your buck into camp and everyone crowds around to help you hang him.

Finally, opening day is your best chance to provide meat for the family and, if all goes well, be a proud and safe hunter, and a good sportsman. That's what opening day means to me: a combination of all those sights, sounds, and smells and the shivering expectations of success.

Now in the previous two years we've gone hunting, Grandpa and I started talking about these things at least a month before the season opened. So it seemed strange that he'd hardly mentioned them this year. But, as always, the old fox was testing me, trying to find out how long I could last before I exploded.

The next day, when I came home from school, I decided to confront him. I came roaring into the kitchen, threw my books on the table and before he or Suzy could say a word, I yelled: "Grandpa! Where are we going on opening day? We've got less than five days before hunting starts and you haven't done anything to get us ready!"

The old man looked up and deadpanned it: "What makes you so sure I haven't done anything?"

I swallowed hard. I suddenly realized I had no way of knowing whether he had done anything or not. But I'd come this far and decided I'd better state some reasons: "First, you haven't said hardly anything about opening day. Second, we haven't got our maps out. And third, we haven't even looked at our equipment. All we've done is sight in my rifle and that was ages ago."

With relief I noted a smile playing around the corners of the old man's mouth. "So you think I've just been ignoring the whole thing? Well, would it surprise you, kid, to know we're all set to go huntin' day after tomorrow?"

I sat down, drew a deep breath and tried to save some dignity. "How was I supposed to know? Nobody told me anything and I still don't know where we're going."

Grandpa responded, "That's an easy one, kid. We're heading into the Blue Mountains with Paul Schlosser. He knows exactly where to go and he's got all the equipment. All we have to do is bring our rifles, sleeping bags, and clothes and we're ready!"

Two days later, Grandpa and I jammed our gear into Paul's pickup and headed east from the coast. After driving several hours in which every topic of conversation *except* deer hunting had been mentioned, Paul got to the main point. "Ya know," he said, "this'll be the tenth year I've come over here. Eight bucks in ten years and six of 'em on opening day. That'll tell you how important opening day is in my theory about gettin' a deer."

Grandpa looked over at me and winked. "A theory, eh? Well, let's hear it, Paul. We're gonna need all the theories we can get. I read that the buck count in the Blue Mountains is down this year." Grandpa waited a second and when Paul didn't respond he asked, "What do you think the criteria were for making that judgment? I mean for the fish and wildlife people."

Paul's voice sounded a little hesitant. "I didn't see their study, but they'd be dealing with how much feed there was this past winter and what kind of winter it was. Then there's predators and how many fawns survived. And I guess you'd have to add in the number of bucks taken last season..."

At that point I interrupted. "What do you mean bucks from *last* season? I thought we were talking about *this* season?"

Both Grandpa and Paul laughed. "Kid," drawled Grandpa, "I thought you took biology last year."

"Oh," I said, my face burning. "I know what you mean now. You're talking about the number of bucks left to take care of the does. Right?"

"Rigghhhttt," they said in unison, and then Paul continued, "There're other things I pay attention to when I go deer hunting. For instance, the bowhunters and musketmen.

They're taking big bucks at a time when they least suspect it. Archers don't spook deer. The musketmen, though, make noise and by the time we come along there're not many bucks that don't know it's huntin' season. So I try and go to a place where there aren't too many hunters."

Grandpa turned an admiring glance toward Paul. "Sounds like you've been thinking about this for some time."

———————

THIS REALLY WAS Paul's show. Aside from the groceries and some gas money, he had insisted on supplying everything as well as selecting the place and dates to hunt. He knew what he was doing.

Once we arrived in camp we were doubly impressed by Paul's preparation. He had brought along every conceivable item one might need for a successful deer hunt. The most amazing thing, however, was his knowledge of the area. Not only had he hunted the Blue Mountains for a decade, he had systematically bought every map printed. He even had aerial reconnaissance photos and knew every road, bridge, and canyon in a 10-square-mile area. It seemed Paul left nothing to chance.

From our camp that evening, we looked down on the Grande Ronde, a moonlit silvery ribbon, winding its way along the bottomlands. Each canyon beside us pointed toward the river, and it was easy to imagine hordes of deer walking down each night from the highlands and back up the canyons in the early morning darkness.

After a late dinner Paul suggested we hit our sleeping bags. He loaded up the stove with as much wood as it would hold, turned out the lantern, and said, "Four A.M. on opening day is coming up quick!"

It did. The alarm went off, it seemed, five minutes after I'd crawled into my bag, and I got up reluctantly. But Grandpa's and Paul's enthusiasm soon fired me up and made me eager to get out to our stands. We reached them an hour before daylight and silently peered into the dark canyon below. We had taken a stand that overlooked a small creek running below us. Grandpa and I were spread out, 50 yards apart, and each of us had a view of a hillside in front and a canyon to the left and right.

For the first half hour nothing moved except an occasional hunter who was late getting to his favorite spot. Another half hour went by and still no movement. Light began creeping into the canyons, and what had seemed formless shapes minutes before began taking on definition. For roughly 15 minutes I imagined everything from dinosaurs to grizzly bears drinking from the stream below. But as more light came, their shapes changed into boulders and trees alongside a small creek lined with willows and tufts of marsh grass.

About the third hour I saw a coyote, then two. The temptation to see how my new .270 would shoot was strong, but we were deer hunting now, and I shrugged off the impulse.

We were well into the fourth hour when Grandpa raised his rifle quickly, as if he were going to shoot. I looked and caught sight of a brief movement across the canyon. I realized two deer were working their way up the hill from the creek below. They had been there all along and neither of us had seen them until they were directly across from our stands. Like gray ghosts they blended in perfectly with the brush and timber, and even knowing they were there I still had difficulty seeing them.

After scoping out the area carefully I realized they were does and there would be no bucks following. Minutes later Grandpa made a weak stab at lightening the mood: "Can't say we haven't seen deer today, kid."

"Yeah," I answered. "But they're not the same as bucks." I couldn't hide my disappointment either.

While the appearance of the does had eased the tension, it did nothing to relieve the boredom. After six hours we realized opening day morning was a bust. Nothing was going to happen. The temperature had risen dramatically with the sun and that meant every self-respecting buck had long ago reached a shaded area and was not about to be caught in the open. It also meant that by the time the temperature dropped and the deer started moving again, we'd have less than an hour to hunt.

* * *

ABOUT 11 A.M. GRANDPA stopped pretending he was asleep and suggested we head back to camp. It was a good 40-minute walk, but when we got there we found Paul sitting on a log in the woods near the tent, looking like he'd seen a ghost. Grandpa and I glanced at each other and asked simultaneously, "Paul, are you all right?"

"Yeah," he answered gruffly. "I'm okay. It's just the heat's gettin' me down."

"That's not what's getting me," I said. "I didn't see a buck all morning."

"Me either," echoed Grandpa. "Opening day's a bust this year." Then, looking at Paul closely, he asked, "You see anything or take any shots?"

Paul got a strange look on his face before he replied. "I did, but I sure hate to tell you about it."

Grandpa and I looked at one another and held our breath. Finally I couldn't stand it and blurted out, "Well, tell us what happened."

Then Paul told his incredible story of opening day: "I took a stand about a mile or so below you guys. I'd barely gotten settled in when I saw two nice bucks top a rise about 100 yards away. I raised my rifle and put the crosshairs on the biggest one's shoulder. I squeezed the trigger and nothing happened. I couldn't believe it. So I checked the safety and it was already off. I put the rifle up again and took aim and squeezed the trigger. Again nothing happened. At that point I was going out of my mind and the bucks just stood there. I lowered the rifle and looked at it and suddenly realized my bolt wasn't fully closed. It was open about an eighth of an inch. So I slammed the bolt shut, raised up, and fired four shots as fast as I could pull the trigger. The two bucks turned and dipped back over the rise."

As Paul was talking I looked at Grandpa and he was sitting there open-mouthed. Neither of us could believe it. Paul, an experienced hunter, had gotten buck fever!

"You're kidding," I said.

"No, I'm not," said Paul, shaking his head. "It gets worse. The minute they disappeared I ran to where they had been standing. I looked for blood, hair, anything. I couldn't find a thing. I even looked to see if my bullets had hit a tree or a leaf or something, but I couldn't find anything. Then I began to wonder if I just imagined they were there and I thought I was going crazy. At last I found tracks where they had turned to go down the hill. Darn they were big!"

There was dead silence. Neither Grandpa nor I could think of anything to say. Then Paul, looking pained, began talking again: "That's not all. As I walked back to my

"Paul, an experienced hunter, had gotten buck fever."

stand—not more than two minutes later—two small bucks came flying by me. They couldn't have been more than 20 feet away. I raised my rifle and, of course, the scope was just one big blur.

"The '06 was sighted in at 150 yards. By the time those deer were far enough away so I could see them in the scope, I didn't have a shot."

With that Paul threw his hands in the air and yelled. All Grandpa and I could do was sit there looking at the ground. We couldn't laugh and crying wasn't called for, so we just sat quietly for a couple of minutes. Finally Grandpa said, in a voice that sounded raspy: "Well, don't worry. We'll hit it this evening and we're bound to find something." I could tell it didn't help.

When evening came, instead of going to our stands we decided to walk some meadows and flush the deer out of thick clumps of willow. We spread out and systematically stirred every bush and thicket for more than a mile. Nothing but one rabbit came out. It was an omen. After an hour it was too dark to shoot and we headed back to camp.

On the way back the mood lightened considerably.

Grandpa said it was a darn good thing he hadn't gotten his buck on opening day because then he wouldn't have anything to do for the rest of the week. Paul added he wasn't going to really start worrying until the last day. And I made both promise to buy me a sundae for every day we went without a deer. By the time we reached camp the good natured remarks had re-created the optimism that had been missing during the heat of the day.

Then Grandpa said, "By the way, Paul, you never did explain your theory about getting a buck on opening day. What was that theory, anyway?"

A big grin spread across Paul's face: "My theory? Oh, that! Well, it's simple. After twenty years of deer hunting I've decided people who get their bucks on opening day are just plain lucky. The real hunters are the ones who stick it out till the end. And that's why I didn't tell you the whole theory. I didn't want either of you to think that you were just plain lucky."

"There's no worry about *that!*" I added. And for once I had the last word.

THERE IS THE REST OF THE YEAR . . . AND THERE IS WHITETAIL SEASON.

The
MEASURE
of Our Lives

*I*N THE STRICTEST SENSE, NO ONE NEEDS to hunt; we have farms and ranches and supermarkets to supply us with meat. But if you look beyond the human stomach, you encounter the human spirit, and that part of us needs to hunt as much as it needs to compose music, or write novels, or record history, or worship a higher being. Hunting, as much as anything, made us what we are, and the week or two we spend with a rifle is the pivot on which the rest of the year balances.

To most of us, hunting season means whitetail season. We can dream of the distant and the exotic, but it is the whitetail that draws us to the woodlots and the forests and the swamps. There are two reasons for the whitetail's pre-eminence. It is abundant and, as a trophy, it is second to nothing. No animal, anywhere, can dance you around the woods with such ease.

Years ago, I asked a master whitetail hunter, a man who had written the best book to date on the subject, how to outsmart the really big ones.

"You can't," he said with a wry smile, "not really. About the best you can do is arrange to be around when an old buck runs out of luck."

Maybe that's what brings us back year after year— the thought that this time, luck will be on our side, and we will see awe and envy in the eyes of our fellow hunters. There is a magic to whitetail hunting that keeps us at it for fifty and sixty seasons, as long as we are able. And it is why hunters who are at the end of the trail can still tell you every detail of the day they took their biggest buck.

Whitetail season is the calendar by which we mark our lives.

David E. Petzal

IN RURAL NEW ENGLAND, deer hunting is a fifth season wedged between winter and fall. It is part of the rhythm of life, a time to renew one's acquaintance with the big woods, to walk over familiar ground and see how things have changed, to get way up in the mountains, which afford a fine year-end perspective on the land below and on life in general.

We are not a deer factory like the South, nor do our bucks wear those big Texas racks. A trophy here is any buck. Body size holds more sway than a head full of calcium, which any Yankee will tell you doesn't eat worth a damn. "Get your deer this year?" is the perennial end-of-season question, and a man who answers "Eh-yah!" year after year is a talented hunter indeed.

The whitetail is the king of our woods, despite the occasional bear or moose. I'll hunt for days, sometimes, without seeing one; for years, sometimes, without seeing a buck. People ask "Why?" and all you can say is this:

"Because it's deer season, and in deer season hunting deer is what you do."

Lionel Atwill

AS A TEENAGER I was hiding against a tree in dark East Texas squirrel timber and turned to see a huge buck staring straight at me, so close I could see the coarse hairs on his chin and the eerie glow of dawn light on gnarled, massive antlers. In the same instant he whirled and disappeared into the shadows. . . casually leaping a 4-foot brushpile. He was the most arrogant, majestic creature I had ever seen.

There were far fewer deer then, and even seeing a track was worth a serious conversation around our local barbershop. Most piney-woods hunters knew little about the life cycles of deer, and oldtimers told wonderful tales of wise old bucks that lived in the same forbidding thickets where their grandfathers had seen them. They were impossible to outwit, and carried names like "Ol' Crumplehorn," or "Splayfoot," or "Rockin'chair." Hunting them was like hunting spirits, and the mystery and the anticipation was far more important then any hope of meat.

Now there are many more deer, all across America, and they're hunted for venison, vanity, and because hunters just like to be in the wild places where deer live. But the magic and the mystery, the dreams and memories of great bucks seen but never taken, remain as precious and timeless to me as those spirit bucks of my youth.

Bob Brister

Whitetail Insights

It has often been said that, of all the big-game animals in North America, a mature whitetail buck is the most difficult to successfully hunt. That is true not only because of the whitetail's extremely sensitive sense of smell, keen sense of hearing, explosive speed, and seemingly constant state of alertness, but also because of its incredible ability to avoid detection.

Whitetails are natural survival experts, and a big buck seems to know almost intuitively when a hunter is in its home range—which it knows better than you know your own living room. When you're hunting such an animal, you can afford few mistakes.

Perhaps these qualities are also what make whitetails such fascinating animals to hunt. The trick, if you can call it one, to improve your odds of getting a deer is to know the basics of whitetail biology and behavior, and then to understand how conditions—time of day, season of year, weather, forage, hunting pressure, even herd size—affect the deer in the area you hunt, and how they respond to those conditions. If you know all that—and the following stories will help you learn how—then you're on your way to filling your tag.

By Sam Curtis

BODY LANGUAGE

ALL ANIMALS MAKE CERTAIN GESTURES THAT REVEAL WHAT THEY'RE THINKING. DEER HUNTERS TAKE ADVANTAGE OF THIS PHENOMENON BY LEARNING WHAT THESE MOVEMENTS MEAN.

A N ANIMAL'S BODY LANGUAGE conveys social etiquette, courtship, and signals of alarm and flight. Knowing how to interpret a deer's movements—the way it holds its neck, head, and ears, its stance, and its gait—will let you know whether to shoot fast or relax and wait for a better shot.

Although both mule deer and whitetails have similar mannerisms that convey the same meaning, whitetails are more flamboyant and showy with their gestures than muleys. This is in keeping with the temperament of the two species.

When a deer is going about its daily business, several mannerisms indicate it isn't considering anything except the task at hand. It will frequently flick its tail and ears, walk slowly with evenly spaced steps, and lower and raise its

head, remaining alert, yet relaxed. This deer is not about to run off.

In the company of other deer, however, you may notice gestures that look like signs of alarm but are, in fact, expressions of social courtesy. When moving past one another, deer often lower their heads and flatten their ears. They may also crouch and curl their tails between their legs. These are signs of submission, which may even be expressed by the dominant deer in a group. It means "Hey, everything's cool" or "Let's keep the peace."

WHEN DEER BECOME alarmed they don't slink; they jolt to attention with their head and neck erect, ears forward, and nose pointed in the direction of their concern. Mule deer often stand in this rigid position with one front leg raised, periodically stamping their foot to the ground. Whitetails embellish this routine by explosively blowing air

through their nostrils with a loud snort. These acts usually mean that the deer senses your presence, but it isn't exactly sure where you are. The snort and stomp are attempts to make you move so the deer can establish your location. Such behavior indicates that the animal is very alarmed and may bolt at any second.

I've been so close to deer before they've bolted that I could see the hair on their rump rise and their tail stick straight out behind them. These are sure signs that your game is about to go.

On the other hand, if you remain perfectly still and the wind is in your favor, a deer in this alarmed stance may suddenly wag its tail and lower its head to a normal relaxed position.

If the deer runs off, however, certain gestures can give you a clue as to how alarmed it is. The whitetail, of course, signals with its tail. If it is really scared, the tail will be upraised and waving frantically. If the tail is only partly raised, the deer may not be too upset, and you may be able to keep hunting it. The muley shows his concern in his gait. A mule deer that trots off is not really alarmed. It's the stott—the stiff, four-legged bounce—that indicates a scared muley. He may travel for quite some distance before settling down.

important movement is a buck's tending posture, just before he mates with a doe.

Approaching or following a doe from behind, a buck will stretch out his neck, hold his head low, flick his tongue, and avoid looking at the doe directly. This fawning posture is quite unmistakable. At this point, the buck is quite preoccupied with other matters and not at all aware or concerned with your presence. That's why some of the biggest bucks are taken during the rut.

A NUMBER OF gestures are used in courting routines including shows of dominance and submission, threats and sparring matches, and fighting postures. But the most

By Jim Bashline

Are Whitetails
WISING UP?

AS THEIR HABITATS
DIMINISH, DEER SEEM
TO BE EVOLVING INTO
SMARTER ANIMALS.

IT'S WIDELY AGREED AMONG experienced outdoorsmen that some animals are more intelligent than others, and some individual animals are smarter than others of the same species. Many hunters and more than a few game biologists, however, now are beginning to believe that deer as a group are brighter and better able to evade hunters than they could just a few decades ago. Those who did not bring home the venison last season, of course, will probably embrace this theory wholeheartedly.

Still, theories surrounding the reasons for increased deer wariness often conflict. Some folks who profess to care a great deal about animals insist that deer (and most wild creatures) did not display great wariness before man—the hunter—came on the scene. Common sense says this is pure poppycock. Long before the human predator stalked the wilds, meat-eating animals ate other creatures when they could catch them. So, being alert to predators was already a well entrenched habit. The hunter, therefore, is only a recent factor in the rise and fall and general wariness of deer populations. This is not to say that the modern hunter is *the* major factor. He's certainly one of them, but closer proximity to all humans, their buildings, and their highways has brought about changes in how deer react, whitetails in particular.

About five years ago I mentioned my "smarter deer theory" to a couple of biologists. They agreed, adding that deer are smarter because all of the stupid animals are killed before the brighter ones. This leaves the more wary of the species, the bigger, older bucks, to continue adding to the gene pool. The cumulative result, say the biologists, is that big, smart deer beget big, smart deer.

More recently, I asked the question again but couldn't beg a concise quote from most well-traveled deer researchers. Either they've changed their minds or don't want to become embroiled in the current deer intelligence debate. I can't say that I blame them!

One expert was willing to offer his views. According to Dale Sheffer, Chief of Research for the Pennsylvania Game and Fish Commission, studies undertaken jointly between the commission and Penn State University prove to him that deer are capable of learning. In the experiments, scientists placed desirable deer foods in certain drawers and undesirable foods in others and found that the deer could remember which ones to push open meal after meal.

"In fact," said Sheffer, "the deer were even able to adjust when the researchers switched the good food with the bad, barely missing a beat."

To further support my theory about deer smarts, I began searching for some tangible evidence. Highway-killed deer provided some clues. When Interstate 80, which traverses northcentral Pennsylvania, was completed about a quarter century ago, deer/auto collisions were frequent. Two thousand deer deaths per year were ordinary, an estimate that is probably conservative since many deer stagger unseen into the woods to die after being struck. As the years passed, however, fewer dead deer were counted along 1-80. At the same time, the hunter harvest remained the same or increased in counties the highway bisected. It was obvious that the deer learned to avoid the sound of cars and semi-trailers in the night.

Other evidence shows that deer are becoming wiser. Spot checks of deer killed last year on 1-80 revealed that the majority were fawns or young adults, not older, more experienced animals. Many mature bucks are indeed hit on highways during the November rutting season, and, of course, adult deer are chased across the road during open seasons or by feral dogs. When they are not being pursued, however, it appears that older bucks are learning to change their course to avoid dangerous roadways.

Bear biologist Gary Alt, who spends more time in the outdoors in six months than most of us do in a lifetime, is continually amazed by the intelligence and adaptability of wildlife.

"In many parts of the Pocono Mountains," Alt said, "summer cabin dwellers are dumbfounded when they learn that a bear den can be as near as 50 feet from their back door. One big female raised two sets of twins over a five-year period within spitting distance of a big picture window . . . and the occupants never knew she was there. The mother bear adjusted her comings and goings to coincide with the times no one was at the cottage."

Although some may claim that bears are simply

smarter than deer, there's little difference in brain size. Besides, bears will come back time after time to plague a farmer's pig pen or cornfield in spite of being yelled at, shot at, and even trapped and carried many miles away. Spook a whitetail deer badly enough, on the other hand, and it will avoid a specific locale for a long time.

Two years ago, I cleared a small brushy area on my property that covered a well-used deer path. The trail was the most direct route between a large area of cropland and the protective cover of 60,000 acres of state forest. For two weeks, the deer continued to use the old trail, which was now an open vista. Then, as if at a signal, they began to skirt the area, creating a new trail 100 yards away to take advantage of thicker cover.

Such an abrupt change in daily habits did not take place initially at the Lincoln Hunting Club in Pennsylvania some fifty years ago. According to camp records, the deer in this Lycoming County area continued to use the same convenient trails for over sixty years, even after the club's leased acreage was severely logged. It wasn't until off-road vehicles and snowmobiles became common in the late 1950's that the deer reluctantly changed routes. Today, the well-pounded deer trails are still there . . . they're just not in close proximity to the tire tracks. Have the deer learned? I think so, and studies prove this out.

Records kept over many years often show evidence of learning on the part of deer, but so do events occurring in a single season. In heavily hunted locales on opening day, for example, deer tend to make deadly mistakes with great frequency. But after a few hours of seeing hunters behind every tree smelling their scent on every bush, and hearing the echoes of rifle or shotgun shots, a strange phenomenon takes place—the vanishing deer trick. At these times, it seems as though every deer in the state has crawled down a woodchuck hole, nowhere to be seen. Following the frenzy of the season opener, the successful hunter really has to hunt.

In some highly populated areas even opening day provides no guarantee of stumbling onto a trusting deer. The big bucks in the farm regions of Ohio, Illinois, Indiana, New Jersey,

and other states never stand around like milk cows waiting for feeding time. These deer are used to the human silhouette and the accompanying aroma, but familiarity does not mean a lack of caution. They know exactly where humans are, and staying out of sight (or gun range) is their chief mission. That's how they got to be big bucks.

As much as I'd love to teach a magic formula or secret trick that would somehow increase readers' odds of tagging one of these big, educated deer, I haven't learned one yet. There just aren't any sure-fire methods.

Caution, stealth, reading the "signs," scouting the area before the hunt, and practicing better marksmanship are heavily stressed by most experienced deer hunters today. I believe this is because experienced deer hunters have come to understand that deer today *are* smarter. After all, most deer hunting states have reported increases in deer populations for several years. Why, then, are deer so tough to get a bead on?

If the deer are becoming smarter, then we must become better hunters to outsmart them. This means spending more time studying them in the off season as well as hunting them. Clearly, despite what anti-hunting folks would have you believe, deer don't stand around chewing their cuds until they are bisected by the crosshairs of a telescopic sight.

By Sam Curtis

WHITETAILS
Up High

IT'S COMMON KNOWLEDGE THAT HEAVY
SNOW DRIVES BUCKS TO LOWER ELEVATIONS.
EVERYONE IS AWARE OF THIS FACT...EXCEPT
THE DEER THEMSELVES.

HERBIE GUTMAN AND I HAVE been friends since our fourth-grade music teacher made us play a tuba duet at Connecticut's Fairfield State Hospital. That was forty years ago. I've spent over half that time in Montana; Herbie has moved to Vermont. But we still write.

Herbie likes to tease me about how good the whitetail hunting is in New England, how the deer get big and fat eating ornamental trees in people's backyards, how the whitetails back East are truly sporting game because they do things you wouldn't expect them to do—things Western whitetails aren't smart enough to do.

Take the "up high" whitetails Herbie wrote me about last year.

"You'd think that a good fall snowstorm in these parts would send all the mountain whitetails scampering for lower elevations. You'd think they'd get down in those old softwoods—the red spruce and the balsam fir, the white pine and the hemlock—down along rivers and streams where the snow isn't so deep. That's what you'd think, and I bet that's what your Western whitetails do."

I had to admit that when serious snow starts to set in during hunting season in Montana, I watch for whitetails to start moving downstream, out of the foothills where I live, into lower, more open country that doesn't get as much snow. It may be a move of only 2 or 3 miles, but it's enough to take them completely out of country where they have congregated in numbers during the summer and early fall.

I wrote Herbie that I thought the equation was simple for both Eastern and Western whitetails: the more snow, the

lower they go. Herbie wrote back and said that that wasn't the case with his whitetails, that when it snows in Vermont they sometimes go up high. He's *seen* them up there.

It seems Herbie had taken a bunch of Scouts on a three-day fall backpacking trip along one of those Eastern trails that follows the skyline over hills that look like sleeping giants. Given Herbie's luck, snow fell through the first night, ending around noon the second day. Although the sun came out, it didn't do much to melt the foot of snow that covered the trail as it wound along the northern side of the ridge.

But Herbie and his Scouts were prepared; they plowed on, stopping occasionally to rest in the sun where the trail broke out on the steep southern side of the hills. At one of these stops, Herbie was right in the middle of wishing the trail was on the *south* slope, where the sun had already melted the snow to half the depth he and his Scouts had been hiking through, when they spotted the whitetails.

There were a dozen deer. They were moving easily along the steep southern slope foraging on sumac and hop hornbeam. It was an unexpected sight, Herbie admitted. He figured the whitetails had just been caught off guard by the sudden storm; they were probably trying to make the best of a bad situation. But before the backpacking trip was over, he'd seen dozens more deer hanging out up high on steep south-facing slopes, apparently not at all concerned about getting down to lower elevations where you'd expect them to go when faced with snow.

Before Herbie had got the last Scout home, he'd decided where he was going to hunt when the next snow fell. His Eastern whitetails were no fools, he wrote; they didn't like to wallow through deep snow. So they found places where snow dissipated the fastest—steep open slopes facing south or west.

Herbie has a way of making things sound very simple and straightforward, but I had my doubts. Those high, open slopes might be sunny, but they were also windy. Without any cover, whitetails weren't going to set up permanent housekeeping with a stiff wind knocking down their ears.

⊷⊶⊹⊷⊶

I WROTE HERBIE about my doubts, but before I got an answer, some Western whitetails showed me they were just as smart as those back East.

It was two days after the first good snow of the hunting season, just long enough, I hoped, to have pushed some elk down out of the alpine bowls into the foothills where they'd be easier to hunt. But after five hours of slogging through snow, I hadn't even crossed an elk *track.*

The fastest route back to my truck took me through an old stand of fir on the east slope of the ridge I'd been working and then opened out onto a steep meadow on the west side before descending a half-mile to the creek and the gravel road.

I spooked the whitetails at the top of the meadow— two bucks bedded down in the sage and grass where the snow was the shallowest I'd seen all day.

I thought of Herbie. Although no wind was blowing, I knew that all the whitetails would have to do for cover was walk over the ridge into the natural windbreak of the old-growth fir that I'd just come through. The move might take them a couple of minutes at the most. The deer could easily

move about and browse on sage and snowberry in the shallow snow on the steep west slope and still have quick access to shelter and escape cover on the forested east side.

In my head, I was composing a letter to Herbie when a hunter stopped by my truck to admire the buck I was wrestling into the back. He'd been hunting all day along the creek looking for whitetails that he thought would be pushed lower by the snow. He hadn't seen any deer. When he asked where I'd found the buck, I waved vaguely upstream and mumbled something about having hunted a little higher.

My letter to Herbie was short. I told him our whitetails out West are smart too; I had an "up high" whitetail hung in the barn to prove it. As for the wind thing, I told Herbie Western whitetails knew exactly how to handle that. I couldn't resist ending my letter with: "How do *your* whitetails cope with the wind on those high, open slopes?"

It was a month before I heard from Herbie. He'd clipped a note to a copy of a twelve-year-old article from the *New York Fish and Game Journal.* The note read: "Got a 10-point on top of Mount Homer. Please read the enclosed. Guess we aren't the first ones to figure out what those tricky whitetails are up to."

The article, by Nathaniel Dickinson, was titled "Observations on Steep-Slope Deer Wintering Areas in New York and Vermont." It spilled the wind out of my and Herbie's sails because it let us know that what we thought we'd discovered about whitetails had already been recognized by someone else.

It appears the whitetails all through New York and Vermont and other hilly states where it snows (even western states, Herbie) often move up to steep southern, southwestern, and western exposures to get away from deep snow. Where whitetails in the West can find easy protection from wind in nearby north or east slope stands of fir, Eastern whitetails can slip into the cover of hemlock and white pine on slopes of the same aspect. (Herbie had underlined this part of the article.) These trees also provide forage for deer, along with foods such as striped maple and witch hobble that grow on the sunnier slopes.

⊷⊶⊹⊷⊶

THE ELEVATIONS OF these up-high whitetail gathering grounds may be from a thousand to several thousand feet in the East. The steeper the slopes, the more use they seem to get, because the rays of the sun shine more directly on these areas and melt the snow faster. In the West, elevations are more difficult to pinpoint. However, whitetails often move 1,000 to 1,500 feet up into the foothills that border the creek and river bottoms where you'd expect them to seek refuge from the snow.

Because the quickest access to north- and east-slope cover is found at the tops of hills and ridges, this is where the deer tend to congregate. It suggests some specific hunting tactics that even Herbie and I agree upon.

Since daybreak and dusk are the best times to catch whitetails out on these slopes (especially during hunting season) these are the times to take a stand near the tops of the hills or ridges. Timber edges and rocky ledges are good spots to post when the hillside is mainly open. Sometimes, however, these southern slopes are covered with sparse tim-

ber that will allow you to conceal yourself at a number of good vantage points, depending on the wind and the lay of the land.

During windy days, the deer will probably take shorter forays into the open to forage, but they will make more frequent trips, and they may continue their comings and goings later in the morning and start earlier in the afternoon than they would on a calm day. The increased whitetail movement is to your advantage. But sitting out in the wind may call for packing along an extra layer or two of warmth.

By midday the deer will probably be back in the cover of north- and east-slope timber. Where the cover is sparse and allows snow to accumulate readily, whitetails won't go far down the slopes, especially if snow gets much over a foot deep. Just a short way into the forest, they usually seek out snow "wells" at the base of trees where snow depths are shallowest and where wind protection and thermal cover are greatest. Along these north- and east-slope forest borders a skillful still-hunter can find whitetails in their beds during the middle of the day.

However, where thick old-growth timber prevents a great deal of snow from reaching the forest floor, the deer may range quite a distance back into the cover, making it more difficult for a still-hunter to know where to concentrate his efforts.

Although the tops of steep slopes usually get the most whitetail use when it's snowy, don't overlook other adjoining areas, especially if they have some cover. The sides and the bottoms of steep sunny hillsides may also have vegetative and topographic features that block wind and provide good places for deer to hide.

Because these up-high whitetail refuges from the snow are often visible from considerable distances, scouting likely looking areas with binoculars or spotting scopes can save you a lot of leg work and time.

Herbie doesn't always do things the easy way, however. He has already planned another trip for his Scouts for this fall. He calls it his annual Scouting outing, but I know it's more than a Boy Scouting trip. It will be a *deer* scouting trip, too. He'll be looking for those up-high whitetails.

I think I'll write to Herbie and tell him I've discovered our Western whitetails have started climbing trees to get away from the snow.

By John Barsness

Ways of the WESTERN WHITETAIL

THE DEER OF THE HARDWOOD RIDGES AND THE TRUCK FARMS ARE ALSO THE DEER OF THE PRAIRIES AND THE VAST, FLAT RIVER BOTTOMS, AND THE FOOTHILLS OF THE ROCKIES.

*L*OOK DISTANTLY, ACROSS THE river bottom. The flat land below could be anywhere—Arkansas, Minnesota, Pennsylvania—the brown meander of the big stream bordered by thick timber, leaves just turning, the lines of trees edged by square after square of alfalfa or corn or "amber waves of grain." Between the squares run dusty lanes that lead to turn-of-the-century frame houses surrounded by red farm machinery, barns, corrals made of rough-sawn lumber, and chickens scratching in the dust.

As the evening shadows from the trees ease the heat, a family sits in back of the nearest, white-peeling house, eating barbecued chicken, perhaps, with fresh corn and toma-toes from the garden. It must be edging into fall; otherwise they'd be eating inside the screened porch, away from the mosquitoes. Feeling a little guilty about such eavesdropping (though even through 7X binoculars you can see little more than white shirts back under the cottonwood shadows), you lower the glasses.

As you look closely at your feet to ease the strain of long watching, you realize this place couldn't be mistaken for Arkansas or Minnesota or Pennsylvania, because beneath the giant sandstone mushroom you sit on—3 tons of sea bottom left from perhaps 50 million years ago—prickly pear and yucca and sagebrush slant off toward the edge of the bluff. A white-tailed jackrabbit moves slowly out of the sage shadows, its huge ears laid back as it watches a ferruginous hawk circling a mile away along the jumbled edge of the badlands that border the broad river bottom, which extends as far as you or the jackrabbit or the hawk can see.

The sun eases down another slow notch and you lift the glasses again. There, to the right and beyond the farmhouse, in the intense green of an alfalfa field, six reddish rectangles move out from the timber, away from the river. Occasionally you catch the flicker of movement at either end of each rectangle, and you wait. Three more, no, four, move from the haybales, and the sun moves downward, shadowing the edges of the cottonwoods. Another rectangle pauses in the blue shadows under the trees, a rectangle twice the size and clarity of your binocular's lenses, antlers sweeping up and back along the outer edge of the ears, bone still creamy, not yet stained by the skinning of trees. Your heart does hunted jackrabbit things though you are the hunter here, looking across the Dakota river bottom at what you are seeking: the Dakota subspecies of the whitetail deer.

I stopped by the farmhouse at 1 P.M. the next day, hoping to find the landowner at home, but hoping not to interrupt his meal. He didn't quite remember my name—

we'd met just once before, introduced by a friend, a cousin of this man, and at the time I hadn't been wearing camouflage. But his handshake was firm, the calluses along his palm leaving small impressions on my softer hand, and he said sure, go out and hunt that field. Just park on this side of the irrigation ditch, because there's some pipes out there in the alfalfa that wouldn't be helped by eight-ply truck tires.

Four hours later, I approached the haystack from the backside, away from the timber. I made a rough staircase out of six bales and climbed to the top. Several bales had been taken from the side of the stack facing the timber, their absence forming a little platform, so I placed three more bales around the edge of the platform, forming a blind, then lay back against the sun-warmed hay, took an arrow from the bow quiver, nocked it, then placed the bow at my feet. Flies occasionally buzzed around my painted face, and sweat tickled my neck, but still it felt a lot more comfortable than the beginning of bow season

three weeks earlier, when the still-irrigated fields gave off clouds of humidity and mosquitoes. Those who think of Western big-game hunting as days of riding horses through snowy mountains have never lain in a hayfield irrigation ditch in early September, with mosquitoes flying into their earholes and sweat, mixed with face paint, dripping into their mouths.

It was just a few miles upstream that a Montana game biologist, in the cool rain of June, had shown me stands of timber where he'd counted seventy whitetail deer per square mile—meaning that any tree stand erected in that area should have a deer within 100 yards. Here, just across the state border in North Dakota, he thought there might be even more deer, something I kept in mind as another fly landed on my drooping eyelid. In fact, there are hundreds of whitetail deer along all the big Western rivers and their tributaries; even the ranchers along the lower Big Hole Valley, hard against the high mountains of the Continental Divide, complain that whitetails are eating them out of house and hay. The state game department keeps awarding more and more antlerless permits, and the hunters in the haystacks of the Big Hole say the deer come out in the evening like— well, like jackrabbits.

The deer create trails that could be mistaken for cattle paths, leave the hayfields trampled but enriched with the soft droppings of summer, and in general insinuate themselves so far into the Western landscape that they, not buffalo, might be the new symbol of the high plains. But even with so many deer, the bigger bucks aren't common, because although these are supposedly naive whitetails, there is really no such thing. That's why I sat on the balanced sandstone knob the evening before, searching 4 square miles of bottomland for one of the 250-odd deer living there, hopefully one that grew big antlers.

And even then I blew it, perhaps because after being eaten for three hours by flies I felt the need for some sustenance, something from this land to put back the protein that had been taken away. A half hour before sunset, my back itching like a shedding buffalo bull's, microscopic bits of hay sticking to my sweaty face like a layer of tiny spider legs, four does and their assembled young moved out into the field. They kept moving, their heads dipping to feed then jerking upright, bobbing in the sea of alfalfa like giant red-brown mallards in a green pond. I waited, one doe feeding within 30 yards, and the sun sank slowly and my back itched and the buck never came. Eventually, twenty deer were feeding in the field around my haystack, none of them antlered, and as the sun touched the top of the badlands to the west I decided, in one itchy instant, to take the nearest doe. In that same instant my lazy heart began to shake, and as I held the bowstring against my mouth and tried to make the bowsight dance just behind her shoulder, even as the arrow flew, I knew somehow that I'd made the wrong choice. The arrow went through the top of her right ear, catching on the fletching, and she crabhopped sideways, shaking her ears, the arrow flipping around her head. The heads of all the deer in the field came up, staring, and the doe shook her head once more, then ran toward the timber. Beyond her for just a moment, above the high rosebushes that bordered the field, I saw the head of the buck like a face at a window, his antlers shaped like the white frame of a heart, and then he was gone. The doe shook her head at the edge of the roses and the arrow fell out. That was almost a decade ago; maybe now I could go back and do it right.

Just a few miles back from the rivers, the land becomes a mosaic of dendritic havens, the winding veins of the land holding thigh-deep rosebushes and dwarf ash and occasional patches of chokecherry and serviceberry, tiny "forests" where whitetails hide until the hills rise too far above the rivers—or wander too far west into the rainshadow of the Rockies—and the cover thins. Such land becomes home for mule deer and pronghorns.

There aren't as many upland, open-country whitetails as river-bottom deer—my biologist acquaintance counts only as many as a dozen per square mile—but they seem more common, perhaps because their few hiding places between the shortgrass hills are so recognizable. This is especially true in early fall, when the leaves are still on the serviceberry bushes and heat keeps deer in the shade. But once the leaves drop, the big deer hide in places almost incomprehensible to hunters from Minnesota and Pennsylvania, like the sinuous depression in the middle of a flat expanse of knee-high roses. It's odd to occasionally realize that the branches sticking above that bowling-green expanse aren't a dead chokecherry but rather the antlers of a whitetail buck that's watching you, its eyes level with the roses. The deer will bed in uncut dryland wheat, or the piles of glacial rocks that farmers gather from their fields. The rocks form a haven for weeds and brush and desert cottontails—and sometimes a whitetail buck, which jumps and runs across the dry earth, kicking up dust clouds like some antlered version of the Pony Express.

The common hunting method in that country is to drive around, hunting all the likely spots, until some piece of cover spews forth a buck, usually with the aid of a few well-placed rocks. I killed a few bucks that way, after practicing running shots on tires rolled down hillsides, but after a while the method came to seem imprecise, as if I were taking part in some sort of prairie lottery.

That's why I remember my last upland whitetail best. He came on a cool morning in late October, one of those perfect days between the first frosts and leaden November snowstorms, when wisps of high cirrus clouds seem to turn above you as you turn, like the Hide-Behind in Paul Bunyan stories, always pulling at the corners of your vision. The sun was just barely up, slanting beneath the clouds, as if the earth and clouds formed layers that trapped the light, both cirrus and shortgrass backlit by thick orange. I hunted the border of a big plateau, the edge dropping off in shortwicked coulees filled with buffaloberry, heading toward a tributary of the Missouri 3 miles away. I hoped to catch a buck "standing up," feeding in the low serviceberry patches at the edge of the plateau, above the raw badlands. I'd ease up one small ridge, glass quickly, then cross the coulee below and climb to my next vantage point, leaving precise footprints in the dewy, shallow sand, prints that seemed as

if they'd either disappear in the midday breeze or stay forever—nothing in between.

The buck and a doe were already dropping off the plateau edge when I saw them, perhaps three coulees over. We were all in little swales just below the flattest land, the beginnings of the deep draws, the deer visible from the knees up, almost luminous in the thick low light. Beyond them a triangular butte, banded by a line of coal, caught the same light. The range seemed all of 300 yards, and when I lay in the grass, sling tight, I held the crosshairs of the .270 steady on the upper half of the buck's chest. At the shot he leaped forward, heading down the slope, the doe following. I found him in the brush below; the distance must have been a bit farther, perhaps 350 yards, because the bullet just barely caught his heart. It's always seemed rather odd to me that the longest shot I've ever made on a deer didn't kill a mule deer, but a whitetail.

I learned to hunt whitetails on the riverbottoms and prairies, so when, like the early explorers and fur traders, I followed the big rivers toward the Shining Mountains and first encountered foothills whitetails, they puzzled me, for how was a prairie hunter to hunt when he couldn't glass? Once in a while there'd be a bare south slope where someone could sit and hope for a young deer to show himself, but the larger bucks in the canyons and draws of the Bitterroots and Absarokas seemed impervious to my hunting methods. Even tree stands were of no use, because these whitetails usually lived in the steepest, noisiest draws, where even a midday approach to a carefully placed portable stand betrayed me to every deer on the mountain.

———— ✦⊠✦ ————

AND THEN ONE summer I ran into a prairie hunter who said he liked to rattle up bucks, something I'd half-heartedly tried a few times with no results. But that fall I got a good pair of "horns" and went up to the National Bison Range after reading everything I could find on the subject. It was November 18, just after the peak of the rut, and in one morning of rattling I brought in five bucks, one from a half mile away. Now, admittedly these were "tame" bucks, but even the Bison Range's bucks are rarely seen except during the rut, preferring instead to hang out in thick cover along Mission Creek. I fiddled around with various techniques until I had it reasonably right; the only problem was that my tag had already been filled on a mule deer.

The next November came as one of the coldest on record throughout most of Montana, weather more like January, with nightly lows of 20 and 30 below, and midday seeming nice if it hit 10 above. My wife, Eileen, and I camped up Rock Creek on the 13th during one of those nicer moons, up the road from a cottonwood flat. Above the cottonwoods, the hillside rose across a talus slide for 100 feet—an approach as noisy as New Year's Eve—before flattening out into a pine and aspen pocket that ran perhaps a quarter mile across, leading to an avalanche chute which extended to the top of the mountain. We scouted quickly along the mountain's base, in the alders below the talus, and then searched the paths between the cottonwoods. Our

effort yielded innumerable small tracks and one set of prints as long and splayed almost as wide as my palm, but no scrapes. I suspected the scrapes were in the pocket above; since there was no way to get close, we flagged a couple of likely deadfalls for blinds, then glassed the hillside from a half mile away that evening, trying to perceive movement. We saw only one doe feeding on the edge of the aspens below.

And yet in the morning, after the ice had built another inch across the bottom of the fast creek, there were fresh tracks on the road as we waddled, swathed in wool and down, to our flags. I used the flashlight sparingly, because a buck could be watching from the hill above.

Eileen went into the timber 200 yards above my trail, moving very slowly through the starlit snow and trees. She said later that she figured if she survived that morning, that hour and a half of sitting on a dead tree as the cold deepened with the rising sun, she could survive another few years with me. I sat and wondered many things, mostly about ice and mortality. Luckily my watch didn't freeze, and at the legal hour I took the horns from around my neck and held them firmly, glad to have something solid to wiggle my fingers around, and brought them together twice, hard, then paused as if two bucks had backed off. I crashed them together again, grinding the notches between the tines, the hard cold making the sound seem to leap out from the brown bone almost too loudly, echoing off the talus above. I waited as long as I could, and when my fingers began to numb through the heavy gloves, I rattled again, then waited some more. I thought I heard something in the ghostly light, as if the earth had cracked just a bit. I heard nothing more until the buck snorted behind a line of willows perhaps 40 feet away, and then I heard him walking beyond the brush. I saw his antler tips once between the slender gray branches, then heard him cross the talus, far to my left and out of sight.

The buck had crossed behind another lie of willows 30 feet from Eileen. She heard him, but saw only one foot before he walked up to the sound of the horns, probably standing behind the willows until my scent pool edged into his nose and he snorted. We backtracked his line down the mountain and found where he'd come out of the trees above, where we'd seen the doe the evening before.

Maybe this fall I can go back and do it right.

By Norman Strung

The First Snow of
AUTUMN

WITH THE CHANGE OF SEASON COMES THE PROMISE OF RENEWAL AND THE CHANCE TO SEE THE WORLD IN A WHOLE NEW LIGHT.

THE FALL OF '87 WAS ONE OF the driest on record in the West. Arrowleaf crackled underfoot like rice paper, temperatures that should have hovered close to freezing hit 60 every day, and meadowlarks were still warbling in November.

It didn't feel like big-game season, and I didn't feel like hunting; but deer and elk represent sustenance as much as sport to my wife and me, and the weather patterns that caused the drought showed no signs of abating.

Two, perhaps three, times a week I would course the mountainsides that rise above our cabin and return sweaty, discouraged, and emptyhanded. The sighting of so much as a doe was cause for celebration; the woods seemed barren, boring, and without promise.

Then, one mid-November night it snowed. It was not a heavy fall, but upon awakening that morning, there was palpable change in the air. It smelled swept clean and new, and for the first time that season I felt the electricity of anticipation. When I struck the woods there was a new snap to my step.

I crossed my first trail at sunrise, and a half hour later I had four muley does and fawns in my sights.

They were feeding beneath a big Douglas fir on a south-facing slope, and they never saw me. I left them and went over the ridge, striking the trail of a good-sized herd a mile away.

When I caught up with the deer, they were bedded down at the head of a black coulee. A doe jumped up, and led eight does and fawns by me. They passed one by one through a gap in the timber like sheep jumping a fence. A forkhorn brought up the rear, and I considered taking him, but declined. I wanted a heavier animal.

As noon approached, my legs began to tire. I turned homeward, working downslope on a gentle incline that led me over a series of terraces and through dark pine hollows. I slipped up on two other skinheads who never knew I was there and killed a four-pointer where the forest met the canyon floor.

On that one day I had seen more deer than during the previous three weeks of hard hunting. The temptation is to owe their sudden appearance to migration, but the snow depths were insufficient to create the kinds of conditions in the high country that would force game into the lowlands. The deer had actually been around all season long; it just took a little snow for me to see them.

There are both physiological and psychological reasons why this happens. Most important is the effect the first snow of the year has upon a deer's perception of critical zones.

Most whitetails and muleys develop a sixth sense regarding how close they will allow a human to approach before becoming evasive. This critical zone amounts to a circle of terrain and its diameter varies with the kind of cover they inhabit—the thicker the vegetation, the tighter the circle. Critical zones are largely determined by a visual limit called the forest curtain. This is the distance you and they can normally see into the forest. It is not a wall, but more like a veil, a gauzy haze of brush and trees. At the inner limit of the curtain you can see objects clearly. At its outer limit everything is obscured. However, between those two points, a sharp eye can usually pick out the ill-defined form of a deer.

Perhaps taught by the actions of older deer, or by signals of human recognition—hunters or hikers staring, pointing, yelling, making excited motions, or shooting—

deer learn at what point within that curtain is safe to watch a walking hunter without being seen. Snow, because it reflects flat light into the darkest woodland corners, and because of the contrast it provides, moves the forest curtain back. But deer don't realize that at first—remember, the animals have spent six to eight snow-free months with the woods on their side, warned by sounds and scents and hidden in dappled shadow patterns—and as a result, they stay put and are easier to spot.

Even light snow cover can short-circuit a deer's early warning system: it muffles and absorbs the sound and shock of footfalls, helps cover and diffuse human scent, and silhouettes the deer's telltale outline. All in all, the first snow of autumn brings a dramatic change in a deer's environment that the animal is unprepared to cope with and that makes it much easier to hunt.

On the other side of the prey/predator relationship, snow has a positive effect on hunters and their habits. Perhaps the visual change wrought by a blanket of white suggests to our subconscious that the slate has been wiped clean. Perhaps it is the invigorating effect of cold, crisp air. Whatever the reason, the sight of fresh snow seems to call up a new reserve of human energy and resolve. You are more eager, more confident, and, as a result, you hunt harder.

Tracks play a part, too. Not so much because they lead directly to game, but because a fresh track is incontrovertible evidence that a deer passed that way recently and that it is somewhere nearby. Cutting tracks pumps you up psychologically. It keens your senses and forces all of them to focus upon one thing—serious hunting—and that edge often accounts for the difference between success and failure.

I remember one particular fall—back when I was a guide and outfitter—when the weather conditions were similar to those I experienced in 1987. Indian summer lingered like a curse, and except for the flurry of activity that always occurs on opening day, the meatpole behind camp held neither elk nor deer week after week.

Many times watching a football or baseball game, I have sensed a lack of spirit on the part of the losing team. It is not an identifiable fault or flaw, just a kind of negative aura that hangs over the heads of the players and the way they execute their parts. An equivalent dark cloud hung over my clients every day we went up into the mountains, an overbearing sense of "the game is already lost."

Then one morning we awakened to three inches of snow that had flurried in during the night. I can still recall stepping out of my tent to greet that day. The scattering clouds were tinted pink by the first rays of the rising sun and they wreathed the distant peaks like cotton candy. Snow clung to every branch and bough so lightly that it seemed a sharp breath would blow it all away. Suddenly it was a whole new ball game.

Like a key play that sparks a rally, you could feel a change at the breakfast table. Conversation was more animated, everyone ate with more gusto, and where clients had lingered over their coffee before, they now left the table to get suited up immediately.

The presence of tracks urged them deeper into the timber that day. They complained less about being winded and tired. They went the extra yard, and that afternoon we shot a fine muley buck, then a spike elk the next morning, and the rest of the week went well.

Although a fresh snowfall is a powerful ally, hunters do need to adapt to some of the changes it brings about. It's always a good idea to use binoculars when big-game hunting, but it's a virtual necessity when there's new snow.

Clinging to boughs, branches, and the trunks of fallen trees, cottony snow combines with the forest tones to create the illusion of an animal—the right balance and shape of white, brown, gray, or buff that suggests things like the white throat patch on a whitetail or muley, or the butt of an elk. With a pair of binoculars, these illusions can be sorted out quickly. Before I got that figured out, I spent a lot of time stalking stumps or, more embarrassing, watched the object I had positively identified as a blow-down get up and run away.

Wool pants, recommended hunting apparel because they are quiet, are a must when hunting in snow. Every other material forms ice around the cuffs, which then whiff and wheeze as you walk, warning every creature within earshot. Wool stays supple and soft.

Lastly, I have found that game learns to adjust quickly to the changes brought about by the first snow: the harder they are hunted, the sooner they extend the critical zones to encompass the new forest curtain. Hunting the same area with no competition, I figure I have four days before whitetails or muleys move farther back into the brush. In heavily hunted areas, I've seen them do it the second day.

When that happens, if I have the gift of time, I hang up my rifle until a truly severe storm blows in from the North, with all the physical stresses attendant to knee-deep snow and bitter cold. That kind of a snow changes game habits once again, and in other ways. But that is yet another story.

By Sam Curtis

Early-Bird
WHITETAILS

You've got to get up pretty early in the morning to fool a whitetail buck.

I SUPPOSE EVERY KID LEARNING to hunt whitetails had some old duffer tell him at one time or another that the best time for hunting is during dawn and dusk. But by the time you reach my age, you've heard that axiom so often, and you've gotten so many whitetails at other times of day, that you begin to question its wisdom.

So, presumptuous as it may seem, I'd like to suggest being even more specific and say that the best time to hunt whitetails is between 6:00 and 8:00 in the morning.

One of the reasons I make this recommendation is that over several decades of hunting and observing deer those are the two hours of the day I've seen the most whitetails. Another reason, and probably the more convincing, is that a number of tracking studies have concluded that in the fall (during hunting season) whitetails are more active than at any other time of year, and are most active between 6 and 8 A.M.

I would also add that a whitetail on the move is probably the easiest whitetail to hunt.

So what's the story? Why would whitetails want to move around the most early on a fall morning?

Generally speaking, it has to do with fall as a time of changes—changes in weather, changes in food, changes in hormones. And movement is a response to those changes.

In the fall, weather is in transition. Where I live the harbinger of winter comes with an equinoctial storm that hits like clockwork between September 1 and 10. Suddenly, the warmth of summer is broken by two or three days of temperatures in the 30s accompanied by snow or rain on the verge of snow.

That storm has an effect like no other storm of the year. My neighbors and I start the final harvesting of our gardens, hurry to get in firewood, and run around trying to finish outside projects. The days may turn warm and balmy after that first storm, but we know winter will close down around us very soon. We want to be ready.

The response of whitetails is very much the same. Summer is a lazy time for them. They have plenty of forage and don't have to worry about the weather. But with a hint of winter in the air, deer go on the move to stock up on food to make body fat for the lean months ahead.

As fall progresses, morning temperatures get cooler, often reaching lows just before dawn when radiant heat loss from the ground is at its greatest. This nippy morning air, combined with increased wind caused by the rising sun, stirs deer from their beds. Movement and food help raise their body temperatures and chase the chills away. The approach of dawn with its increasing light also has an energizing effect. The deer can see better so they start to move around more.

Then there are the changing locations of the most nutritious deer foods. All summer whitetails have had their pick of a wide variety of foods within a relatively limited area. But as grasses and forbs dry out or get frosted in the fall, the best foods are fewer and farther apart. Whitetails go on the move to find acorns, beechnuts, and other mast crops that are beginning to fall to the ground. They search out fruits such as apples, grapes, and cherries, and head for agricultural lands where nutritious leftovers remain even after harvest.

Morning is the prime time for food-related movement, and whitetails really do move when they eat. Rarely do you see deer standing for any length of time in one spot to feed. They take a bite here and then move on several steps to take a bite of something else.

This food-related activity is even more pronounced if one of their fall staples is in short supply. In areas where the annual acorn crop is poor, whitetails may be more visibly active than usual because they are forced to leave the cover of trees and spend more time out in the open where cultivated crops provide the best food.

Because of the restricted availability of food in the fall, whitetails will go to considerable distances to get choice foods. For instance, two ancient apple trees provide a limited source of high-powered food in an area I like to hunt in the morning. The trees are in the middle of a field ⅛ mile from the nearest cover. Local whitetails come from up to a mile away—usually in the early morning—to get at the apples on the ground and on branches within their reach. Often I will see a number of them moving in single file over well-worn trails to get to these trees.

Whitetails often use one part of their range at night and another part during the day. Typically, they'll frequent open areas at night under cover of darkness. In the morning, they move to safer wooded or brushy areas. If the ter-

rain is hilly, deer may spend their days at higher elevations and come down to lower-lying land to feed at night.

The hours between 6 and 8 A.M. represent the height of the morning deer traffic going between bedding and feeding sites. In some habitats this may only be a matter of moving a few hundred yards. In other places the deer may move up to a mile.

While all deer are active on fall mornings, bucks are the most active because of the influence of the rut. Hormones drive them to find females. They're on the move to freshen scrapes and check them for doe scent, and to follow doe trails. And sometimes bucks move simply because the more they move, the greater the chance of bumping into a female.

The home range of a buck is greater in the fall than at any other time of year. So he is traveling greater distances in an attempt to check the entire area for receptive does.

The rut can cause some bucks to do crazy things. But there are a fair share of males—the ones that grow to be trophies—that spend much of the day undercover despite the passion in their veins. These old veterans chase does all night, and by early morning—say between 6 and 8 A.M.—they move off to some remote patch of marginal habitat. There they spend the day hiding from hunters until after dark when they go on the move again.

I was once alerted to the presence of such a buck by his big tracks in the dirt of a moist draw. It was at the height of the rut, and other bucks were out and about in the full light of day. But I knew this fellow only by the hoofprints he left. Then one morning I decided to take a stand by his tracks.

Just before 7:00 I saw the buck moving at a steady pace up through the aspens. He was in a poor position for a good shot, so I was back at the same spot that evening. I stayed until the end of hunting hours without seeing the buck again. But the next morning at 6:30 he was moving out of the bottomlands toward some secret daytime hideaway. And I was situated perfectly.

Hunting these early-bird whitetails is best done from a stand or by standing or sitting still. The deer are going to be on the move, so you shouldn't be. If you are in a good spot, the deer will come to you.

The best locations for taking a stand in the morning have to be keyed into what the deer are likely to be doing at

that time. In the case of the big buck in rut, the tracks were the tipoff to a good place to stand. The tracks might have been made at any time of day, but because they led from bottomland to higher elevations, they were probably made on morning moves to the buck's hideaway. And, because of the whitetail's habit of making trail networks and using them frequently, numerous fresh tracks are also indicators of a good stand location. But they may only be useful to the early-bird hunter if they connect feeding and bedding sites.

Your best bet is to locate choice fall foods—things such as nuts and fruits—and then look for trails radiating out from these prime feeding locations.

You don't want to put a stand too close to these areas for fear of spooking deer before you even get to the stand. So, stay back a few hundred yards from obvious food sources if possible. It's also wise to stay back somewhat from the trails themselves. You may be well hidden and per-fectly silent, but your scent can make deer disappear if you're too close to where they walk.

Don't ever try to place a stand or find a good spot for one on the same morning you want to use it. The successful early-bird stand requires some advanced planning. Scouting out a stand location can be done days in advance, but make sure the deer have first settled into their fall patterns of habitat use. Lots of changes can take place between August and October.

PERHAPS THE GREATEST tactical problem after locating an early-bird whitetail stand is to get to it in the dark, since you should be in the stand well before shooting hours in order to let things quiet down after your arrival. Decide on the specific route you're going to take. You may even want to remove snags and downfalls from the path. The route should be as direct as possible without going right through areas that whitetails are likely to be using at that time of day.

To get into your stand, don't be afraid to use a small flashlight, keeping it pointed at the ground directly in front of you. While using a flashlight I have passed deer in the darkness, and they have either remained motionless or sim-ply moved off a few yards. Then I've been able to get into my stand and sit quietly awaiting the time when whitetails really do go on the move—6 to 8 A.M.—the whitetail hours. Try them.

By Christopher Michaels

Living with
WHITETAILS

BY OBSERVING DEER EVERY DAY AND WATCHING THEM CLOSELY, YOU LEARN THINGS OTHER HUNTERS NEVER DREAM OF.

ON A BRIGHT FALL AFTERNOON the day before deer season opened several years ago, I sat in my office, working and intermittently looking out the windows, observing two whitetail deer that were combing the areas under oak trees in our yard. Curious about what they were after, I picked up a pair of binoculars.

Under the oaks, I discovered clusters of large, fat, brown bolete mushrooms had pushed up. Boletes are of several species, most of them edible and delicious to humans as well as deer. In numerous areas they are among the most abundant fall mushrooms. The deer, out foraging in broad daylight, seemed to know the boletes would not last long. Some would quickly decay, and insects would riddle others. Various mushrooms, I knew, were relished by deer; as one hunter friend puts it, they serve as a kind of seasonal dessert.

As I watched, I was envisioning horse trails along woods edges on our ranch, a remote piece of land 20 miles from our home place, where my office is. Deer regularly follow the trails made by horses. During falls when boletes are abundant, these mushrooms invariably spring up in patches and rows along the travel routes. If boletes were appearing right now in our yard, they were undoubtedly popping up along those trails on the ranch.

The next morning at dawn I was out there on a stand where I could scan one of the trails, having verified the previous evening that indeed the bolete crop was showing abundantly here. Signs indicated that some early ones had been eaten. Ample numbers were left, and probably more would appear before morning. At exactly 8:00 A.M., a fat forkhorn came tripping along the trail, picking off boletes as he traveled. Shortly after, he was hanging from the meat pole in our old creekside camp.

Obviously this is not an experience one is likely to repeat year after year. But what it demonstrates is that close and constant observation of deer may turn up deer habits that can be applied to hunting. For more than twenty-five years I have practically lived with whitetails. Hardly a day passes when I'm home that I don't have the opportunity to watch and wonder about what the deer are doing. Our home place consists of 27 heavily wooded acres, with two ponds. For years, subdivisions from our nearby growing city have been crowding in on the area. Our land has become a kind of oasis for resident deer. Year after year we have from six to a dozen. They wander off this reservation at night, but most of their lives are spent in our small woods because all around us the cover has been stripped.

Although we give these deer supplemental feed in winter and during droughty summers, they're not tame. We purposely avoid trying to make them so. Thus I can observe wild whitetails on a small range, day after day. One lesson I've learned from this constant contact is to be wary of pronouncements on the nature of whitetails, whether from biologists who do studies or oldtimey hunters who claim to know all about deer.

Much *has* been learned by specific research, but deer are infinitely complicated creatures, and the "final secrets" of whitetail behavior and hunting success are still being learned. Just when you begin to think you have whitetail lore down pat, some behavior will astonish you, and try as you might, you won't be able to explain the why of it.

For instance, in the hilly country where we live, we get abominable TV reception most of the time, and have no opportunity for cable hookup. One noon I switched on the TV to watch the news, and here was a sharp, clear, stable picture. We were into one of our "good TV" periods, which usually last two or three days.

I happened to look out the window while the news was on, and saw deer wandering all over the yard. Suddenly I wondered: was there some correlation? The following noon, a Friday, I switched on the TV, found the picture still sharp. Again the deer were moving around. That evening both my sons got home for a hunt down on the ranch the next day. I told them about the TV and the noon activity of the deer. When they came back from the ranch on Sunday evening, they related that deer had moved most of the day, both days. They each had easily filled tags. Monday noon I checked the TV. Bad. I also checked the deer. Not a one showed.

I don't pretend to know what relationship there is between excellent non-cable TV reception and deer movement. The TV service people blame both good and bad reception on "atmospheric conditions," whatever that means. I do know that further checks over several seasons showed that the phenomenon occurred quite consistently. We always try nowadays to get a chance to hunt on good TV days, and are seldom disappointed with deer movement.

One of the problems with patterning your hunting on research is that it may not be universally applicable. This is not to put down research, but only to caution you about accepting any too-pat theories as your bible.

I recall some years ago a study done in the East "proving" that whitetail deer do not eat grass. Following it, one writer rehashed the report and warned hunters to shy from grassy situations and hunt only where browse was available. In my area. where deer and Bermuda grass are both abundant, it is not unusual to see several dozen deer gorging themselves in fall on lush and succulent Bermuda. Where the study was done, the statement that deer don't eat grass might have been valid, but not where I live. "Always" and "everywhere" take in a *lot* of territory. What's important is to know the habits of deer in *your* area.

As an example, on numerous occasions in fall when the rut is starting, I've had opportunity to watch a buck making a scrape. Recently, near dusk, I saw a six-pointer within 60 steps of the kitchen windows. A wide-spreading live oak there has some branches that droop to within less than 4 feet of the ground. The buck reached up to nuzzle twigs and leaves on a branch and gently stroke them with his antler tips, then began to paw out a scrape.

Later he fiddled with a large cedar, nuzzling and stroking it with his antlers, but he did not paw the ground. I have checked scrapes many times in our area, and seldom are they made anywhere except under live oaks, where a branch droops within nuzzling reach. Never have I found one under a Texas cedar. Both trees are tremendously abundant in my area. When I set out to look for scrapes, I check the live oaks. It's a shortcut, quite often, to a successful hunt.

Whitetails are also selective, my home-place observations have taught me, about what tree or shrub species they use for rubs. We watch for rubs here at home to keep a check on where the bucks are hanging out, hoping they don't move off the reservation and get shot. With few exceptions they select small cedars—actually Ashe junipers. On the ranch, that's where we search for rubs of bucks we hope to get a chance to shoot.

But I carried rub observations farther. I remembered that in northern Michigan, where I once lived, most deer used small balsams for rubbing. However, I once found an area there where witch hazel bushes were abundant, and for some reason bucks used those, in that location, more than they used conifers. Out of curiosity about whether Texas deer would do something similar, I scoured our home place, seeking rubs on other than cedars. One hillside has an abundance of Texas persimmon, a tough, smooth-barked shrub. I discovered that our home bucks often made rubs on these. I thereafter scanned persimmon patches on the ranch because there were

not many of these, but thousands of cedars. I caught a buck in the act and whacked him. Once more what I'd learned by living with deer had paid off.

Not many hunters will have a situation comparable to mine for deer watching. Most can, however, find public lands, even wildlife refuges (which are often excellent locations), where they can make a hobby of observing deer off and on all year. Fall and winter are the best times, because deer habits change with the seasons. Months that coincide with or bracket open season will be prime times for learning much that will apply to hunting success.

Always be alert for unique activities. You can bone up on basics by reading books and magazines. A classic example of what I have in mind concerns two gems learned from deer in our yard. Whenever there is unusual deer activity during daylight hours, I always try to ferret out what may have caused it. Several years ago during a time when the deer seemed especially active much of the day for several days in a row, I was browsing through an almanac and suddenly realized that these activity days had fallen during and immediately after the equinox.

This got me fired up and wondering also about what might happen during the winter solstice. Sure enough, the same kind of activity occurred. We've checked these periods on the ranch for several years, and so far, deer movement has matched that of the home deer.

The amount of *movement* of deer is directly related to hunter success. The more they move, the more they are visible, and the higher hunters score. The greatest amount of movement is during feeding periods. It has been said many times that whitetails eat such a variety of foods that seldom does any one variety tie them to a specific place. Meticulous observation of feeding deer disproves that.

I've watched deer feeding in a small open valley near our house for long periods. It is grassy, and my first assumption was that they were indiscriminately eating grass of several varieties. However, I was skeptical.

I studied what was going on through binoculars. The deer would take a bite, move a step or two and take another. I was able to see wads of grass in their mouths. There is a tough, abrasive grass in my area locally called "wire grass." That, and only that, is what the deer were eating. Applying that to hunting. we've staked out (twice now successfully) grassy areas on our ranch where bunches of wire grass are scattered. On every whitetail range, I'm sure, a keen-eyed hunter can discover certain obscure forage that deer relish. This advanced lore reaches far past the basics of acorns and hardwood browse, and if diligently pursued, sometimes can make the difference between success and failure.

Classic examples occur where certain foods occur erratically; a heavy crop one season and none at all for the next several years. In my area wild grapes make a good crop only now and then. We have lots of wild grapevines at

home and my wife likes to make jelly when they bear. We have to check closely in order to beat the deer to them.

Another most interesting phenomenon I've observed is that there are distinct individual tastes and food habits among deer. The cedar, or juniper, that covers the Texas Hill Country where I live bears masses of bluish berries in some years. I've watched our home deer around them many

times. Certain individuals that we easily recognize seem simply addicted to them. Others totally spurn them. I've killed deer and opened paunches that are packed with these berries, and while others in the same season have none.

Looking back over the many years of living with these deer and their progeny, I realize that they've taught us countless lessons. When relative humidity is low, the deer move more than when it is high. On days when the temperature is normal for that time of year, or lower, movement is greater than when it is higher. A hard, chill rain dampens our deer movement. but a mist or drizzle, especially at normal temperature, sees them moving about, and not as wary as on bright days. When winds blow, we don't see deer.

Indeed, according to my observations, weather undoubtedly has the greatest influence on deer movement. I sometimes wonder if these home-place deer, which have it pretty good, are aware of all they've taught me about how to bag their ranch brethren. If so, maybe one day they'll begin passing me false leads!

By Byron W. Dalrymple

ESSENCE
of Deer

DEER LIVE BY THEIR NOSES.
UNDERSTAND THAT, AND
YOU'RE READY TO REALLY PUT
DEER SCENT TO WORK.

DEER HUNTERS NOWADAYS use scents as standard hunting equipment. Some of these mask hunter odors. Others supposedly attract deer, and there is substantial evidence that occasionally these scents actually do the job. Few hunters, however, know much about how deer use scents of their own, and how important these are in the animals' social lives, during the rut, in marking trails, helping them find their way, announcing their presence to other deer, warning of danger, or indicating fear. Hunters can use this knowledge to their own advantage.

The senses of deer have been carefully studied. Although hearing and sight are keen, scientists point out that the sense of smell is the keenest sense deer possess. There's a logical probable reason for this. In often dense cover, deer can't and don't see each other or properly identify possible danger by sight over long distances. They may listen to each other moving about at close range, but they seldom communicate vocally. In a lifetime of deer hunting and watching, I've rarely heard deer produce vocal sounds, and most hunters would agree.

I've heard a fawn caught by dogs scream much the same as a young domestic goat in similar anguish. A doe caught in a fence may blat as she struggles. Strayed fawns occasionally bleat softly and mothers may reply. Several times I've heard a rutting buck following a doe in heat utter a series of low, guttural grunts. However, vocal utterances are uncommon. Most deer communication depends upon odors the animals produce.

These are chiefly from secretions of paired skin glands. Among the most important of these to the daily life of deer are the interdigital—between the toes—glands. These are present on all four feet. Many hunters aren't even aware of these glands and what they do. Each is a fold of tissue forming a sac that produces a yellowish, waxy substance. Openings are located along each hoof section. At every step, the odor of the secretion is deposited. If you get a close-range whiff, you'll find this odor extremely unpleasant. Interestingly, I discovered by examining the interdigital glands of several whitetails and several mule deer that they're much larger on the former. Biologists have suggested that whitetails, which dwell in cover, require more scent secretion than mule deer, which are able to see each other more readily on open slopes and also are more gregarious.

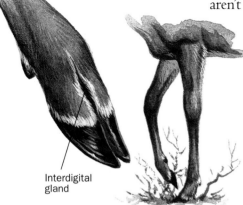

Interdigital gland

Here's an illustration of how important trail scents can be. A rancher friend of mine has a permit to keep whitetails in a pen. He occasionally releases them. They roam widely, but because they're quite tame they come back toward evening to be fed. One day he graded a ranch road after he'd turned them out and they'd crossed it.

"When they returned," he told me, "they milled around by the road, confused. I suspected it was because I'd wiped out their scented trail. Sure enough, when I repeated the routine, the same thing occurred."

There's a lesson here for hunters about scented deer trails. Study the feet of deer you've shot, and you'll discover that there's no way the animals can take a step without leaving scent from one foot or another. This strengthens the indication that trail marking by the interdigitals is extremely important. I've watched a doe trail her own half-grown fawn that had wandered away. Many hunters have seen bucks put their nose to the ground to trail a doe during rut. He may be using several of her scents, but where numerous deer tracks are cluttered on a trail, a buck unerringly puts its nose close to the ground to pick out the one he's following.

The most noticeable glands on deer are the metatarsal glands, located low on the outside shank of each hind leg. These are horny ridges bordered by stiff hair. Size and shape differ among deer species and some subspecies—so much so, in fact, that the metatarsal alone can be used to identify deer species: whitetail, short, about 2 inches, pear shaped; mule deer, up to 5 inches long, narrowly elliptical; Columbian blacktail, slightly over half the size as on mule deer. These glands exude an oily, odorous substance. Some biologists believe fright triggers metatarsal secretions. To date, research hasn't substantiated this, nor precisely how the metatarsals relate to deer communication. Scientists note that, curiously, small metatarsals are found on the less gregarious whitetails, larger ones on the more social mule deer.

The paired scent glands with which hunters are most familiar are the tarsals, located inside each hind leg at the hock. The tufts of long hair surrounding these glands easily mark them. Few realize how many uses musk from these glands has. Whenever a deer is fearful and suspicious, or shows evidence of hostility toward another deer, the tufts of hair surrounding the tarsal glands are elevated. At these times there may be no musk visible on the hair. But the glands are visibly wet and also smelly during the rut.

Tarsal gland

Endless arguments ensue among hunters over whether or not the tarsals should be removed before field dressing or skinning. The musk cannot get into the meat on its own. But if you inadvertently get it on your hands and then handle the meat, it may be offensively tainted. If you are skeptical about the power of this musk, get some on your hands on purpose, and then try to wash it off. You'll be smelling it a week later! As a precaution when field dressing, I remove tarsals, along with a wide swatch of surrounding hide.

All deer, even small fawns, try to urinate on the tarsals tufts, pressing their hocks together to accomplish it. This combination musk and urine scent is used year-round. Does use it to locate fawns that have strayed. Fawns use it to locate their mothers. Does also warn fawns by discharging tarsal musk, which can be done at will. There may be different strengths of the scent for different purposes.

The most abundant use of tarsal musk is during breeding season. Bucks make scrapes and urinate on their hocks and thus wet the scrape with this mixture. Does visit scrapes and do likewise, advising the buck of their availability. As they move about during the rut, both sexes leave the scent on trailside bushes and in the air along their routes. Although little known to hunters, sudden tarsal discharge in any season by a spooked deer warns and puts others to flight. These glands thus serve as a prime source of year-round scent communication.

Another pair of scent glands, the preorbitals, are at the corners of the eyes.

Preorbital gland

For unknown reasons, these are much larger on mule deer than on whitetails. Part of the purpose of these glands is to lubricate and clean the eyes. But recent research suggests more complex uses. Does angry at other does have been observed flaring these glands as they strike out with their forefeet. Although the secretion of these glands is not as odorous as that from the others, observers believe it is used by bucks to mark twigs or limbs above scrapes during the rut.

On numerous occasions I've watched a buck make a scrape, always with a limb overhanging it within reach. The animal then reaches high, nuzzles and nibbles at leaves or twigs, and hooks at the limb with its antlers. Close observation shows that during this activity the twigs or leaves are passed across the preorbitals. Numerous observations of this behavior led scientists long ago to conclude that the preorbital secretion is used as a marker. Some believe it is also deposited for the same purpose on twigs along trails as a buck marks off his territory.

More intriguing, recent research suggests that when a buck makes a rub on a sapling, it's not all for the purposes—as was once thought—of cleaning off velvet and polishing antlers. Preorbital secretion is deposited on the rub. Suspicion has grown that this secretion may not be as important during breeding season as another from the skin of the forehead. As a buck rubs and strips bark from the sapling, the forehead is vigorously employed in a kind of mock goring action. The buck, it is thought, thus leaves a scent marker of his specific identity. Studies of deer scalps before and during rut tend to indicate some glandular activity.

Without question, each buck has an individual standing in the deer community of a given territory and leaves individual scent markers proclaiming his dominant—or submissive—status.

On two occasions while on stand, I have watched whitetail bucks examine and sniff a rub and a limb above a scrape that I knew had been made by a "boss buck" of the territory. In one instance the deer was a young forkhorn. In the other it was mature, husky, heavy-antlered six-pointer. On each occasion the bucks appeared nervous and sneaked off. They seemed to know from the scent that this was no buck with which to tangle.

Hunters who've had the opportunity to watch undisturbed deer know that at any season they routinely identify each other by sniffing. Does identify which fawn is theirs by scent. One doe sniffs another and decides to give her a swipe with a front hoof. A strange deer wanders in, is given the scent test, and is promptly run off or accepted. Remarkably, when one or several deer have been startled and have fled, another that wanders into the area right afterward often becomes suddenly alert, suspicious, sniffs the air, and decides to leave. Certainly much is still to be learned about deer communication via their odors. However, hunters who properly interpret what's already known can apply the knowledge to enhance their hunting success.

By Sam Curtis

Whitetails
UP & DOWN

STREAMSIDE HABITATS ARE MAGNETS FOR DEER, BUT HOW FAR UPSTREAM YOU'LL FIND THEM DEPENDS ON HOW MANY ANIMALS THERE ARE.

WHITETAILS HAVE ALWAYS favored streamside habitat with its abundance of deciduous vegetation and water, which provide plenty of food and opportunities for escape. So, a map of the river and stream courses of the country where whitetails live could easily double as a map of the major whitetail populations. What the map would *not* show, however, is the expanding and contracting nature of whitetail dispersal as it responds to local highs and lows in the deer population.

Put simply, the bigger the whitetail population along a river or stream, the more some deer will push up into small tributary stream courses where hunters are not used to finding them. On the other hand, the smaller the deer population, the more deer will concentrate down where rivers and streams are larger.

Here's the reason. The closer you get to the headwaters of any river, the more restricted the riparian habitat becomes. High up in the hills or mountains where a spring marks a stream's source, streamside habitat is only a few feet or a few yards wide. The water's descent starts out narrow and fast, but as it collects more water and reaches lower ground, it starts to widen and slow down. As the river widens, so does the riparian habitat, which attracts whitetail deer.

These lower areas, with their wider flood plains, are the first areas to be colonized by whitetails. Such areas are the traditional centers of population stability and growth, with mature does passing on "family" lands to their daughters.

However, as population densities increase and reach the edge of riparian habitat, some deer start migrating upstream in search of less crowded conditions. At the height of a population boom, whitetails may be found way back along narrow streamside habitat where you normally wouldn't think of finding them.

The majority of these deer will be bucks, since bucks traditionally disperse from family groups while does tend to stay closer to the areas in which they were born. So these narrow tributary habitats are ideal spots in which to hunt deer when whitetail populations are on the increase. But when disease, harsh weather, or even overgenerous hunting regulations put whitetail populations on the decline, deer may become conspicuously absent from these tributary areas as they drift back downstream to more spacious riparian living quarters.

There is a corollary to this upstream-downstream movement of whitetails. As a deer population grows, the home range size of individual deer decreases. And as a pop-

ulation decreases, individual home range size increases. Looked at another way, the more deer there are in an area, the more the individuals get in each others' way, and the smaller they make their home ranges in order to avoid social stress.

As a result, those bucks that push up into foothill tributaries when deer numbers are high are going to live in fairly restricted areas. Those areas are going to be long and narrow.

Let's say a buck has taken up residence along a tributary stream where the riparian habitat is only ¼ mile wide. And let's say his home range has been limited to ½ square mile by the population squeeze. He can still wander back and forth along 2 miles of stream before he reaches the limits of his turf.

Keep this long, narrow living area in mind the next time you have your sights set on a big buck that you've discovered back along a dinky stream where other whitetail hunters don't think to go.

By Eileen Clarke

WATCHDOGS
of the WILLOW PATCH

BUCKS OFTEN USE DOES AS BIG-MOUTHED
BODYGUARDS THAT WATCH EVERY MOVE YOU
MAKE, BUT THERE ARE WAYS TO GET PAST
THESE NOTORIOUS TATTLETALES.

ASIDE FROM HIS NOSE, EARS, and two or three hunting seasons under his belt, a whitetail buck's most effective means of defense is the suspicious nature of whitetail does. He uses her—herds of her, in fact—as a decoy, and since whitetail herds are growing both in numbers and range, there are a lot of does out there watching every move you make. Want to hunt a buck? First get past his bodyguards.

There are three separate buck seasons: the pre-rut, occurring in September through mid-October, when bucks run together in small bands, often loosely associated with doe groups; the early rut, running from late October until November, when bucks scatter and wander along; and finally, the full rut, beginning sometime in November in most Northern whitetail range, when bucks are chasing does. In most states the pre-rut period is bow season. Most rifle seasons coincide with the early and full rut.

At first glance the pre-rut period would seem to be the worst possible time to hunt a mature buck. He's always surrounded by does and immature bucks. On the other hand, he's less wary this early in the season, not having been hunted hard, and he's out feeding early in open meadows, sometimes as much as three hours before dusk.

One of my early-season bowhunting spots is a transition area between a heavily wooded and brushy river bottom and 1,000-yard-wide grainfields. Early every afternoon, eight to ten bucks come out of the willows and cottonwoods, settling into the edge of tall grass beside the field. This past season there were three heavy-beamed 4x4s and a collection of younger, light-antlered four-bys and forkhorns amid a herd of does and fawns.

I glassed them, scouting before the season started, and discovered the bucks always followed the does from cover, sidehilling several hundred yards along a brushy embankment below the field, then emerging at field level where the cover ran into a fence corner. On opening day, I knelt in the center of a large, wild rose patch in what I thought was the best possible stand—10 yards into the field, facing the spot where the deer jumped the fence—with the wind blowing directly in my face.

Quickly, I learned two lessons the hard way. First, the does would top the cutbank, stop, look square into my eyes, then disappear. Lesson one: never sit directly in a doe's line of sight. The few does that were naive enough to jump the fence anyway pointed out my second mistake: they quickly grazed downwind, behind me, all within sight and hearing range of the other deer—both does and bucks—that were waiting for the "all clear" signal.

The next time I went out, I used another patch of brush along the fence line 20 yards southwest of the fence corner, keeping the wind quartering from the northeast.

The deer crossed the wind at a 90-degree angle. A doe would have had to double back behind me along the fence line to catch my scent.

The largest buck that showed up that season was a 3x5 with tines 8 inches long on the right side of his antlers, but only 4 inches long on the left. He came out of the brush and stood at the fence line watching the does just long enough for me to see that shorter, far-side antler; and instead of shooting, I let him go, hoping to run into his more symmetrical big brother later in the season.

Many times, you can use the terrain to keep bucks from seeing the doe's warning signals. My favorite stand is an ancient, gnarled cottonwood tree situated in a bend of the old riverbed over a heavily used deer trail. Close behind my stand, a cutbank extends 200 yards on either side, leading to a flat bench covered with fields of winter wheat. The deer feed there each evening.

One sunny September afternoon, with the wind quartering from my right front, I settled into this stand facing the river. The deer live in the willow bottoms along the water, 200 yards from the tree, and in the evening emerge from a finger of brush to the left of this stand, walking a diagonal path directly to my grizzled tree. There, the path straightens out and skirts the cutbank for 20 yards, then slowly climbs up to the grainfields.

It wasn't long before the does started coming out. They stopped briefly at the tree, since it was the last cover, and fed there, watching before moving out onto the field. Seconds behind them a 4x4 buck emerged from the willows. The does trotted toward me and then past, not stopping to graze, running out onto the field as if they lived in a very safe suburb and had friends waiting for them. The buck came slowly and stopped to graze—looking up every now and then, his mouth chewing, turning his ears toward an imagined noise, then putting his head down again to feed.

In the meantime, one of the does had worked her way downwind of me. I barely heard her stamp and huff, but the buck didn't hear her at all, and because of the height of the field and the depth of the old river bottom, he couldn't see her either. That's the second good thing about that stand. Bucks emerging from the willow bottoms can't see or hear what happens on the field. This evening, despite the doe scenting me, the buck walked along the trail undisturbed and stopped to graze broadside 10 yards away, giving me an opportunity for a spectacular miss. Just as I drew back a rooster pheasant, which had walked within 10 feet of me, suddenly realized I was there, saw me draw, and flushed. The arrow flew 2 feet over the buck's back.

The second season occurs as the rut nears, when few does are in estrus. The buck herds split up and individuals scatter. The does seem to be feeding by themselves, but the bucks are still there. They just don't come out until twilight, or even full dark, and they're not always where you expect them to be.

For instance, a couple of years ago, my husband and I spotted a nice 4x4 buck that was bedded down along a barbed-wire fence. Only his antlers were visible above the grass, and to the naked eye, his antlers looked more like a bunch of sun-bleached weeds. He was 500 yards away, across an open field and facing us, with the wind at his back enabling him to scent anyone coming up on his blind side. For insurance he was surrounded on all four sides by does and fawns, some as much as 200 yards off. Their heads moved like charmed snakes in the afternoon mirage, but

had we moved, they would have alerted the buck to our presence.

There's only one way to get close to a buck bedded down on a fence row, and that is to plan your hunt for the noonday sun, when the does are bedded down and there is almost no possibility that they will interfere with your stalk. Then you have only one animal to try to outwit, instead of armies of eyes and ears. So it pays to glass the short cover and other unexpected places for bucks, then hunt them midday when the bucks are isolated from their sentries.

I shot my first big 4x4 during the pre-rut in the opening week of rifle season. At that time of year the bucks spend their nights looking for does that might be in estrus early. Bucks move as much as 5 miles in a night, and once in a while you can intercept them on the way back to their bedding areas. This particular buck was as wary and watchful as one pair of eyes and nostrils can be—but he was alone, and that is a great disadvantage.

I'd been out six mornings in a row, and on the seventh morning, in full dark with the wind out of the south, I set up a stand in a stubble field north of the river, 100 yards from a trail that takes a short cut across an oxbow of the river. The oxbow is full of shoulder-high rose bushes, but for a stretch of 50 yards along the bottom of the wheatfield the trail follows a barbed-wire fence, out in the open. My plan was to take the first doe that passed within my range. The does would walk along the trail in front of me and cross the river into the next oxbow where they could feed.

It was that funny, early-dawn light when hunters are likely to see those two other varieties of deer—stump deer and rock deer—except that this stump deer moved, though at first I wasn't even sure of that. I leaned forward, squinting hard, trying to make out movement—a tail twitching, anything. The buck cooperated by coming closer, his head dipping to grab a bite or two of grass, then rising again, approaching the trail. Not a doe in sight. I waited for shooting light, thinking it would never come, and readjusted the rifle on my knees several times. Then, just as the buck reached the trail, turned parallel to me, and started to walk toward the brush, I settled the crosshairs on his chest and shot. He was my first big buck, and it was several minutes before my knees stopped shaking and I could fill out my tag.

After the pre-rut, most of the does come into estrus,

and the bucks follow them like puppy dogs. The does are as alert as ever, but the bucks just don't respond as quickly to their warning signals.

Three years ago, I was hunting a new whitetail area. The first day I set up, I decided to sit back on a hill above the river bottom so I could glass several possible buck areas at one time. In the following days, I planned to move in and make a play along the likeliest trail.

That's not the way it turned out. I waited an hour and a half above the thick willow and cottonwoods that bordered the farmer's cornfields before one lone doe emerged to graze. Since it was the heart of the rut I began to wonder if there were enough does in the river bottom to attract a large buck. But a few minutes later, five does loped out of the brush. Right behind the last one trailed a buck. I took a quick look through the spotting scope before deciding I had to move in closer. Staying out of sight was no problem; all I had to do was sidehill for 50 yards away from the deer, then walk along a cutbank that would hide me from them. I could get within 150 yards, then take another look.

Five does, one buck. When I'd seen them last, the does were quietly grazing and the buck had just caught up with them. I slowly peered over the edge of the cutbank. The buck was in the center of the grazing does, sniffing them one by one. His neck was swollen full in rut, and up close, the antlers that had looked tall and skinny had filled out into a 5x5 with tall tines and brow points. They had grazed on a little farther in the corn stubble, and two of the does and the buck stood broadside to me.

I lifted the gun slowly to my shoulder, resting my left hand on a clump of brush and the rifle's fore-end firmly in my hand. That little movement alerted the does. They looked up sharply, like a school librarian looking for spitballers. I watched through the scope, afraid to make any more movement. The does stamped, blew, and then ran. The buck, now in my crosshairs, hesitated a second too long.

My first choice of deer hunting tactics is to be in a stand and have the animals walk to me, giving me all the time in the world before making the shot. But sometimes that's just not possible.

I had a buck picked out one year and set up my stand along his trail, away from the does—I thought. One afternoon, I snuck in, sat down behind a tree, and prepared to wait 4 hours until the buck came out. I'd been there 5 min-utes when I looked up to see a lone doe walking right for me. She stopped and gave me that old "You weren't here yesterday" look, and I realized I had two choices. I could either shoot her and forget about a buck for that year, or pack up and go home for the day. Then I thought again. I could fool her eyes if I held perfectly still. I could even fool her ears if I didn't move. But eventually, if she kept walking in the same direction, she'd end up downwind, and there was no way to fool her nose. She had to stay upwind, and, before the bucks came out, she had to move on. Calmly.

She came closer, took a bite of greens, and watched me while she chewed. She took two steps toward me, then three to the left. Chewed. Stared. For 15 minutes I kept perfectly still, trying to bore her into moving along. Deer don't bore. Like dogs, they thrive on routine.

Another 15 minutes, another few steps closer. Too close. If the wind swirled just slightly, she would pick up my scent. I waved a glove at her, gently. She took a step back. I waved it again. She stood her ground. I picked up one foot and waved it in the air, like I was doing the Hokey-Pokey upside-down. She turned, slowly walked over a little rise, and disappeared long enough for me to take a deep breath and stretch briefly. Then, as I sat there thinking what to do next, those beady little eyes reappeared and I decided it was best to get rid of her once and for all.

I watched for a moment. She was not alarmed, just looking hard as she took the occasional bite of fresh green grass and moved closer. When she bent her head down behind a tree to feed, I groped carefully for a small rock and lobbed it at her flank. That did it. She jumped sideways, looked around her, and then took off at a crisp trot over the rise. But she was still not panicked. It was just something she didn't understand. She went back into the herd and immediately began feeding again.

One last word of caution. In the final third of the season, when the does are in estrus and the bucks hot on their trail, before you lob pebbles or wave your glove, let the doe take five or six steps out of the brush. If there's a buck in hot pursuit, he'll be just a few steps behind her. And while she may not see the hand that tosses the rock, that buck, standing just inside the line of brush might see it and never come out. This is a solo performance with very small movements, for only one pair of eyes to see, and for those eyes not to see too much.

By Norman Strung

Creatures of
HABIT

THE GOOD NEWS IS THAT EVEN THE SMARTEST WHITETAILS HAVE ONLY A FEW TRICKS. THE BAD NEWS IS THEY'RE VERY GOOD AT THEM.

FOR ALL THE NATIVE INTELLIgence that hunters attribute to whitetail deer, the fact remains that they are creatures of habit, with responses that are programmed from birth. And though a lot of attention is paid to the ways exceptional bucks polish these routines to outwit pursuers, a solid grasp of basic whitetail behavior remains the key to finding the wisest of them.

Whitetails belong to a class of creatures called skulkers. This ominous-sounding classification simply means that they instinctively seek the protection of some sort of cover. For example, when traveling between two points (which can range from hundreds of yards to several miles), whitetails will always skirt a woodland clearing rather than step into it; will follow a hedgerow around an open field rather than cross it; and will feed inside a treeline rather than expose themselves in a green, grassy pasture.

This concept of cover extends to more than just woods. Canyons, cuts, and ditches typically harbor their runways, and they are especially at ease in the cover afforded by subdued light and deep shadows.

The whitetail's affinity for hiding places defines where and when to look for your quarry. Like the deer you seek, avoid wasting time watching or walking through big, bright openings with a commanding view, or tall timber with little understory. These places appear to be happy hunting grounds because they are so open and you can see so far, and they are even more seductive when they are crisscrossed by trails. But whitetails will cross them only under the cover of darkness.

A more productive place to post or still-hunt would be in a thatch of willow, a bottleneck of blowdown, or brushy dips in the landscape. Although the confines of such terrain make spotting distant deer unlikely, the security it represents to a whitetail will often lead it right into your lap.

One of the finest bucks my wife ever took fell in just such a place—a narrow tangle of briar that connected two big woodlots. Dumbbell in shape, the "handle" of the two woodlots was bisected by the spidery trunk of a huge, fallen cottonwood. The tree also made for a tempting place to be suckered into the big view syndrome because the perch at each end of the trunk offered a clear field of vision and fire across 20-acre pastures, but from either vantage, you could not see into the narrow strip of brush at your back.

Laying out a game plan, I suggested that Sil straddle the midsection of the tree while I bumped around in the timberlands. She couldn't see either opening from her perch, but her resolve was rewarded not an hour after we parted company as a husky five-pointer I'd unknowingly pushed from its bed came sneaking down a trail that wound through the middle of the brushline.

Since subdued light is akin to dense brush to whitetails, their need for cover also indicates *when* to hunt them. Periods of lowlight early morning, late evening, and cloudy, overcast days—always rate as the most likely times for deer encounters. Deer know they are harder to see in the dim and dark, and move about more often under these conditions, making them more likely to cross trails with hunters, and vice-versa.

The startling effect diminished light can have upon whitetail movements was well illustrated one afternoon on a Western riverbottom. I was bowhunting from a tree stand in Indian summer weather replete with the buzz of flies, and after an hour or so of fruitless watching, I dozed off.

Awakened by the distant rumble of an approaching thunderhead, I cussed the fact that I'd forgotten to bring raingear and was about to descend the tree when something caught my eye. In the lowering light of the black-bellied clouds, a doe whitetail lurched to her feet, followed by her two fawns not 50 yards away. To me, the intrigue of archery is that the watching is nearly as exciting as the hunting, so even though I didn't care to take a doe, I figured I'd stay in place a few minutes more, just to see what would happen next.

I cannot say whether those whitetails walked up on me while I was sleeping, or if they had been bedded there all day long, and I had walked by them, but like ghosts emerging from the wispy brush, seventeen skinheads materialized around the tree and paraded within range of my bow. It was like someone had flipped a switch: as light levels hit a certain point, the deer felt safe enough to roam and feed, and threw caution to the gathering dusk.

Another inborn whitetail trait is a natural inquisitiveness. Quick to detect even small changes in their environment, whitetails tend to be suspicious about manmade fixtures such as newly constructed blinds. These habits can be turned to your favor by intentionally creating a diversion or distraction to direct whitetail curiosity away from you.

One of the cleverest tricks in this regard I've ever heard of is employed by a hunting buddy who simply finds a well-used deer trail, blocks it with some fresh-cut brush, and waits nearby. Deer approaching the unfamiliar roadblock stop and sniff and slowly pick out a new way around the obstacle. Totally preoccupied with this change in their world, they are oblivious to my friend waiting near the trailside.

An even easier way to create a similar diversion is to hang a slip of bright-colored cloth or shiny foil from a branch within good range of a trail, rub, or scrape. I've watched a whitetail "stalk" a strip of twirling foil for 5 minutes, snorting, stomping, and on full alert, yet utterly unaware of my presence.

Although whitetails have a reputation for acute senses, they react to sounds, sights, and smells in predictable ways. Sound amounts to their first line of defense. Whitetails are tuned into every noise in the woods; grazing or bedded deer will flick their ears at the caw of a jay, stare down a squirrel breaking branches until they are sure of the source of the disturbance, and cock their heads at a distant car horn or the lowing of cattle. But noise alone does not alarm deer; it just whets their curiosity.

If sounds don't lead to the sight of a hunter, they are either soon forgotten, or become a deadly curiosity. Twice I've been able to take a buck because I paused and remained motionless for several minutes after I inadvertently stepped on a branch. The deer heard the crack but couldn't identify what made the noise, and their natural inquisitiveness got the better of them.

A whitetail's vision isn't all it's cracked up to be. Their eyes are adept at picking up motion, but poor at sorting out objects from backgrounds. This points to the wisdom of wearing clothes that break up your outline (remember the classic black-and-red deer hunter's plaids?) and the practice of simply waiting animals out or creating an unfamiliar diversion to play upon natural instincts.

These creatures excel, however, when it comes to their sense of smell. Smell represents the ultimate test of what's what, and when deer ears and eyes confront a threat, they will always circle downwind to affirm any suspicions with a whiff. To take advantage of this "habit," always stalk into the wind, use scents that mask human odor, watch your backtrail as carefully as the terrain before you (especially when you jump a deer upwind), and when you are hunting in a party, stagger your drivers so one or more of your group brings up the rear to intercept inquisitive bucks.

There are two other conditions that determine whitetail habits. One is that as pressure mounts, their defensive habits become more ingrained and fine-tuned. More hunters encountered and more activity in the woods result in the deer seeking deeper cover, feeding earlier and later, becoming quickly alarmed by sounds, sights, and smells. Expect to hunt harder when you hunt later in the season.

People are a lot like deer—creatures of habit. Hunters tend to follow the same trails, take stands in the same places, and generally establish predictable patterns of behavior that whitetails quickly perceive and learn to avoid.

It follows then that figuring out ways to break existing habits is as important a hunting tactic as knowing deer hangouts and checking your backtrail. One of the best whitetail hunters I know regularly gets his game by busting through thick brush as if he were after pheasants, rather than stalking along established runways. Another acquaintance claims the secret to his success is to hunt near road-ends, popular parking spots, and other areas of concentrated human activity. . . places other hunters typically storm by in the pre-dawn rush to find distant and secluded stands.

All these practices illustrate the underlying savvy that has tagged nearly every whitetail ever taken—a knowledge of their nature. Once you have some idea of what these deer will do and why they do it, you'll be ahead of the game whenever you enter the woods.

By Jerome B. Robinson

WHITETAILS
on the Move

KNOWING WHERE DEER GO WHEN THE SNOW GETS DEEP CAN MEAN VENISON INSTEAD OF BURGER ON YOUR DINNER TABLE.

WHITETAILS ARE NOT generally thought of as migratory animals, but when snow gets knee-deep, widely scattered bands of deer move to winter range, often traveling more than 20 miles to get there.

Though migrations of 5 to 10 miles are common in most states, telemetry studies in Minnesota have tabulated deer migrations of as much as 55 miles. Deer in the Upper Peninsula of Michigan are known to move as much as 32 miles to reach their winter range, while migrations of 25 to 35 miles have been recorded in Montana and in the mountains of western South Dakota. In the South, whitetail migrations average 5 to 6 miles in the mountains of northwest Georgia and western North Carolina.

From a hunter's standpoint, this shift, which can happen within a 24-hour period, means that a large portion of what has previously been considered good deer country suddenly empties. Even if the deer move only a mile from where they have been, you are not going to see them unless you move, too.

Migratory shifts usually occur at the very end of the hunting season or after it's over, so when deep snow does come during hunting season, what happens is often misinterpreted by the hunter. An area that had previously shown a normal amount of deer sign suddenly shows none, and it is often thought that the deer are holed up someplace, refusing to move, when actually the sign has disappeared because the deer have moved out.

IN MAINE, NEW HAMPSHIRE, and Vermont, where I do most of my deer hunting, deer commonly migrate from summer dispersal ranges where the population may be only six to fifteen deer per square mile, into winter ranges that may harbor 100 to 200 deer per square mile. Unless you knew where they go when they head for winter range, you would think there wasn't a deer left in the woods.

It is important to understand the difference between winter range and a winter "deer yard."

In northern parts of their range, whitetails commonly congregate for 12 to 20 weeks (depending on the weather) between January and March in traditional sheltered areas known as "deer yards." These offer protection from wind and extreme cold temperatures, but may hold little forage of good nutritional quality.

The "winter range" is a much larger area, often adjacent to a deer yard. It is a center of deer activity during times when deer are not actually confined to the yards by extreme temperatures or deep snow. The winter range contains food sources (such as hanging moss and lichens, low-growing cedar, fir or hemlock browse, or hardwood tops dropped by logging operations) that remain available long after the lush summer foods are gone and after snow has covered mast crops that have fallen to the ground.

The first knee-deep snow of the year motivates whitetails to move to their winter ranges simply to assure themselves that a winter food source is still available there. Once having attained the winter range, they often drift back out of it if the snow depth decreases, but will stay nearby should heavy snow come again.

According to Gerry Lavigne, Maine's Deer Project

Leader, the depth of the snow is an impelling factor because foraging for food becomes less energy-efficient once deer have to push through it with bent knees, instead of stepping over it. A snowfall of 10 inches reaches the knees of most deer and goads them into shifting their range.

TEN MILES SOUTH of my cabin in northern New Hampshire there is a major deer yard that attracts deer from as far as 20 miles away. They don't usually move into that yard until after Christmas, but a 10-inch snowfall in November is all it takes to cause them to head for their winter range.

If we have 6 or 8 inches of snow during deer season, tracks show that deer continue to move randomly from feeding areas to bedding areas without following any particular system of trails. But once the snow reaches 10 inches, everything changes.

Random movement stops and deer begin moving in parades, one behind the other, creating trails that quickly become hard-beaten paths. Most of the tracks point in the direction of the nearest winter range. Scattered deer tracks practically disappear, and migratory trails show up.

Often these migratory trails follow major drainages, and the sidehills above waterways may show signs of heavy use while nearby hills are suddenly barren of all sign.

After years of observing the migratory routes that deer follow in my hunting territory, I have developed a pretty good idea of where I ought to be when a 10-inch snowfall comes. Several years ago I discovered a spot where three hardwood ridges come together and form a little bowl. During the migration period, deer coming off these ridges pass through the bowl. Their trails are not evident until the first deep snow comes but then these deer highways get busy.

I went in there at dawn on the first deep snow last November and didn't cross the track of a single deer until I had completed the mile hike. When I reached the bowl, however, it looked like a sheep pasture with hard-packed trails intersecting where deer had poured through from the surrounding ridges. I scooped out a hole in the snow, propped some fir branches around me to break up my outline, and settled in, knowing I was in the right place.

Minutes later the first deer appeared. Two does, each

trailed by a pair of offspring passed through, headed south, stepping high in the deepening snow. Later, two more antlerless deer came in off another ridge and drifted through the bowl. It was only a matter of time before a good buck was sure to come along, and soon he did—a nice 6-pointer that dressed out at 194 pounds.

SEVERAL YEARS AGO I canoed into a remote piece of country in northern Minnesota with some friends and camped in an area that was rank with deer sign. We spent the first day getting the camp set up, cutting a good supply of firewood, and delighting in the snow that had started falling heavily. Judging by all the sign we had seen before the snow began, we were sure we were in for a memorable hunt and the snow would make spotting fresh sign easy.

All the next day the snow continued. We hunted anyway, but saw no deer. "They're holed up," we assured ourselves.

When the storm finally passed, more than a foot of snow covered the ground. We headed out to hunt, expecting to find a carnival of deer sign, but instead we found none. At first we told ourselves that the deer that had left all that sign we found when we arrived were just bedded someplace and not yet moving. By late afternoon, we knew better. We were camped in a good summer deer range, but the deer had moved out during the storm.

Women and children first

WHEN THE MIGRATION begins, does and their offspring move out first. Adult bucks seem more reluctant to change their ways and you will often find their tracks striding through the deepening snow, usually alone, criss-crossing the heavily used trails rather than traveling on them. Once they find sign of a doe in estrus, however, they go where the doe goes, so there is a general tendency for most bucks to follow the does toward the winter range.

Last to leave are the old bucks, many of which have passed their peak years as breeders and are therefore less compelled to follow the does. Instead, they often hang on in secret hiding places while the deepening snow protects them from the approach of hunters. Perhaps they will migrate to winter range later. If the snow gets chest-deep and does not recede, these old bucks can be prevented from migrating and must face the hardships of winter under difficult circumstances.

Even in regions where deep snow does not usually last long and deer migrations are less pronounced, a shift from summer dispersal range to a more concentrated winter range still occurs. In the mid-Atlantic states deer move to steep, sunny hillsides when deep snow falls. In flat country, they move to heavy, protective cover. In all mountainous regions, deep snow at higher elevations drives deer downhill into heavy cover.

The secret to deer hunting success is being able to put yourself in a place where a deer is about to appear. Knowing where deer go when deep snow comes to the country you hunt can make the difference between seeing deer and just seeing snow.

By Norm Nelson

PRESEASON SCOUTING–
Down Payment on Success

If you find acorns, you've struck gold. Deer depend on them for their winter's fat supply. Where the mast is, the deer will be. Guaranteed.

*I*N OVER HALF A CENTURY of whitetail hunting, the most important thing I've learned is this: Successful gun or bow hunters are familiar with the areas they hunt and how the deer use those areas. Preseason scouting is the key to this familiarity. If you try to get the lay of the land while the season is on, you'll waste most of your time looking where the deer aren't and the deer that you do see (if any) will give you the slip because you'll be playing on unfamiliar turf.

THEY AREN'T EVERYWHERE

HERE'S THE PROBLEM: If there are sixteen deer in a square mile (640 acres), that does not mean there is one deer every 40 acres. They may be using only the most habitable 120 acres for room and board, leaving the other 520 acres empty. And neither tree stands, calls, rattling, scents, drives, nor still-hunting will work where the deer aren't.

Deer concentrate where there is food and shelter (which includes security cover). If you can find where the deer are feeding, you can then find the trails linking these areas to their bedding grounds, and you can bet that the latter will be somewhere up the prevailing wind. (Deer don't like to travel very far crosswind or downwind.)

Deer don't necessarily return to the same bedding area day after day. They'll have alternative sites, largely based on existing wind direction and weather conditions. Weather dictates how deer use an area. In a dry autumn, swamp hay and cattails provide good beds. But heavy rains will eliminate such sites as bedding. New beaver dams can do the same thing. Normally, rain or snow pushes deer into younger stands of evergreens or thick brush, and lots of snow forces them down from higher elevations.

THEY DON'T STAY PUT

IT DOESN'T PAY to do your scouting long before the season opens, because conditions change. Logging, storm damage, or changes in farm crops can cause deer to move. If a farmer replaces a hay pasture with a new stand of alfalfa or winter wheat, they will switch their bedding grounds to be close to this new Fat City. A new clearcut will rapidly develop enough browse to make it a deer cafeteria, but in a few years it will fill with young trees, changing from a prime feeding area to a good bedding area. Older patches of timber that once had good deer populations can lose them because the tall trees prevent the growth of ground-level plants.

In forested country, a new road becomes a magnet for whitetails. First, they find it convenient for their own travel outside of broad-daylight hours. Second, the new road's raw-earth edges quickly develop lots of new plant life that appeals to deer.

SCAN THE MENU

WHITETAILS ARE HIGHLY adaptable and have varying diets in different parts of the country. When scouting an area, find out first what the food resources (both natural and agricultural) are. Deer often pass up natural browse for such farm goodies as winter wheat, corn, cabbage, beans, alfalfa, and timothy hay, to name only a few.

Natural foods vary greatly from one part of the country to another, and it's important to remember that food choices change with the season. In a mild autumn, Northern forest whitetails (for example) will feed on grasses, mushrooms, shrubs like wild rose, and shallow-water plants. But when a killing frost removes some of that food supply, they switch to mountain maple, dogwood, and sucker growth of black

ash and aspen. And switching to a different diet often means feeding in a different part of their range.

WANNA BED?

DON'T ASSUME THAT deer always look for beds near their feeding areas. During hunting season, protection from poor weather and hunter activity are the top priorities, and deer will commute some distance, particularly in cover-shy farm country. Given an easy travel route or a tougher one, they'll choose the former if it has some protective cover. The exception is smart, older bucks. If they're not crazed by the rut, they'll usually stick to travel in thicker cover even if it means tougher going.

Ridges or knobs with southern exposure are midday favorites in chilly weather, and severe cold finds whitetails holed up in thick, lowland evergreens which turn the wind better and maintain a warmer microclimate. Unseasonably warm weather in late fall makes deer (with their autumn fat and winter coats) seek bedding in cool places like north slopes or shady, lowland evergreens.

OTHER FACTORS

AS LONG AS it's not too distant, a water supply for whitetails need not be large. A tiny stream, spring, or even bog puddles are often all that's needed. However, prolonged dry weather can eliminate these sources, and a bad drought

year will find local deer moving to wherever there is water.

Hunting pressure is a factor, too. A deer-wise uncle of mine always said that on opening day, just the steady roar of hunters' vehicles before dawn on normally quiet rural roads was in itself enough to alert whitetails that The War was on again. This may partly explain the vanishing act that deer seem to pull as soon as the season opens. That's why it's important to know in advance where their "Condition Red" hideouts are, complete with escape trails through concealing cover. Big bucks will pick the spots that you are most likely to avoid—the ones where the going is toughest.

Here's something else I've learned in decades of hunting deer in the flatland Lakes States and mountain whitetails in the West. Because eyesight isn't all that useful in thick brush and timber, whitetails who live there do not seem to use their sight all that well. But those living in open hill country with its distant vistas have more opportunity to use their eyes—and believe me, they do very well at it. Thus in rolling or hilly country, bucks like to bed on higher ground to add eyesight to their detection systems. They're not the equals of mule deer, but they're no slouches, so when working uphill, use concealment.

Flat country's senior bucks often choose to hole up in the swampy places because they have the thickest cover. Big ol' swamp bucks are usually realities, not just hunting-camp myths, and they can be the toughest of all trophies.

GET THE POINT

BIG BUCKS GROW big antlers, and then they're thoughtful enough to shed them to show you where they hang out. The best time to find them is in the early spring before they're gobbled by calcium-hungry rodents or concealed by new growth. The best places to look are along fences where a buck's leap often knocks loose a ready-to-shed antler. Sheds are good clues to whether bragging-size bucks have been around, but they're not guarantees. Its

owner may not have survived predation, or a hard winter.

The surest indications of current buck presence and approximate size are rubs and scrapes. Big bucks make big scrapes and rub bigger saplings than lesser bucks.

TAKE NOTES, GET MAPS

IF YOU SCOUT properly, you will be accumulating much more information than you can remember. So take notes, either written or dictated on a small recorder. Get your hands on every map you can and mark them. Also, regional, state, or federal forestry agencies may be able to furnish direct overhead aerial photos of the area you want to hunt. These are invaluable once you've learned to read them.

Good scouting is serious work and takes plenty of time and effort to do it right, but look at it this way: You're sunk without it, and it does a marvelous job of psyching you up for the season ahead.

By Sam Curtis

Wind and WHITETAILS

WHETHER IT'S A BREEZE
OR A GALE, YOU CAN MAKE
IT WORK IN YOUR FAVOR.

THE WHITETAIL WAS WINNING. I'd watched his shenanigans for an hour from a knoll overlooking the creek bottom. Along with the local up-canyon breeze, three different hunters had slowly worked upstream. The whitetail had outmaneuvered each one of them. As soon as a hunter was within 200 yards, the buck would make his move. It was never very far, but the hunters never saw the deer. What I saw was a clear lesson in wind and whitetails.

Most hunters I know pay lip service to air movement as a consideration in their hunting tactics, but few of them pay much attention to it in the field. Yet we hunt whitetails at much closer range than we do most big game. So wind direction, velocity, temperature, and moisture levels all influence how and where we should hunt these deer.

Wind makes whitetails nervous. It can cause erratic behavior in their movements or it can cause them to sit tight. Wind influences where whitetails bed and where they feed. Wind can carry your scent to the deer you hunt or it can whisk your scent away. And deer react differently to dry wind and moist wind, cold wind and warm wind.

Your scent, carried on the wind, lets whitetails know you are in the woods or fields faster than anything else. I think of the times I have been caught out in the open by a whitetail's gaze. If the wind is in my face and if I don't move, the deer stares and fidgets, trying to decide what I am and what I'm doing. He stamps his hooves and he snorts. But chances are good that he will stand his ground or even come closer.

Yet put the wind at my back and the deer is all leaps and bounds at the far end of the field. Or he is simply gone before I ever see him.

Under ideal conditions, whitetails can catch your scent up to a quarter of a mile away. That means you may stink up half a whitetail's home range the moment you step into it.

Ideal conditions for a whitetail's sniffer means there is a light and steady breeze (perhaps 8 to 10 miles per hour), the temperature is in the 50s or 60s, and the humidity is above 50 percent. Air moving at this speed carries your scent and also lets it spread out over a large area. Moderate temperatures enhance scents and make them more noticeable. And humid air helps moisten the deer's nasal membranes and lets them detect scents more efficiently. These conditions stack the cards against you.

But there are other wind conditions that work in your favor. And you should watch for them to provide good whitetail hunting. A gusty wind tends to break up your scent and send confusing signals to a deer. This sort of wind makes a whitetail nervous, but it isn't always sure where it should run even if it does get a whiff of you. A strong, steady wind, on the other hand, will carry your scent in a narrow corridor directly downwind from you. It doesn't have a chance to settle and spread out over a wide

area. So, you may be upwind from a deer but removed from the direct flow of the wind to the deer, and your scent will be blown past him undetected.

Much of the importance of wind to whitetail hunting, however, is not related to your scent and the deer's ability to detect it. Deer respond to different kinds of wind in different ways whether or not you are present. And understanding their response is the key to knowing where to hunt whitetails.

The most typical whitetail response to wind is to bed down. Whitetails know they are vulnerable on windy days. There's a lot happening to distract and confuse them. Predator scents come to them in crazy patterns and then suddenly disappear. Boughs and branches wave and sway in a distracting manner. Trees creak and snap with alarming sounds.

All the commotion makes whitetails very edgy, so they look for places to escape the wind. Abrupt leeward slopes provide the best protection: steep, narrow valleys and draws in wooded terrain; washes, coulees, and cutbanks out on the prairies.

Years ago I was hunting whitetails in New York on a day so windy it had me headed back to my car without any hope of seeing a deer. I'd tramped up and down hills for several hours, but the firs and the spruces were waving and moaning so much that I suspected any sensible deer would be hunkered down out of sight.

Then, seeking a shortcut out of the bluster, I stepped off a ridge into one of those very quiet leeward slopes where you suddenly realize you've entered a sanctuary from the wind. Before I had walked a half a dozen steps into that stand, deer were starting to stand up out of their beds by twos and threes. The hollow was crawling with whitetails.

Yet there are times when whitetails will seek out places where it is windy. Insects often send deer onto exposed ridges and outcroppings where the wind will give them some relief from the biting bugs. And heat is moderated somewhat if a whitetail can find a shady spot where the air is moving. On those warm Indian summer days in October when the temperature reminds you of August, I often look

"Yet there are times when whitetails seek out places where it is windy."

for whitetails at the base of lone trees on sunny, open slopes. But when the thermometer falls, deer don't want anything to do with windy slopes. Finding refuge from a *cold* wind is a matter of survival.

Constant exposure to wind in cold weather causes heat and energy loss that eats up a deer's fat reserves by the end of winter. Deer have a survival strategy of going into winter with as much fat reserve as possible. Because their winter diet is often not nourishing enough to give them a positive energy balance, their bodies draw on fat reserves to make up the difference. Any conditions, like a cold wind, that cause them to draw on that fat reserve may make the difference between life and death come late winter or early spring.

So, whitetails take refuge from a cold wind at any time of year. In studies conducted by Alan Wood on the prairies of eastern Montana, the sheltered bedding sites whitetails selected during windy days had wind chill indexes over 60 percent lower than nearby exposed areas.

Deer seem to put up with more wind when they are feeding, but only when temperatures are moderate. In very cold conditions, the energy gained by feeding can be offset by the energy loss caused by exposure to the wind. At these times, whitetails are better off not eating at all, and they remain bedded in sheltered spots.

Wind has its pros and cons for hunters, too. On a calm day whitetails can be just about anywhere. But when the wind comes up they will congregate on leeward slopes or behind windbreaks. If you know how to read the terrain and you understand how whitetails respond to windy conditions, you've got a whole lot fewer places to look for them.

Working against you is the fact that deer gathered on those leeward slopes are very alert. They're in their beds or they're up feeding, but they know they are more vulnerable because they are packed into smaller areas.

One windy-weather whitetail hunter I know says, "I've watched them feeding on those leeward slopes and they'll eat a few bites and then just throw their heads back in a real exaggerated fashion and look around. Then they'll feed a little more and then wheel around and look over their shoulder. They're just totally on edge. When you find these quiet spots on a windy day you've got to enter them like you're stepping into a church, because all the deer are looking."

Scouting for local windbreaks in the area you hunt is something you can do at any time of year. I remember look-ing for a Christmas tree several years ago and finding a deep, narrow draw that provided a dandy tree. It was also a quiet relief from the wind that was going wild in the rest of the forest. In hunting that same draw the following season, I confirmed its use as a windy-day whitetail hangout by bagging a big buck during a blow that could tear your socks off.

In forested land, draws and hillsides and even thick timber offer good windbreaks. When hunting agricultural land, look for hedgerows and eroded banks made by rivers and streams. Out on the prairie, whitetails are going to seek the most rugged country they can find. They'll tuck themselves up into cutbanks and washes and behind gumbo knobs.

When you find one of these sites, you should enter just the edge of it and then sit down and wait for 10 or 15 minutes. After a while you'll start seeing ears twitch, or a deer will get up and make one of those short little feeding circuits before he lies down again.

Although you'll want to sit for a few minutes at the edge of each likely windbreak, this is not a time to use the traditional deer stand approach. Since whitetails are not up and moving very much when it's windy, sitting in a stand for hours at a time isn't productive.

The trick is to keep checking out those windless sites. If you don't find deer in one, study the terrain and figure out where the next leeward slope or windbreak is and go to that.

Whether you're sitting or still-hunting, the old adage of keeping the wind in your face remains the golden rule. You're just wasting your time if you're walking with the wind at your back. You can quarter into the wind—have the wind coming at one side of you or the other—but forget about hunting the downwind side. Just concentrate on looking for deer on the windward side.

As one of my friends says: "Hunting whitetails in the wind is a real opportunity. You've just got to go from one leeward pocket to another and hunt those pockets very carefully once you locate them. There's no question that you're going to find deer after you've walked into two or three or four of them."

The Challenge of the Hunt

Even the most experienced whitetail hunter in the world will admit that he learns something new about the sport, and about his quarry, every time he goes afield.

Then again, perhaps it takes a lot of whitetail hunting experience to fully realize how humbling the pursuit can sometimes be. It happens sooner or later: You take a buck or two a few years in a row, and just when you think you know all about deer hunting, and are maybe considering passing up smaller animals from now on—"six points or better for me this year, boys"—along comes a season when you just can't get a shot at a buck. Or even see a buck. Not even a spike. And that, of course, is going to be the season when all your hunting buddies get deer. Nice ones, too.

Successful deer hunting boils down to two factors: luck and skill. The more hunting skills you gain, the less you have to rely upon luck to get a buck. Although you can't completely eradicate the luck factor from whitetail hunting (which is why the pants pockets of so many deer hunters bulge with assorted charms and talismans), you can increase and hone your skills. And the following stories will help you do just that.

SINCE 1895

FIELD & STREAM

THE SOUL OF THE AMERICAN OUTDOORS

TAKING A STAND AND HAVING WHITETAILS
MOVE IN ON YOU IS A TIME-HONORED TACTIC,
BUT WHEN THE DEER HOLD TIGHT, A DIFFERENT
APPROACH IS CALLED FOR.

By Sam Curtis

Whitetails
THE OTHER WAY

"JUST *WHAT* ARE YOU DOING?" THE VOICE CAME from above me as I stalked a hillside near a patch of brush in the middle of the afternoon. Looking into the bordering trees, I could see a splash of orange 10 feet off the ground. The hunter sat in his stand fuming.

"I'm hunting whitetails," I said.

"Then you're an idiot or an imbecile or you don't know a hill of beans about hunting whitetails."

"Thanks," I said, figuring politeness and humor were the better part of smoothing ruffled feathers. It got the guy to chuckle.

"Look, just go someplace and sit still. You don't *go after* these deer," the man said, "you let them come to you."

I waved my hand in acknowledgment and skulked off through the trees. Two hundred yards farther on a whitetail buck bedded down at the base of a lone fir offered an easy shot. I have to admit, it gave me a little cheap satisfaction.

Take a stand for whitetails. It's a strongly held attitude. Whitetails are nervous. They spook easily. So, most hunters have been brainwashed into thinking the only way to hunt them is to sit in a tree and wait. It's a tactic that works well when whitetails are on the move, but when they're holding tight, you want to be stalking.

What follows is a primer for whitetail stalkers, developed through a lot of trial and error. In short, these are tactics that have worked for me.

Best time to stalk: The time to move around for whitetails is when they are not moving. This is usually in the early afternoon or during windy or stormy days.

For generations, hunting lore has told us that whitetails become less active during the middle of the day, but not until recently has field research shown their most inactive time to be between noon and four in the afternoon. That's when a lot of whitetail hunters have lunch and take a siesta, but it's prime time for stalkers.

Also, a windy day will find a large percentage of whitetails hunkered down behind tree trunks or hummocks, hiding in the lee of hills, or down in protected hollows. A friend of mine claims that some of his best whitetail hunting in open country comes from walking slowly into a strong wind and carefully scanning the terrain for small windbreaks. He has come across numerous whitetails in a single day in this manner. And though the deer are invariably looking in his direction, they seem to hold longer than usual, perhaps because the wind completely masks his scent and sounds.

Stormy days also keep whitetails down. Snow or a cold rain often keeps deer under the cover of dense canopies of deciduous or coniferous trees. However, rain in warm weather doesn't seem to make a difference.

In Northern states during the hunting season, a prolonged snow may even encourage deer to congregate in and around yarding areas where they may spend days without moving much at all. These heavy concentrations of relatively sedentary whitetails make for excellent stalking opportunities.

A heavy mid-November storm three years ago caused a whitetail vanishing act where I was hunting. Suddenly, there were no deer in the areas where I'd been seeing at least five or six a day. But the next day I spent stalking the periphery of a local deer yard, and I counted twenty-seven whitetails while I moved slowly through the trees.

Best habitats to stalk: I've found my most successful stalking in places that are wooded or hilly. Where these two habitats are combined, it's even better.

Whitetails are most at ease in brush and thickets and amidst the trees. Vegetation breaks up their silhouettes and screens their movements. But the same vegetation that camouflages the whitetails can conceal a careful stalker.

Whitetails, especially bucks, are hiders. A whitetail will hold tight in the presence of danger until it gets too close for the deer's comfort. Then it will bolt. Chances are, a deer that bolts in this manner has been in a place where you could have spotted it *before* it spooked had you looked carefully enough.

One of the all-too-rare but nonetheless breathstopping aspects of stalking is that instant you see a set of eyes looking at you through the trees. The last time it happened to me I was just putting my foot down in the wet leaves on the far side of a log and my gaze was rising to search the branches of a dogwood thicket. At first, there was only a maze of branches, but then I was face to face with eyeballs and antlers.

Hilly terrain also allows you to move in close to white-tails. The crests of hills and ridges will hide you completely from deer that are on the other side, and you can ease over the crestline, revealing only your eyes and the top of your head, while you check the terrain on the other side for game.

The more closely spaced the hills and ridges are, the easier the stalking will be. And when hilly terrain is forested, you have additional protection from early detection.

Best places to stalk: Depending on the weather, three places seem particularly productive for stalking whitetails.

Before, during, and after a storm, the meeting zone of coniferous and deciduous vegetation seems to attract an unusual number of whitetails. With hardly any movement at all, the deer can take advantage of two different habitat niches. Usually, the deciduous vegetation offers the best food and escape cover, and the coniferous vegetation provides the best shelter from rain and snow and protection from radiant heat loss.

I rarely fail to see whitetails when stalking the meeting edges of aspen and fir stands in the West. And the best tactic seems to be to stalk as close to that meeting line as possible. Just before and just after the storm, I'll see most of the deer feeding in the aspens, and during the storm, most of them will be bedded under big firs. This is the typical pattern of use in adjoining deciduous/coniferous stands across the country around the time of a fall storm.

Another good place to stalk during any weather is a patch of favorite food. At night, whitetails may have bedding sites that are removed from feeding grounds, but during the day the deer are often quite content to rest and ruminate right in or near the places they like to feed. So, moving slowly through a stand of aspen or stripped maples or oak will often be the best way to find whitetails in the afternoon.

However, the all-time favorite and most productive whitetail stalking grounds for me are hillsides above brushy thickets. Because whitetails are especially jumpy during hunting season, they may spend their days in thicker cover than usual, making them particularly difficult to see. But, if you can stalk above this cover and look down into it, you may be surprised at how many whitetails can pack into even a small patch of brush.

The strip of hawthorn I like to hunt is so obnoxious I would never try to hunt *in* it. But it comes with a steep hillside at its back and a narrow, yet relatively level, game trail on which I can stalk parallel to the brush. On my best day ever, I saw five bucks in less than 100 yards. Sometimes, I don't see any deer at all though I never doubt that they're hiding there. It's a place any whitetail stalker would like to keep a secret.

Best conditions for stalking: It's amazing what a little moisture will do under a falling foot. The twigs, leaves, stems, needles, and husks that make such a racket when they're dried crisp start to calm down with even a good dew. Light rain quiets them even further. And a real drencher can make ground litter so wet and pliable that even a heavy stomp through the woods and fields can seem relatively noiseless. So, the rainy-day stalker has a definite advantage.

Snow can also help muffle your footfalls, but it depends on what kind. Crusty snow is crunchy, and snow at very cold temperatures is squeaky. But given 6 inches of snow at moderately cold temperatures, you can cover up all but the biggest mistakes in fancy stalking footwork.

Snow also lets you know if the deer have been around and how recently they have passed. Aging tracks in falling snow is a matter of checking the amount of snow in the tracks and estimating accumulation rates per 15 minutes or half hour. Aging tracks after the snow has stopped is a bit more subtle. For about an hour after it was made, a track will have the consistency of the snow around it. After that it begins to harden. I've found it helpful to make a fake track with two doubled over fingers, and compare the consistency of that with the real deer track. If the consistency of the

two tracks seems almost the same, you've got a very fresh deer track—one that's worth following.

Best method of stalking: At the heart of successful stalking tactics are the way you move and the way you observe the surroundings. Stalking for whitetails requires very slow, fluid movements. The biggest problem most hunters have is pushing the pace, and that defeats them from the start. I've found it helpful to keep in mind that the home range of a whitetail is typically very small—1 square mile or less is not unusual. Remembering that keeps the rush out of my movements and helps me concentrate on looking for deer. If you get used to thinking that each step you take will be *the* step on which you'll see a whitetail, you'll also find yourself slowing down.

Last year I was stalking whitetails in a dogwood patch when I realized I was moving much too fast. So, I consciously tried the next-step-will-be-the-one trick. After 20 minutes of that, I took the next step and did see a four-point that was totally unaware of my presence. The next-step gimmick had slowed me down enough to allow stalking to work.

Another trick you might want to try is the 100-steps-and-stop routine. Stalk slowly for 100 (roughly, you don't have to keep exact count) steps, and then stop for about 3 minutes. This has the tendency to make any hiding whitetail very nervous without actually causing it to bolt. What the tactic does, however, is goad the deer into making small movements—a flick of an ear, a turn of the head, or a shift in weight. It may even cause a bedded deer to stand up. Any of these movements could alert you to a deer's whereabouts, if you're watching the terrain carefully.

That's the other "must" for successful stalking. You've got to scan the whole scene at each step. It's something you learn to do with your eyeballs, not by twisting your head around and craning your neck. What you're looking for are any changes in shapes, colors, or densities that might alert you to the presence of a whitetail—a horizontal line among vertical trees, a hint of tan in a gray thicket, or a thickening of light behind some leaves. Any of these might be a whitetail upon closer inspection.

It's the careful, unhurried movements and the alertness to subtle changes in the looks of the landscape that ultimately let you stalk close to whitetails. So, the next time the deer aren't moving in on you, try hunting whitetails the other way.

WHEN THE WHOLE WORLD USES FEET AND WHEELS TO GET WHERE THE DEER ARE, THE WISE MAN PICKS UP A PADDLE.

By Jerome B. Robinson

Hunting Where Others
CANNOT GO

ALONG THE BANK OF EVERY brook, river, lake, and swamp in the wild lands of North America there is a game trail. That should tell you something about where big-game animals are often found. The edges of waterways are natural territorial boundaries as well as common travel routes. In deer country in late autumn these trails are always heavily marked by bucks; trees where bucks have rubbed their antlers and ground scrapes where they have left sign are exceptionally abundant along the edges of waterways.

For many years I have concentrated my hunting efforts close to water. Sometimes we travel a long distance by water to reach a remote area; on other trips we use a boat only to get to the other side of a stream or lake in order to get away from roads. Crossing water is the best way I know to get beyond other hunters and find a territory where the deer are moving according to their natural inclinations instead of being pushed around by people.

The best trips are when we go in for a week or so and set up a tent camp and hunt the remote back side of the country hunters can reach from roads. We go in November, just before the freeze. At this time, bucks are in full rut, searching day and night for receptive does, and resting only briefly now and then.

"Bucks like to bed on high ground near the sound of water," an old Maine deer hunter once told me. I've remembered that advice and over the years I've become satisfied that he had discovered something. When I hear the sound of a rapid, a little babbling brook, or the wash of waves along a shoreline, I look for high ground nearby. Often I find a buck's bed there, and sometimes he's in it.

Once we were camped on a remote northern Maine river in a good patch of deer country several miles downstream from the road. The flood plain was thick with alders in the bottoms, but where the ground was a little higher there were big patches of high grass and scattered ancient poplar trees. In back of that were miles of spruce and fir so dark and thick you had to pry your way through.

If the deer had sensed danger in the woods, they could have gone into the dark growth and never been seen, but we

had canoed into country too remote for road-bound hunters to reach, and the sign showed that deer were regularly crossing and feeding in the open areas.

That first afternoon I followed a game trail along the riverbank, checking sign and the lay of the country. The tracks of at least one big buck were evident, and the frequent ground scrapes and rubs on thick trees indicated that I was in an important piece of his real estate.

When I heard the rill of a little brook coming down off a hillside up ahead, I stopped and studied the terrain. A little fir-covered knoll caught my eye and I remembered about bucks bedding near the sound of running water.

With the breeze in my face I crept toward the knoll, stopping in the shadows every few steps and watching. The buck and I saw each other at the same instant, and my rifle spoke as he rose to his feet. He was a big eight-pointer, and I had him in the canoe and back to camp before my companions came in at the end of that first day's hunt.

There is a road to my streamside camp up in the New Hampshire-Quebec border country, but if I canoe across the stream, I enter a huge roadless block of woods that few hunters bother getting to. Just the simple act of crossing 20 yards of water separates me from the competition and puts me into country where the deer are moving on their natural schedules.

The deer pull the same ruse. When hunting pressure gets heavy, they simply cross the stream and go on about their business undisturbed. I've shot several nice bucks in that country, but the best was a heavy-bodied old eight-pointer with a rack that spanned 22 inches.

A group of us did a canoe hunt in Wyoming a few years ago and scored with six good bucks in two days of hunting. Actually, I think we could have killed all six the first day, but we didn't have room for that many deer in the canoes.

The cowboys we met in a saloon the night before the season opened laughed when they saw our canoes on the trucks.

"You need horses in this country," they chuckled. "Horses and a four-wheel drive. The bucks are high, up around the rimrock. Nothin' but does and fawns down along the river…"

They thought our canoes were silly little toy boats, just what they'd expect of people from Back East.

But the next morning, when the cowboys were all four-wheeling their horse trailers into the high country, we slipped our canoes into the river and went downstream to some big, brushy river bends that were on publicly owned BLM land. There we found a mother lode of deer.

There were lots of does and fawns, just as the cowboys had said. But have you ever known a buck in full rut that could stay out of a big piece of unhunted heavy cover that holds herds of well-fed does?

Once again, we had gained access to a deer hunting paradise by simply taking to the water.

Another year we went out to Minnesota and canoed a river that led us into some big swamp country that was beyond the reach of road hunters. You can check road maps and find these places. Just look for a blank spot in timbered deer country with a lake, river, or stream going in or coming out of it. Any such place is worth checking.

This time we were attracted to a low, boggy area with a river running through it. All that water assured us that men on foot would never go there. After a few miles of paddling we stopped to check the riverbank and found so much deer sign we elected to make camp right there. The whole place was tracked up like a sheep pasture, and there were half a dozen big buck rubs within sight of our chosen campsite.

That night we went to bed sure that this would be a short trip—we'd each have a good buck the next day.

But you want to watch out for overconfidence, which has a way of playing tricks on you. That night it started snowing, and by the time the storm stopped three days later, the snow was deeper than our knees and the river had clogged with slush and frozen solid, bank to bank.

"Well, we can't leave, we're frozen in," Jim said. "Nothing to do but hunt and hope the river opens up in a few days."

That was a rough hunt. The boggy country covered in snow looked smooth and walkable, but wherever we went we broke through thin ice beneath the snow and sometimes had to slog out through knee-deep ice water with deep snow on top.

Wet, miserable, and cold, we were fearful that the river might stay frozen and force us to stash our outfit in the woods until spring and walk out through those awful swamps. The second night after the big snow, Jim was late coming back to camp. Darkness came, another hour passed, and he was still out there. We fired signal shots, but heard no reply. We worried, but there was nothing we could do before daylight.

Two hours after dark, Jim stumbled into camp. He looked awful, all sweaty and covered with snow and debris and wet to the thighs. But he was smiling, and in his hand was a bloody plastic bag containing a deer liver and heart.

"How big is he?" we demanded.

"Twelve points, probably about 230 pounds dressed," Jim answered. "He was bedded with a doe on a little knoll above the river a couple of miles downstream."

Next morning we went out to help Jim drag the big buck the rest of the way to camp. On the way out we walked right into a six-pointer moseying along the riverbank.

That night rain came and the river began to rise. The ice would go out now, and we decided to go out with it in the morning. As we did, we realized that once more the canoe had enabled us to discover a fine piece of deer country we could call our own.

Water's Edge

When you hunt in country you haven't seen before, staying close to the edge of a waterway gives you a reassuring knowledge of where you are. You can't get lost following trails along riverbanks and lake shores, so you tend to hunt with extra confidence, and your mind is free to concentrate on observing the sights and sounds.

Using a boat to reach deer country also makes you a better deer hunter because it encourages you to study deer year-round. Every fishing trip in remote country becomes a deer scouting venture as well. Most of the boat hunts I have made have been conducted in areas we discovered while fishing in the spring and summer.

On early spring trout trips into remote country we are always alert to signs of where deer wintered. We make midday sojourns through the spring woods looking for deer sign—places where deer gather in the winter are usually in tall spruce and fir close to water. These deer concentration areas remain spotted with profuse droppings well into spring, and we make note wherever we find them.

We know that deer will be migrating toward these yarding areas when autumn snows coat the hills.

On later summer fishing excursions we note the development of foods deer will be attracted to come autumn. Will there be a heavy crop of acorns or beechnuts? Are there signs of heavy browsing on striped maple and raspberry bushes in the clearcuts?

We check the game trails close to water and assess the amount of deer traffic they are carrying. In early autumn when bird hunting, we continue to study the deer sign, checking for rubs when the bucks antlers harden and they begin to polish their tines.

When we finally choose a deer hunting destination, the decision is made on the basis of firsthand information and real knowledge of where to expect deer to be, as well as the discovery of places we can reach by boat or canoe that hunters will not get to from the roads.—*J.R.*

By Bob Robb

Tactical TREE STANDS

SUCCESSFUL TREE STAND hunting requires much more than buying a stand, randomly picking out a tree, and climbing aboard. *Here's how to do it right.*

Scout: You must locate areas where the sign is hot before choosing a stand site. They can include preferred-food sources, active trails and trail junctions, funnels, green field edges, fencelines, crops, scrapes, rubs, and the like. Look for fresh deer droppings, tracks, and signs of feeding activity, like fresh acorn caps, half-chewed corn cobs, and browse such as honeysuckle that's been nibbled on. During the pre-rut and rut, look for fresh rubs and scrapes.

As a general rule, the best stand locations for whitetails cover trails leading from food sources to bedding areas in the mornings, and are close to food sources in the afternoons.

Watch the Wind: Even if you're 20 feet off the ground, you have to hunt with the wind in your favor. It's important to set your stand so that game will approach upwind or crosswind of your stand, and for you to walk to the stand with the wind in your face. For example, when hunting a fresh scrape it's better to set up 30 to 100 yards downwind, and not right on it. Just how far depends on whether you're hunting with a bow or firearm, the terrain, and the thickness of the brush. Bucks usually approach the scrape on the downwind side to scent-check before walking to it; you don't want them coming in downwind of you.

Cover: Contrary to popular opinion, deer do look up! Set your stands so that you have as much cover around you as possible so deer and other game won't spot your movements or your silhouette. A backdrop of leaves and branches is minimal. When the leaves are off the trees, set your stand in a small clump of trees so the multiple trunks offer cover.

Don't Trim Too Much: When pruning branches (both around your stand and on the ground) to create shooting lanes, remove only the minimum amount of foliage to get the job done. Too much pruning and the game will be on to you before you know it.

Don't Move! Just because you're off the ground and in full camo doesn't mean game won't spot your movements. They will. To control my own fidgeting, I bring a paperback book to read while on stand and place cut branches on the edge of my stand so game can't see my feet shuffling. The less you move, the more game you'll see.

Beware of Hollows: If you set your stand in a hollow, you must be aware that deer may be moving on your level on the adjacent hillsides regardless of how high you set your stand. This makes it easier for them to spot the slightest movement.

> JUST BECAUSE YOU'VE GAINED SOME ELEVATION DOESN'T MEAN YOU'VE GAINED ANYTHING ELSE.

Stand Height: Choose stand height according to conditions. On flat, open ground, 12 feet may be enough. In thickets, 20 to 25 feet may be necessary for optimum stand placement. Do what's necessary to achieve the optimum compromise between cover, visibility, scent control, and your own fear of heights.

Be Quiet! When setting up a stand, traveling to and from the stand site, and sitting on stand, noise is a red flag to game. Secure all rattling stand parts, such as chains and exposed metal surfaces, when hauling the stand in. Before the season, lubricate stand parts to remove squeaks and groans. An old piece of carpet cut to fit makes a warm, quiet foot pad.

Minimize Your Gear: Some hunters aren't comfortable unless they pack the entire Cabela's catalog on stand. Come on, you're only going to be there a few hours! The less you bring, the less there is to get in the way.

Be Flexible: If you're seeing game from your stand, but it's out of range, be prepared to move the stand to the area where the game is moving. If there's no action by midmorning, or the area's been dead for days, climb down and scout for hot sign. When you find it, hunt it that afternoon or the next morning.

Ground Odor: Game, and especially whitetails, will smell where you've walked and avoid your stand site unless you take great pains to minimize the odor you leave on the ground. Wearing knee-high rubber boots is a huge first step; so is not walking directly on trails you think the deer will use to approach your stand. Not touching anything with bare skin is another. Washing your hunting clothes in no-scent detergent, storing them in a clean plastic bag, and putting them on in the field is another smart move.

TREE STAND TYPES

Portable or Fixed-Position Stands: The most popular stand type, these feature a platform and seat joined by metal poles, all of which are attached at the top to the tree trunk by either chain or nylon webbing, and supported on the bottom by either T-screws or built-in spikes. Tree steps or ladders are required to climb the tree when using portable stands.

There are more different makes, models, sizes, and styles of fixed-position stands than any other. They are also the most versatile, as you can use them safely with virtually any type, size, and height of tree. Many bowhunters like smaller fixed-position stands because they present a smaller outline against the tree trunk. Many fixed-position stands have a large support arm that wraps around the outer edge of the stand at chest height when the hunter is seated. This serves as both an added safety device and an excellent gun rest.

Climbing Stands: Climbers are popular in areas where there are lots of tall, straight trees with few limbs, like oak and birch. They are designed for quick, quiet climbing without the use of tree steps or ladders. They generally have two pieces, with the hunter raising and securing the top piece with his arms, then lifting and securing the bottom piece with his feet. They are usually heavier and bulkier than fixed-position stands.

Climbers are excellent when the hunter is scouting on the move, and prepared to set up and hunt hot sign that day. They are quick to set up, allowing the hunter to find his tree, assemble the stand, and climb into position in a few minutes. This makes changing stand location easy, but the downside is that they are impractical to use in trees with lots of large limbs or crooked trunks. You must also remember to connect the bottom section to the top section with a safety rope or cord. If the bottom portion slips off your feet and falls to the ground without the safety cord, you'll be left hanging—literally.

Ladder Stands: These use aluminum ladders secured to the tree, with a small seat/footrest built into the top of the ladder. Ladder stands are easy to climb, and are most popular on private land, where their bulk and weight are not a factor with hunters who leave them set up all season.

Ladders are growing in popularity each year because of their easy-to-set-up nature, and because they are generally very safe. When you begin securing the ladder to the tree, you must take care that it will not roll off the trunk at the top, a potential problem on small-diameter, slick trunks. Ladders generally permit you to get no more than 12 to 14 feet off the ground, with many only rising 10 feet up. They also create a large silhouette against the tree trunk.

Tree Slings: Generally used with tree steps or Step Stix, tree slings permit the hunter to sit in a sling held in place by several nylon web straps and/or rope. Slings allow the hunter to remain close to the tree trunk, reducing his outline, and also quietly maneuver around the tree trunk and change his shot angle, depending on the direction game is approaching from.

These are graduate-level stands that take some getting used to. They are popular with bowhunters because of their versatility and the small outline generated against the tree trunk. Most hunters use a pair of screw-in tree steps as foot rests once the sling has been set up, which makes waiting more comfortable.

Tripod Stands: Most popular in Texas and portions of the Southwest, where the tall trees needed to use more conventional tree stands are few and far between. Tripods are just that—three legs joined at the top, on which a rotating seat or shooting house is placed.

Tripods are monstrous stands, and stick out like a sore thumb unless they are set up inside or adjacent to a small tree such as a cedar. If set up and left for a long period of time, though, game will generally get used to their presence. Hunters sitting in an open-area tripod with a seat on top must take great care not to fidget, as they have little or no cover around them. Tripod stands are very stable, very safe, and easy to get in and out of. They work well when set overlooking large green fields, feeders (where legal), and open-country water holes.

Homemade Stands: These stands are constructed by hunters of wood, nails, and whatever else they may have lying around. Extreme caution should be used before climbing into a homemade stand you're not familiar with, as rotting wood and loose steps have been the cause of more than one serious accident.

ACCESSORIES

BESIDES A SAFETY belt and a means to climb into the tree, you'll need a small amount of other gear to successfully and safely hunt from tree stands. This includes:

1. Day pack: Keep it as small as possible.

2. Pruning shears: For snipping off small branches.

3. Compact saw: For trimming large branches. Brown-

ing, Uncle Mike's, and Game Tracker, among others, make good ones.

4. Pull rope: For hauling your gun or bow and day pack up and down the tree. Nylon parachute cord works well.

5. Bow or gun holder: Either hooks that screw into the tree trunk or holders that clamp onto the stand's platform keep the weapon handy and your hands free.

6. Headlamp: Better than a flashlight, it keeps your hands free for climbing up and down the tree in the dark.

7. Flagging: Can be used to flag a trail into the stand so it's easy to find in the dark. Fluorescent stick-on dots also work for this.

8. Wind detector: Talc-filled puff bottle or butane lighter works, but tying a piece of thread with small downy feather on a tree branch will allow you to constantly monitor subtle wind changes.

9. Pee bottle: 'Nuff said.

TREE CLIMBING AIDS

IF YOU'RE USING A fixed-position-type stand, you'll need some way to get up and down the tree. These include:

Tree Steps: Both screw-in and strap-on steps are available. When using screw-in steps, make sure they are screwed in tightly, with no gap between step body and tree trunk. Never set the steps so you have to take overly large steps from one to the next.

Both solid steps and steps that fold in the middle for compact carrying and storage are available. Several footrest sizes are also available, with the larger steps being the easiest and safest to use in cold weather with pac-type boots. The best screw-in steps have long, large-diameter screws that will bite deeply into the trunk. On trees with thick bark, you may have to chip the bark away to ensure that the step digs into the trunk itself.

Ladders: A series of lightweight aluminum ladders that come in sections, adjusting height as needed. Most are secured to the tree trunk by rope or nylon web straps. They are excellent when used on tall, straight trees. Two basic styles are available—those with sections that are made to be fitted together, and separate sections that are strapped to the tree trunk, one over the other. Both work well.

Ladders are gaining popularity because they are quick and relatively quiet to set up, very safe to climb, and cause no damage to the tree. Stand height can be adjusted up as long as you have more sections. When broken down, most ladders can be easily backpacked, with a stand, into remote areas.

Spikes: Similar to a telephone lineman's spikes. You attach one to each boot, then use them to dig into the tree as you climb with the aid of a climbing belt. Definitely a graduate-school tool, and used most often with tree slings and some fixed-position stands.

ARE YOU FEELING LUCKY?

WHEN DIRTY HARRY asked the would-be robber, "Do ya feel lucky? Well, do ya, punk?" he might also have been talking to the hundreds of tree stand users who refuse to wear a safety belt or harness. And each year, dozens of those "lucky" hunters come home crippled or dead.

Using a safety belt improperly can result in serious injury, too. Tree stand manufacturers have done tests with dummies dropped just a few feet, and the results are an eye-opener. "Most people aren't aware that for every foot they fall, they multiply their body weight by seventeen in terms of the pressure exerted when they hit the end of their belt or harness," said John Louk, president of Ol' Man Treestands. "That's the reason people who use safety belts improperly may not hit the ground, but are injured or killed anyway."

The best safety device is a harness, not the belt often provided with tree stands. If you fall while wearing a harness, you'll remain upright, not upside down or sideways, making it easier to get back under control. A harness will also distribute the shock and load better. If you wear a belt-type safety device, fasten it under your armpits, not around your waist. If you fall with it around your waist, the pressure of the belt can rupture internal organs or your diaphragm.

A safety belt or harness should be fastened around the tree trunk at head height when standing on the stand's platform, not at waist height. Then you can still maneuver to the edge of your stand, but if you do fall, you'll drop less than a foot, minimizing the load and keeping you in an upright position.

By Ross Seyfried

The Last
SECONDS

THE ONLY THING THAT CAN DEFEAT YOU IS YOU.

I N THE OLD WEST, THERE were two things that separated the winner and loser of a gunfight. The winner was mentally committed to the task. And, contrary to what popular Western lore would have us believe, he went for his gun first. The last few moments in a big-game hunt are a bit like an old-time gunfight. Some of us get it done . . . and others dither.

I've had the privilege of stalking game with some great African hunters, men from tribes who had, for many generations, depended upon hunting success for survival. While I employed them as trackers, many became friends and mentors. Perhaps the most valuable lesson I took from them was their almost universal belief that the game could

"feel your eyes upon them." When we stalked they always admonished me not to look at or even think about the animal we were trying to take.

While at times they carried this to the extreme, it makes sense. First, if you are looking at an animal he is very apt to see your eyes. Eyes play an extremely important role in communication, human and otherwise. Further, there is a sixth sense, a wild thing that we humans have mostly lost. A lion, on his way to a kill or to get a drink, can stroll past hundreds of antelope without drawing their notice. Take the same lion and the same antelope, but change his mental and physical posture to hungry and hunting, and pandemonium results. If, as we stalk, or as game approaches, we concentrate on things other than the animals, we are less apt to alert them, and we can use the time to set up a shot.

To see how it works, let's stalk a buck, a big buck, the chance of a lifetime. Imagine him with great sweeping beams, five rough points on each side and a gnarled drop point on the left side. He's old, buckskin-colored, and heavy, perhaps 300 pounds. He's the kind that makes the coolest hunter go blind and stupid. He's the kind that gets away. . . unless we do it right.

We found him bedded 800 yards away at the end of a long meadow. The wind is quartering in front, and while there isn't much cover, an old creekbed will conceal us for most of the way and there are some small bushes and a ridge of rock just 80 yards short of the monster.

Now it's time to move, because every moment that passes is a moment for something to go wrong. A shift in the wind, a curious doe, or simply a change in his mood that moves him into the heavy timber could end the hunt. We have the rough path in mind, having studied the ground with our binoculars, as we move down the ridge and slip into the cover of the creek. At the next bend we'll pause, wisely giving into that nagging urge to see him again. The distance is now 400 yards, a good time to "relocate" him and to check the path. Belly up on the edge, behind that clump of grass and look at the great antlers one last time. You won't see him again until it counts. Fix his position relative to the bushes and rocks.

Before you move, make sure: Is the rifle loaded, one in the chamber, safety on, scope clear? Make sure; look at every detail one last time. Now go, not thinking about the deer or looking for him. Think about the stick you might break, the stone you might roll, and about your movement from the creek to the bushes.

Now you are there, 20 yards from the rocks and bushes, 100 yards from the buck. Take a deep breath and really begin to see the terrain in front. Five thick bushes all offer perfect cover. All you have to do is crawl up behind any one of them and the buck is yours.

But when you reach your bush, how will you shoot? They are thick, very thick. If you finish the stalk behind any of them you will not have a clear shot. There! The last bush on the right, and the 2-foot rock beside it. The bush is the main cover, then you can crawl to the rock. It's both the rest for your shaking hands and the elevation to put the muzzle above the meadow grass.

You are 20 yards from the prize. Every second, every sound, every move is critical now. As you crawl, watch the rock, study it; it is the key. The buck will take care of himself, don't think about him.

You've reached the bush and your heart is crashing. Think, think about what you must do. The rock has a perfect fold 3 feet to your right. Slide to it gently and remember the safety. It must come off as you push the muzzle past

the rock. (How many deer have raced away as a hunter bent his trigger with the safety catch locked?) With the safety off and your finger safely beside the trigger guard, slide over the rock with your left hand holding the fore-end. Don't rest the stock, and certainly not the barrel, on anything. Doing so will put the shot high. Rest your hand on the rock.

There he is, and your eyes go to the huge head. No, no, look at his shoulder, see the blade of grass in front of the muzzle. Everything is shot placement now; you must hit the correct spot. The buck senses your presence and is standing. Calculate his stance and position. If he is facing away, you must hold back on the ribs; if he's facing toward you, you must strike well forward on the shoulder. Look past the scope and move the barrel to clear the grass, for even this tiny stem will deflect the bullet. He is facing three-quarters forward. See the fold in the hair on the point of his shoulder; use it as a target. Now focus on the trigger; the trigger is critical. Say it over and over, like a prayer: "Squeeze, squeeze, take your time, do not flinch." You've done everything else, now you must be a rifleman. Gently load the trigger. There is no doubt.

<hr />

IF, INSTEAD OF the long, planned stalk, the encounter was a surprise one, you finish the last seconds in the same way. Make every move slow, deliberate, and efficient. Seek a rest, a clear bullet path, and cover, as you slowly move the muzzle toward the target. Look at the deer with sideways glances, not a direct stare. Study every limb that could serve as a rest or deflect a bullet. Then pick your spot, bring the rifle up, take the safety off, and squeeze.

If you hunt from ambush, many of the same elements apply. Once you're safely in the blind or stand, load your rifle and double check it. Make sure the scope is clean and then look over the ground as you watch for game. Play "what if?" What if he comes from there, or down that path? Point your rifle in the direction most likely to present a shot. Ask yourself where and how you will support the rifle to make a shot in any of these places: on a limb, over your knee, against the tree trunk itself? As the game appears, your first job is to be sure it is game and not another hunter, then decide if it's the animal you want. At the same time, if the barrel needs to be moved into shooting position, study when and where you will be able to make that move without giving yourself away. Don't wait until you want to fire to position the rifle; do it beforehand, gently and slowly, preferably when the game's eyes are looking away. Now release the safety and begin to plan your bullet placement. Pick a clear path to the buck, and remind yourself of the basics of marksmanship.

But what if your carefully laid plans go astray? What if you, a right-hander, are in a tree stand, and the buck shows up behind your tree, on the right side? To stand and turn that way will give you a good view of a pretty white flag bounding through the timber. Patience might bring him in front, but a good ambush hunter is at least partially ambidextrous.

As the deer looks away, gently switch hands and shoot him southpaw. With a little practice, standing shots with a rifle are quite easy from our off side, especially if you've thought it out before panic sets in!

Ultimately, every hunt is different, but the same. Think about the details—what you're going to do in the next 3 seconds and the next 3 minutes—rather than the game. Hunt as a race car driver drives. Brake before the turn, then think about the next curve while you negotiate the one at hand. Seconds are actually long enough to be very useful. If you use them wisely, even the toughest situation can seem easy.

By Byron W. Dalrymple

ZEROING IN . . .
The 40-Acre Whitetail Hunt

DEER DON'T TRAVEL FAR; WHY SHOULD YOU?
IF YOU'RE COVERING MILES, YOU'VE PROBABLY
PASSED BY THE BUCK YOU'RE LOOKING FOR.
HERE'S HOW TO *CONCENTRATE* YOUR SEARCH.

WHEN I BEGAN DEER HUNT-ing, I was forced to learn what is perhaps the most important lesson of the craft. At that time I lived near a vast State Forest. There was a two-week season, one buck only, and hunting was not easy. The local measure of a hunter's expertise was how far he walked in a day. A buck tagged every two or three years was average.

A friend owned 160 acres, single-wire fenced, deep inside the Forest. Four of us hunted there, and for safety, each of us hunted a designated section. We split it evenly, and each hunter had a mere 40 acres. The first year I didn't bag a buck; however, I did learn my assigned plot virtually tree by tree. I could have drawn a map—and labeled every hemlock, balsam, maple, oak, and the easy crossings of the short stretch of creek in my territory. I had sat on every ancient pine stump left from lumbering days, and had noted poplar and birch patches. Each succeeding year for as long as I hunted there, I tagged a buck. I knew that area as well as the deer did.

The taking of one buck during those years is worth recounting. It succinctly illustrates how intimate knowledge of a small tract beats aimless wandering and hoping.

Beech trees were scarce in that region then, but I'd often noted two venerable giants, the only ones on my tract, gracing a low ridge above the creek. I kept hoping that one fall those trees would produce a crop. My wife had once made a delicious beechnut cake, and those trees must have known my wishes. One fall as deer season was about to open, the ground beneath them was littered with hulls.

Sixty paces from the beechnut trees a moss-covered pine stump surrounded by head-high balsams made a perfect hiding place. On opening day I was there before dawn. While the light in the woods was still subdued on that quiet, frosty morning, a stunning 10-pointer walked up the slope from the creek, straight to the special treat of beechnuts. Broiled fillets from its backstrap were topped off that evening by a slice of my wife's beechnut cake.

Consider a deer's routine. Its normal range is roughly a square mile—640 acres. Where forage conditions are optimum, a deer may live its entire life without moving outside its home territory. Whitetails are homebodies. If one wanders outside its established bailiwick, or is disturbed into fleeing out of it, the animal soon returns.

It's doubtful that a hunter could become intimately acquainted with a 640-acre tract, but deer know every square foot, every stick, stone, bush, and tree of their home. During a period of several days, a deer is virtually certain to move over its entire territory. Furthermore, good range will hold several deer per square mile, all of them moving around. Chances are high that one or more deer will spend part of any given day within ¹⁄₁₆th—40 acres—of its home range.

You can study a small area like that meticulously, and

in a short time come to know it as well as the deer do. This approach is especially useful to a hunter in strange territory. By sticking to a small area and working it yard by yard, and slowly hunting through this small plot of land, he learns to be inconspicuous, and disturbs deer far less than he would wandering widely.

On a deer hunt in Maine one fall, I met a native who perfectly summed up the small-area philosophy. He was known locally as a wizard at always bringing in his buck, but he had a bum left leg.

"This leg's a nuisance," he told me, "but I have to say that it's a help in deer hunting. I can't walk fast, or very far, so I hunt a small piece of woods and always know where the deer are, or will be, and when and why."

The choice of 40 acres as a hunting ground, of course, is arbitrary. That Maine hunter didn't know how large his chosen area actually was, but guessed it was about 50 acres. On a Wisconsin hunt one season I was expounding my 40-acre theory to a hunter who scoffed: "On such a tiny piece you'd have to sit. There wouldn't be room enough to move around." I offered to prove that 40 acres was a larger expanse than he imagined. Farmers and many country dwellers know this, but urban hunters, the majority of today's sportsmen, have little concept of woodland space. We went into the forest where we both were hunting, measured our paces to make certain we each stepped off a yard equally. I set a compass course and we paced north as straight as possible. After 440 paces he began to change his view. I pointed out that if we now went 440 paces to the east, and likewise south, then returned to our starting point, we would have walked the perimeter of a square 40-acre plot—and would have traveled 1 mile.

Certainly you shouldn't settle for just any randomly selected slice of habitat. The plot I was assigned as a tyro was different because the 160 acres that the four of us divided was all prime range. What you should do is scout a sizable expanse of woods, looking for specific attributes. Your choice of tract should contain a deer's basic requirements in ample portions. Forage is the most important. Deer spend more time eating than at any other activity. When deer are moving to and from specific feeding areas, and are at those areas, they're more vulnerable than at any other time, since they must show themselves en route and while feeding.

The abundance of food of special seasonal kinds at specific places (such as those two beech trees) presents golden opportunities. A friend bowhunts an area that contains several black cherry trees with low limbs and a thicket of choke cherries. In heavy crop years, deer will gorge on the fruit for a few days. I've hunted a Southern forest where small groups of chestnut oaks occur along a creekbottom. Their acorns, extra large and sweet, are prized by deer. Even with numerous other oaks present, deer will seek the chestnut oaks first. I selected my plot to include several groups of these trees, and took a fair buck on the second morning.

The tract you select should contain plenty of standard browse. Some special seasonal foods are invariably present, and you can find them if you study the area closely. If there is water, especially a stream, great. Water is seldom a problem for whitetails, except in the few arid terrains they inhabit, and they'll travel and feed along a creek or river, which is a focal strip for movement. Areas where safety and comfort are a factor are very important. In hilly country, be sure your hunt area has several draws. Deer commonly travel from bottoms to ridges along these, and the heads of draws

are prime bedding places because they're safe and comfortable. In flat or gently rolling woodlands, dense clumps of conifers, or lower story brush with tall timber above, form resting hideouts.

If the 40 acres you select has all or most of these attributes, and you know the area well, your odds of success far surpass those of the wandering, long-distance hunter. In laying out your boundaries, try to keep the plot as close to square as you can. A rectangle, especially a narrow one, is difficult to hunt unobtrusively, and disturbed deer can leave it too easily. In a square tract, a deer jumped inadvertently may stay within the boundaries.

The most vital part of the small-area scheme is how thoroughly you learn the place. Each tree, each bush counts—even its species and whether or not deer eat it. Every rock, downed tree or ancient log, every minor land contour, and every creek crossing should be memorized. Every deer sign is a key to potential success.

Another buck I took during those early years classically illustrates the effectiveness of putting memorized observations together. At one point on both sides of the creek there was an opening in dense alders. Printed in soft earth on either side were deer tracks pointing in both directions. On the far side from where I observed this, numerous witch hazel bushes, scrub poplar, and maple were present, all of which are relished by deer. I put all this on my mental map.

⟡

FIFTY YARDS FROM this crossing, a low ridge paralleled the creek. Along the ridgeside, I happened to see several dimly printed deer tracks pointing to the right, directly opposite the alder crossing. Idly prowling the ridgeside, I came to a deep, narrow saddle. The thought crossed my mind that deer, which are creatures of habit, might come from the browse patches across the creek, move to the ridgeside, turn right along it to the little saddle, and pass through to the area of large cedar trees beyond. When I checked, there were indeed tracks going both ways through the saddle.

I squirreled away these details. A day later I remembered the dark patch of cedars that I'd studied earlier. It was directly in line, roughly 100 yards into the woods from the

saddle. There I'd seen an abnormal amount of droppings and several places where wintergreen and bracken were flattened, indicating a deer had bedded there. I began putting the pieces together, adding the fact that I'd seen a rub on a small balsam near the saddle.

I imagined a buck feeding through dawn and after across the creek, then crossing around 8 A.M., trotting to its right along the ridge slope, and moving left into the saddle. I could envision it giving the balsam a few rips with its antlers, then moving on to bed down during midday in the cedars.

I had hunted four days without seeing a deer. I decided to play out my imagined scenario. Before dawn I sneaked into the saddle, and took a stand among some small balsams within 20 feet of it. If I moved farther away, I couldn't see to shoot.

Dawn crept in with utter stillness. By 8 A.M. I began wondering if this was just foolish imagining. By 8:30 I was convinced. As I started to arise, I thought I heard a minor splash of water. I eased back and got my rifle ready. I actually heard the *tap, tap, tap* of the deer's hooves as it trotted toward me along the ridgeside, the lightly frost-hardened ground enhancing the sound.

The animal turned into the opening of the saddle and paused to lick its opposite side. I was so astonished watching my imagined drama played out, pieced together from bits of intense observation, that I almost forgot the rifle. It occurred to me that the deer had still done everything I'd pictured except rip the little balsam a time or two, enlarging its former rub.

And then, as if on cue, it did just that—and I shot. It wasn't any trophy, just a modest, narrow-antlered seven-pointer with one tine broken. Or was it an authentic trophy? At any rate, it proved that the 40-acre whitetail hunt is a sound idea. I'm almost embarrassed to reveal that I had the deer's head mounted as a reminder.

> "The most vital part of the small-area scheme is how thoroughly you learn the place."

By Ray Sasser

The Scientific RATTLER

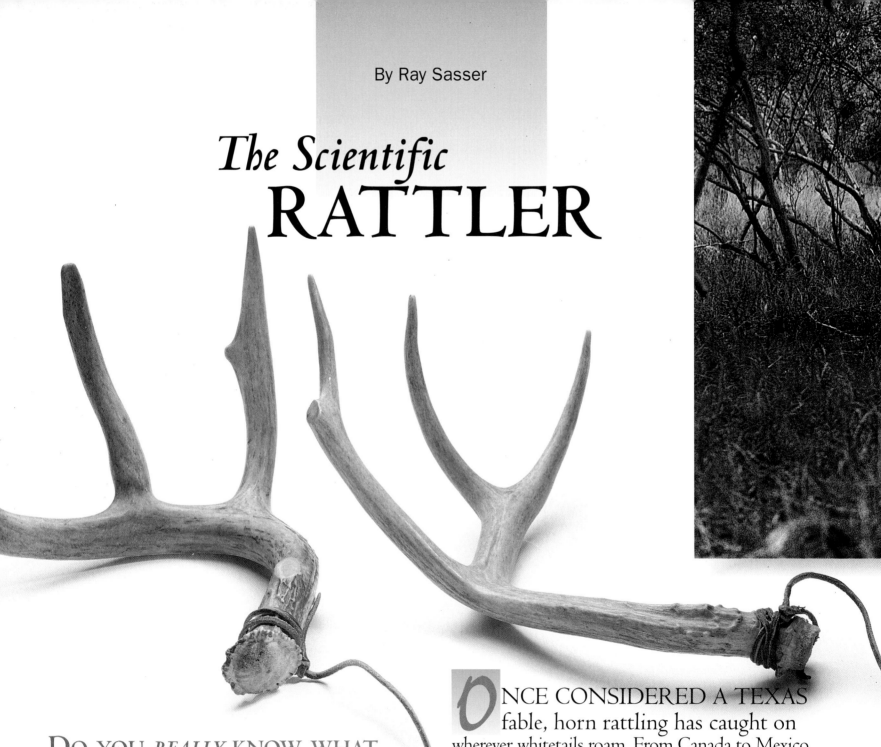

DO YOU *REALLY* KNOW WHAT
HAPPENS WHEN YOU WHACK
THOSE HORNS TOGETHER?

ONCE CONSIDERED A TEXAS
fable, horn rattling has caught on
wherever whitetails roam. From Canada to Mexico,
hunters report success in rattling up bucks with everything
from plastic antlers to dried mesquite branches. Hunters
know that rattling works, but they don't necessarily know
why it works. Mickey Hellickson, a University of Georgia
graduate student working on a doctoral degree in wildlife
science, has spent three years trying to find the answer.
While the primary part of Hellickson's unique study was to

radio-track bucks and determine activity patterns based on age (the older they get, the less they move), he decided to branch out into the rattling study.

The study actually consisted of two parts. In part one, a horn rattler on the ground did the actual rattling in sequences that varied in length and volume. An observer on a nearby 30-foot tower watched for bucks and videotaped the deer.

In the second part of the study, Hellickson located radio-collared bucks of known age and size, rattled where the deer could hear the sounds, and tracked them via radio telemetry. During 197 sessions, 132 bucks were rattled up. On two occasions, researchers rattled up eight different bucks during a 30-minute session.

"The first study was designed to figure out which rattling sequences attracted the greatest number of bucks," says Hellickson. "We also broke the study into pre-rut, peak-rut, and post-rut rattling to see if timing made any difference in which deer responded and how they responded."

What's the best time to rattle? For mature bucks, Hellickson found the highest response during the post-rut period, after most breeding is over. He believes that young bucks are bunched back up into bachelor groups in the post rut and are more interested in feeding than fighting. Mature bucks remain in the aggressive breeding mode well after the primary rut has finished.

The second-best time to rattle up mature bucks is pre-rut. Interestingly enough, bucks during this period are also bunched in bachelor groups. What Hellickson observed is that only one buck in a bachelor group is likely to respond to pre-rut rattling. That will be the group's dominant buck, most likely the oldest.

If you're rattling with the idea of attracting just any buck, the peak of the rut is the best time to do it. That's when Hellickson had the highest overall rattling success. Unfortunately, most of the bucks rattled up during the rut are young to middle-aged.

"Bachelor groups have broken up during the rut," says Hellickson. "Mature bucks are the most efficient at finding and tending estrus does. During the rut, mature bucks are likely to be occupied with actual breeding. The younger deer are not as likely to be tending does. Since they're not in bachelor groups dominated by one buck, younger bucks respond to fight sounds best during the rut."

Even among the ranks of veteran horn rattlers, there is disagreement on why bucks come to fight sounds. There are two theories. One is that rattling is a territorial response. The deer is incensed that other bucks have invaded his territory. The second theory involves estrus does. If bucks are actually fighting over a doe, a third buck, attracted by the sounds of battle, hopes to slip in and make off with her. Hellickson believes that bucks respond to rattling for both reasons.

Hellickson's studies were done on two well-managed ranches with large numbers of mature bucks and good buck-to-doe ratios.

"I have not done these studies on deer herds that are consistent with what most hunters see," admits Hellickson. "In most deer herds, the bucks are much younger than in my study and there are many more does than bucks. In that more typical situation, I don't believe rattling is nearly as effective."

The use of a tower observer in Hellickson's first study confirmed what most veteran horn rattlers already suspected—a lone hunter on the ground never sees the majority of bucks that he attracts. Bucks come to the sounds, circle cautiously downwind, realize they've been duped, and leave without ever being seen. The observer in the tower saw more than twice as many bucks as the hunter on the ground. Hellickson figures that a whitetail hunter actually spots only about one-third of the bucks he rattles up.

It was the telemetry study that revealed the best news for fans of the horn-rattling art. During this phase, Hellickson located radio-collared bucks by electronic receiver. He moved to a downwind position so the deer would not be aware of his presence.

By approaching to within 200 to 300 yards of the target buck, researchers were certain the deer could hear their sounds. They then began the rattling sequence, at the same time electronically monitoring the buck's response. The radio-collared deer ranged in age from three and a half to eleven and a half years. The buck with the biggest antlers scored about 165 Boone and Crockett points, just shy of record book proportions.

"We divided the bucks up into two basic categories, depending on antler size," says Hellickson. "The smaller bucks scored 130 or fewer B&C points. The larger bucks scored 130 or more. Even when we never saw the deer, we knew what they were doing. Seventy-five percent of the trophy bucks responded to the rattling. Only fifty percent of the smaller antlered bucks responded."

The basic response was for the deer to head directly toward the sound, then veer around in a semicircle in an obvious effort to gain the wind. Sixty-five percent of the deer made their final approach to the fight sounds from downwind.

That leaves 35 percent of the deer coming with the wind, thus losing their most important defense mechanism—their sense of smell. "Mature bucks were no more likely than immature bucks to circle and use the wind," says Hellickson. "In fact, we were unable to determine that mature bucks are any smarter about how they approach fight sounds."

Perhaps the most fascinating part of the telemetry study was that the same bucks would respond more than once.

"We rattled to six different bucks more than once and five of them responded the second time just like they did the first time," says Hellickson. "The 160-class buck responded both times. We rattled three times to a six-and-a-half-year-old buck and he responded all three times."

The older deer get, the less they move and the more deliberate are their movements. That's obviously an age-related adaptation to conserve energy. However, extremely old bucks can and do breed does and will respond to fight sounds. Since bucks with the biggest antlers are generally older than five and a half years, that's good news for deer hunters.

＊——＝❖＝——＊

HERE ARE SOME rattling tips that Hellickson proved effective:

Rattle as loudly as possible. You can't make too much noise. Buck fights are brutal.

Rattle with a partner when practical. The hunter should position himself downwind from the rattling sounds, preferably in a tower, tree, or on a hill that provides maximum visibility. It's also possible for two hunters to combine efforts. I like to grind antlers together while a companion pounds the ground with his rattling horns and occasionally mixes in a grunt call.

Set up to provide good downwind visibility. Use an odor neutralizer or place a cover scent downwind of your position. The fresh tarsal glands from a buck will add credibility to the fight sounds.

Wear camouflage (including a face net) where it's legal and there's no danger of other hunters mistaking *you* for a deer. In any case, take advantage of brush or other cover to break up your outline.

Rattle from a spot that's near the thick cover used by bucks for sanctuary and bedding areas. The least productive rattling spots are generally the most open ones.

Pick your rattling conditions carefully. The worst situation is high wind, simply because the deer can't hear the fight sounds well. Hellickson's best rattling success came between 7:30 A.M. and 10:30 A.M. Best weather fea-tured cloudy skies with light wind and low to moderate temperatures. Those peak conditions probably vary from one region to the next.

Rattle during the pre- or post-rut if you're hoping to attract the biggest bucks.

Be patient. Hellickson's rattling sequences required 1 to 3 minutes, followed by silence when he watched and listened for responding bucks. Twenty-five percent of the bucks that responded showed up after the third rattling sequence, a full 20 minutes into the session. Hellickson recommends waiting at least 30 minutes before giving up on a rattling location.

Use other sounds. Hellickson often used grunt tubes to supplement antler clashing. He and his research assistants also rubbed antlers against brush between rattling sequences. Deer responded to the combination. In fact, the rubbing of antlers against brush caused approaching bucks to stop and fight brush as an attempt to intimidate unseen rivals.

Don't give up. Hellickson still doesn't know why horn rattling works one day and not the next. Nor did his research make it possible for him to predict how he'd do on a given day. Always give it your best shot. The buck of a lifetime may be just out of sight, waiting for that one last crack of the antlers before he comes in.

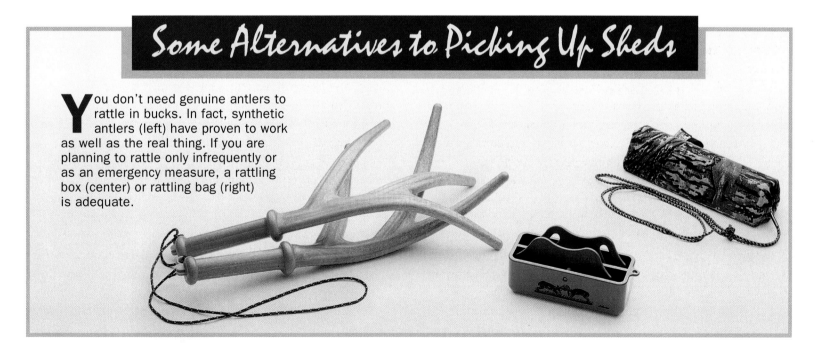

Some Alternatives to Picking Up Sheds

You don't need genuine antlers to rattle in bucks. In fact, synthetic antlers (left) have proven to work as well as the real thing. If you are planning to rattle only infrequently or as an emergency measure, a rattling box (center) or rattling bag (right) is adequate.

By Byron W. Dalrymple

BE READY
When the Deer Is

ARE YOU TIRED OF WATCHING HELPLESSLY AS WHITETAILS DISAPPEAR IN THE DISTANCE? THEN IT'S TIME YOU GAVE SOME THOUGHT TO CHANGING THE WAY YOU HUNT THEM.

ONE FALL WHILE STILL-hunting for whitetail deer, I slowly worked out a strip of timber, gun at the ready every second. Coming to the end of the trees without sighting a target, I swung my rifle sling over my shoulder and started across an open, tall-grass field of possibly 50 acres. On the far side was another plot of likely timber.

Halfway across, I was startled to see a handsome eight-point buck rise from its bed in the grass, way out here in the open. It, too, was startled. It stood for perhaps five seconds, broadside, and stared. Then it ran like blazes. I simply stood and gawked. No buck was *supposed* to be bedded down out here in the open!

Every deer hunter, I'm sure, has been involved in comparable situations. The problem is invariably the same. The deer appears during one of those moments when the hunter isn't ready or is unable to do the shooting. Trying to think of all the situations that might thwart a shot isn't easy. Nonetheless, as most expert deer hunters agree, incessant high-key alertness and detailed plotting are essential to success.

A Wisconsin hunter whose den wall is covered with trophy-size heads explained this the best I've heard. "Many hunters," he told me, "fail to understand the imbalance between hunting time and shooting time. Think of it like this: During deer season there probably will be an average of 10 hours of hunting light each day. If you're fortunate enough to have a week to hunt, that's 70 hours. Maybe you'll get several opportunities for shots. Or perhaps you'll get only one, or at least only one at a deer you really want."

Most chances, he pointed out, come and go in no more than 10 seconds. So given 70 hours of hunting time, there may be only 10 seconds of shooting time buried somewhere in them. Even if several opportunities are presented, and they're longer than 10 seconds, at best you'll have only a couple of minutes out of 70 hours to make it a successful hunt.

"There's no way," he concluded, "to predict when any one of these brief periods may occur. A deer hunter who is successful most of the time has to be ready *all* of the time!"

That buck bedded in the open grass field taught me one of the specific lessons of alertness. General experience, and reams of deer hunting literature, teach that when deer, especially whitetails, are resting, they are always in dense cover. But "always" is a word that should be deleted from the deer hunter's dictionary. *Most* deer rest in heavy cover. However, an individual deer may be, at any time, anywhere it wants to be, which means that it may be…anywhere. The hunter who stays cocked, always expecting the unexpected, is the one who has the advantage when an opportunity arises.

Much of the art of staying ready concerns alertness to small details. A classic example of failing to follow this advice took place during a mule deer hunt I made with a friend in western Texas. We were driving during midday on a large ranch, pausing to glass for deer. I was at the wheel, and my friend was to do the shooting. We finally spotted a big ten-point rack silhouetted against bright yellow grass. The deer was lying in shade beneath a piñon.

The small pine was the only tree in the area. A low, grass-covered ridge ran up to the right. Fifty yards upslope a motte of shinoak not much taller than a deer spread over an expanse of possibly 30 yards. My companion, hopping with excitement, got out, and, hurriedly circling left, began a sneak, hoping to get within close range.

Presently he appeared, bellying over a small hummock not

more than 75 yards below the bedded trophy. It looked so easy, but a critical detail had been overlooked. Because the grass was tall, both he and the buck would have to get up for him to place a shot.

The buck rose. The hunter started to. The deer whirled and bolted up the ridge, behind the single piñon. The hunter by then was moving aside, trying to clear the pine, the branches of which now screened the deer from his view because of the angle of the slope. By the time my friend got into position, the buck had wheeled around the shinoak motte; and before he could move again, the deer was over the ridge.

Afterward he admitted he'd been impetuous, and we discussed how it should have been done. Had he looked the layout over carefully, then circled *right*, behind the low ridge, he could have come back over and downslope, covered by the shinoak patch. A sneak around its end, rifle ready, would have allowed him to shoot from above at close range, over the grass. The buck probably could have been killed in its bed.

Indeed, the lament, "There was just that one tree in the way!" has for years been a minor-key dirge sung by hunters in practically every deer camp in the nation. Few who sing it seem to realize that *they* put the tree in the way by poor planning. Whether you're on a stand or still-hunting, meticulous attention to trees and land contours that could become shot spoilers will help keep you watching, or moving, so you'll be ready when a deer is.

There are numerous other situations of which to be cognizant, and to avoid or use to your advantage. Light direction is one. When my sons, Mike and Terry, were beginning to hunt deer, one of my instructions was a basic rule I've long followed. On bright days, hunt west early in the morning, and east late in the day, unless the breeze direction makes it impossible, in which case, hunt north or south.

I pointed out that there are two reasons for this. When you face bright light from a low-slanted sun, in numerous instances your scope becomes useless, overwhelmed by brightness. Also, if breeze direction, or lack of one, allows you to put the sun directly at your back, you have deer at a disadvantage. Staring into bright sun inhibits their vision just as badly as it does yours.

Mike and Terry were youngsters then, and during that period they didn't think the Old Man was nearly as smart as he later became. They didn't pay much attention, so it amused me when each in turn came to me full of frustration with a tale about a buck that stood and stared as they desperately tried to see him through a scope, looking into the sun. The Old Man's wisdom suddenly was amazing.

Oddly, a surprising number of unready moments occur where they'd be least expected, and most easily avoided, to hunters on stands. Three that I can think of offhand are typical.

"I had built myself a seat in a tree," one sad story goes. "There was one limb I straddled. I had my gun on the right side of it when a deer appeared to the left. When I moved my gun I clunked the limb, and the buck was gone. It was plain dumb not to have cut it off in the first place."

"I was sitting on stand, gun ready, with a good rest," runs the second lament. "A real trophy buck appeared, close. I moved my foot and there was this stick that popped. You can bet I've cleaned every twig from stands I've used since."

The third tale of woe goes like this: "A wet year had resulted in tall grass covering openings. I was sitting down, and not until the deer showed did it dawn on me that the grass was as tall as the deer. I'd have to shoot through many yards of the stuff, and I did. Maybe not every bullet would have been deflected, but mine was. It was a valuable lesson."

It's difficult for a hunter to anticipate all the problems that may crop up. Some you simply have to experience. The best example of this happened to an archer friend with whom I was hunting mule deer in open country. We'd built a small blind of sagebrush on a hillside above a creek waterhole, near which was a welter of deer tracks. Short sage grew around the pond.

The plan was to wait for a suitable buck to come in to drink. When it put its head down to the water, the short sage would be above its eyes. The archer would slowly rise and shoot down on it over the front of the blind.

The first two deer to come in were does. My friend decided to make a practice draw on them. As they started to drink, he made his play. The deer flushed in a panic. We had no idea why. The next deer was a most desirable buck. When its head was lowered, the archer again eased up. The same thing happened. Before he could get off an arrow, the buck all but turned wrong side out getting away.

Not until I went down to the waterhole and had him rise and draw his bow did we dope out what was wrong. His movement and figure were perfectly mirrored in the water. To the drinking deer, he appeared to be rising right at them out of the pool.

Much of deer hunting lore is concerned with thwarting the animals' three keen senses. Most hunters understand this and follow the obvious rules. They hunt across a breeze to keep deer from scenting them. They use various ruses to keep deer from seeing them, and realize that motion, not necessarily the shape of an immobile human form, is what draws the attention of the quarry and often frightens it. Yet there are always those errors, like the image in the pool, that result in the deer being readier than you are.

Among these are *small* sounds. Deer hearing is acute. Animals that haven't yet seen or scented danger are often especially uneasy about noises they don't understand, particularly ones repeated at rhythmic intervals. I hunted one fall with a fellow who wore a squeaky boot. The day was still and damp, and every step he took—*squeak squeak.* I moved off to hunt on my own, and I could still hear him many yards distant. I saw several deer and shot a doe. When we got back together he told me he'd seen nothing.

I recall another still-hunter who carried a rifle with a sling swivel that tinkled and rattled. He was so used to it that I doubt he even heard it. Deer may not be afraid of such unnatural sounds, but you can bet those sounds will direct their attention toward you, which is the last thing you want.

What causes the most ruined opportunities? For several seasons I asked this question of hunters I met, and urged them to tell me their sad tales. The consensus (by a wide margin) was that the majority of foulups were due to lack of a rest, or a poorly chosen one.

A still-hunter friend missed what he claimed was the top trophy of all his hunting years because he tried an off-hand shot. A few hunters, to be sure, are good at shooting offhand. This is not, however, a very sensible or accurate way to shoot a rifle. Most hunters miss more than they hit when trying it, or wound deer.

This hunter now operates as if he's hunting rests as diligently as deer. "I'm constantly aware of vertical saplings, stumps, blowdowns, large boulders, fenceposts—anything that will serve for a solid rest. I still-hunt so I'm always near a quick rifle rest."

Setting up a proper rest on a stand is just as important. Where can a deer appear? What will serve most quickly and efficiently to cover all the possibilities? Some rests may place your barrel too high or too low; others may allow you to steady your rifle only at a certain angle.

The most ingenious rest arrangement I've seen was shown me by a rancher friend in Texas. He sat me beside a small post oak on a low rock bluff overlooking a narrow, wooded valley. He picked up a stout stick about 5 feet long, jabbed one end into the ground at my left and leaned the other into a crotch of the oak on my right side near my head. The stick thus slanted from right to left in front of me.

"If a deer appears far down the valley, grab the stick high up with your left hand and lay the fore-end across the stick and your fist. For any shooting angle that's closer, even to right below you, just slide your hand down the stick and let the rifle follow. You can also move the barrel left or right at any height, to cover the width of the valley."

This rest worked beautifully. In fact, when a buck appeared close below, I slid my hand down, the rifle barrel following. The crosshair settled steadily, and I put the deer down. I've used this rest numerous times since when on a stand. It's always a reminder that no amount of deer hunting lore you may have stored up makes much difference unless you train yourself to be ready…always.

CEASELESS, FUTILE WANDERING IS THE FATE OF MANY A DEER STALKER. BETTER TO PUT YOUR FAITH WHERE IT COUNTS—IN A DEER STAND.

By Joe Doggett

BLIND FAITH

R.C. "COLA" CLARK WAS THE REAL THING—A Texas cowboy born in Bandera and raised on ranching. Despite graying hair, he could still threaten the blue ribbon in any rough-knuckles contest. There wasn't a cutting horse he couldn't ride, a two-step he couldn't lead, and a buck he couldn't hunt. He was a big man in a young boy's eyes.

We were 30 minutes from a cold, drizzling dawn. R.C. Cola waggled a bright beam at a deer blind. The wooden box-type structure was my introduction to stand hunting. I studied the blind and balked. The concept of sitting in ambush rather than searching on foot seemed to violate sporting ethic. I mentioned this sentiment to my mentor.

Clark straightened. "Well, I surely don't want you to be taking no unfair advantage," he said, stained hat dripping, chill breath steaming. "I tell you what. If you get a big buck standing out there, I'll come running right over and shake your blind real hard to give you a nice sporting shot. That way, maybe you can shoot him in the tail, or maybe in the leg. Then we can have a real sportin' time trying to trail your cripple down through them cedar draws." Then he lowered the boom.

"Boy, don't be talking to me about no cheap shot. Ain't many big bucks going to roll over for you. Blind or no blind, you'll earn every one you ever get. And from where I sit, the best shot is the one with no mistakes. Take your time and wait for a clean chance. Then take a steady rest and put that bullet square on his shoulder. There's been a ten-point slipping through here. If I come back and find you've let the air out of a forkhorn, I'll string you up in the tree along with it. Now, it's coming on dawn, so I suggest you tend to your knitting."

The eloquent R.C. Cola introduced me to serious stand hunting, and the longer I pursue deer the more convinced I am of the wisdom of his words. A blind or stand is the best way for the average hunter to bag a mature whitetail.

Sitting may lack the glamour of walking, but the odds of success improve dramatically when a stationary hunter allows game to come to him. Unless your family crest depicts Hiawatha on one escutcheon and David Crockett on the other, the chances are not too strong of slipping up on an unsuspecting warlord of the brush.

And a big deer—not just any deer—is the aim of the trophy hunter.

The proper blind serves two purposes other than the primary one of hiding the hunter. It can give you time to size up an unalerted deer, and it can provide you the support to place a killing shot. Those are high cards in the real world of big bucks and thick brush. Conversely, the aspiring and perspiring buckslayer tangled up on foot often must act quickly, sometimes on the ragged edge of mistake at the fleeting glimpse of a deer. A hasty shot can result in bitter disappointment.

Waiting and watching can be as basic as crawling into a brushpile or as complex as climbing into a portable tree stand. The philosophy is the same. It sounds simple enough, but there's more to "blind faith" than many hunters realize. The ability to remain quiet, motionless, and alert is no small talent. A stand vigil is more intense and demanding than wandering around on foot. You've got to stay with it, even under adverse weather, and you've got to remain mentally up, fixed on the same dead brush when game movement is zero. Not everyone has the temperament for doing this. Fast-lane go-getters accustomed to making things happen get restless. If a twelve-point, drop-tine buck doesn't gallop past within the first hour, the urge to get out and move around becomes an increasing and ultimately irresistible temptation. This wanderlust has spared a lot of big deer.

It takes uncommon resolve to remain still and quiet and beady-eyed for more than four hours at a stretch. Comfort is critical; the hunter must dress adequately, remembering that an inactive person will feel the cold more than an active one. This is true even inside an enclosed box blind. An elevated stand or platform has an increased wind-chill factor to consider, and there are no frozen feet quite like those of an insufficiently dressed deer hunter stuck like a scarecrow under a winter wind. Not being allowed to move and stretch makes the suffering so much harder to bear.

The most miserable session that I have ever endured was on a wretched oak limb under a whipping ice storm. The ordeal occurred in Mexico, not Montana, which underlines the fickle nature of Señor Jack Frost. The brittle twigs rattled and popped under 20-knot gusts, and there was no warmth to be found on the entire Rancho Longoria; and no deer, either, only a wet and mangy coyote that padded past my huddled agony. Neither of us had enough coat, and while he couldn't help his shortcomings, I resolved never again to be without extra hunting clothes.

A firm rule is to take one more warm layer than you think you'll need. It may seem unnecessary in the cozy glow of camp, and it may seem unnecessary on the heated hike to the stand, but it can keep you from blowing your cover during the final 30 minutes of daylight, as the temperature starts dropping, the shadows start spreading, and the big bucks start stretching. If you don't need to wear the extra jacket or parka, use it as a seat cushion or keep it handy for a padded rifle rest.

Even when warm, it is difficult to remain still in a cramped or constrained position. Numb legs and an aching

back can be mutinous; about the time the woods settle and a cautious doe steps out, you've got to change position or risk paralysis. At the start of the vigil, try to establish ample foot and leg room and a firm backrest. Failure to do so will be regretted between clenched teeth about two hours into the hunt. The most comfortable and efficient supports are

considerations in selecting items to pack in. A tote bag rigged with a shoulder strap is a handy way to haul your gear. In addition, this "possibles bag" makes transporting gear in and out of an elevated stand easier and safer.

Climbing into a tower or tree stand demands full attention and both hands. A single false step or rotten plank might mean a 2.5 difficulty dive into the cruel embrace of a prickly pear, greenbriar, or cedar swamp waiting below. Even if you hit the ground undamaged, the commotion will almost certainly spook any decent bucks lurking nearby. Do not overload for the ascent. Make two trips, if necessary, or use a rope to raise and lower extra gear. The rifle should be unloaded during any climb, and the treestand hunter must be especially cautious. The barrel and sling can snag everything but a horned owl amid dark branches, and no less than Spiderman could untangle the ensuing web. When hunting from an elevated stand, I do not recommend wearing a belt knife with a fixed blade that might slash through its sheath. A safe, functional choice for the stand hunter's belt is a heavy-duty folding knife. If you opt for a fixed-blade knife, stow it sheathed in the tote bag.

All potentially noisy items such as flashlights, scent-screen bottles, and rattling horns should be tucked in the bag or placed away from underfoot. Don't get careless in your housekeeping. An eight-point buck once flew over a ravine (and irretrievably from sight) when I knocked over a

tripod stands and box blinds with swivel seats (assuming such devices are legal). Such refinements might offend the purist, but they are far superior to random stumps and tree forks. A Chippendale or Hepplewhite hunting chair might be going a bit far, but a comfortable seat with a backrest can add an hour or two of effective watch to the average hunter's resolve. Regardless of origin, most seats make noise—dramatic, untimely squeaks, pops, and squeals, some of which could spook a Tyrannosaurus rex from a bushed thicket. Test the seat when you settle in, not when you lean forward hungrily as a huge buck steps out.

Do not shortchange yourself on accessory gear. Because proper stand hunting means remaining in one spot, and because most whitetail stands are within easy reach of four-wheel-drive vehicles, weight and bulk are not major metal thermos while reaching for the rifle. In another painful incident, a gnarly horned Muy Grande turned inside out when I hoisted the gun and the barrel struck the tin roof of the blind. That cymbal audition brings up a point that might save ten or twelve: Go through a deliberate drill of grabbing, raising, and aiming the rifle, utilizing all available rests. Find out what obstructions are waiting before you start hunting, when it doesn't cost anything.

The whitetail hunter will spend much more time looking *for* deer than looking *at* deer. The naked eye is the easiest way to scan edges of cover for movement or suspicious "new" bushes, and less tiring than using a glass. By maintaining an open view, the hunter can quickly spot peripheral movement. However, once a deer or possible deer is located, there is no substitute for a pair of quality binoculars that can gather gray light and probe inside shadowed brush. Large, powerful binoculars are the mark of the serious stand hunter. When glassing for game, the hunter should keep the glasses tight to, and in front of, his chest. Even in warm weather, a pair of dark gloves should be worn to mask the flash of hands. Do not use a rifle scope as a spotting tool unless a moving deer is within a few feet of screening cover and a quick decision and shot might be necessary.

Stand placement can be either long range or short range. Ideally, the hunter will have the wind in his face and the sun on his back. The long-range eagle overlooks a broad area, usually from an elevated perch. The blind may cover an open field or a long right-of-way or an expanse of rolling hills and broken cover. Shots may be beyond 200 yards and almost always at unalerted deer. For that reason, the hunter can usually afford to be deliberate and wait for an open shot at a stationary target. He can improve his odds with a scoped, flat-shooting, hard-hitting rifle supported by a padded rest; indeed, he is cheating himself with anything less.

Close placement is for ambush, often intended for a previously scouted deer. For example. a stand might be situated downwind of a "hot" scrape left by a dominant buck to mark his breeding territory. The caution here is for the rifleman not to set up too close and needlessly spook a wary buck that could be taken cleanly at 100 yards.

Long range or close range, the hunter on a strategically placed stand will seldom be in a better position to bag a trophy buck. Once there, impatience can become his worst enemy. It takes determination and conviction to remain on stand hour after hour, perhaps day after day. You get bored, even drowsy, and I have on occasion counted more sheep than deer.

In fact, I have counted animals of all sorts. Once, on the magic hour of the magic day of the magic month, I waited in a blind overlooking a dry creekbed known to hold the biggest buck on Whiskey Canyon Ranch. All conditions were ideal for antlered glory. A soft crunch announced an approach behind screening cedars.

Ah-ha, I thought, how like the wise old warlord to ease past inside the cover. I turned inchmeal to intercept and, not 30 steps away, a large red eye stared through an opening in the brush. Behind the large red eye was an enormous brown bulk.

It was a cow, the vanguard of an entire crunching, munching, mooing herd that ranch owner Sam Douglass assured me almost never ventured into the creekbed. I glared and hissed at the approaching mob and was greeted with a chorus of soulful bellows. The cows were transfixed with the blind, and the entire herd waddled over and hovered close, staring up with wonderment.

I never saw the big buck. You seldom do in the middle of a roundup. Occasionally, the stand hunter has to contend with forces beyond his control. If such a situation does develop, he might be better off abandoning his perch and relocating on foot.

But, random moos aside, R.C. Cola was right. During the past two decades I have bagged 35 or 40 whitetail bucks and, significantly, the largest was taken from a stand.

The trophy rack, which grossed 160 Boone and Crockett scoring points, was a bold exclamation of blind faith. Waiting and watching are patient skills that too many hunters sell short or fail to utilize to full potential. A serious stand hunt means settling in and bearing down, not fidgeting and wandering after an hour or two of inactivity. The restless combination of an abbreviated stand hunt followed by a clumsy still-hunt seldom works as well for the average hunter as a full-on, no-nonsense vigil. Smoke, if you must; eat, if you must; drink, if you must; but stay in position and remain alert, ready to react if Lady Luck and Mr. Buck step together into the open.

And, after the stand becomes the biggest chunk of boredom in all of deer hunting, here is a final piece of advice.

Give it 30 minutes more.

By Sam Curtis

The Native American
DEER DRIVE

ALL TOO OFTEN, MODERN
DEER DRIVES ARE FREE-FOR-
ALLS. TO DO IT RIGHT, TAKE
A LESSON FROM HISTORY.

DEER HUNTING WAS A
serious business for the original
inhabitants of this country. Undertaken mainly
by males, hunting was part of a man's marriage contract; he
was expected to provide venison for the larder. And for many
tribes, successful deer hunting was a matter of survival.

Although solo hunting was practiced, it did not result
in a large enough harvest to satisfy the needs of an entire
tribe. So, people hunted alone more often for ritual and ceremonial purposes. It was the deer drive that really produced
results; Indian tribes from Long Island to Puget Sound used
this technique to hunt both whitetails and mule deer with
great success.

The success of the drive depended largely on the par-
ticipants' intimate knowledge of the landscape and on their
teamwork. In fact, the Native American deer drive is a hunting technique that can be put to very effective use in modern hunting camps when solo hunting is slow and when
there are hunters sitting around wondering how to stir up
some action.

Although some Indian strategies, like fire drives, are not appropriate today, other drive techniques used by Native Americans are as suitable now as they were then.

Perhaps one of the greatest lessons we can learn from the Native American deer drive is the way the Indians used the landscape to their advantage. They knew every nook and cranny of the land they hunted, and they knew that some places were suitable for deer drives and others were not. The success of a deer drive was based on funneling and isolating deer by using driver movements combined with natural vegetation, topography, and deer runways.

Vast stretches of woodland offered poor drive possibilities. Instead, these hunters looked for fingers or peninsulas of brush and forest that were bordered by open grassland, meadows, or water. Here, drivers could work through a confined section of cover, funneling deer in front of them and eventually forcing them into the open where hunters were waiting.

Topography worked equally well for isolating deer in this manner. A brushy canyon or valley bottom having steep sides with sparse vegetation was ideal terrain for driving deer. Even a single flanked landform barrier like rimrocks or a swift river that deer would hesitate to enter were suitable obstacles for making a successful drive.

Another strategy was to use escape runways, made by the deer themselves, as avenues for funneling and isolating game. When whitetails are alarmed and pressured, they naturally head for travel lanes they have made through surrounding cover. Where limited cover bottlenecked these escape routes, hunters could post and await deer that were fleeing before the drivers.

All of these natural drive opportunities are still available to whitetail and muley hunters who know, or take the time to learn, the lay of the land where they want to hunt. It's important that all members of a drive know the terrain and its vegetation well, not only so they know what to expect of the deer that are being driven but so they can get to their individual drive positions easily, quickly, and quietly.

Once you've mastered the lay of the land, teamwork becomes the needed ingredient for successful drive hunting. Tribal hunts were made many times a year, year after year. Members of a hunt knew one another well and developed a keen sense of how to coordinate with one another. Modern hunters should develop the same kind of rapport with their fellow drive members. You'll find that this kind of teamwork is developed only when you drive hunt with the same people on a regular basis.

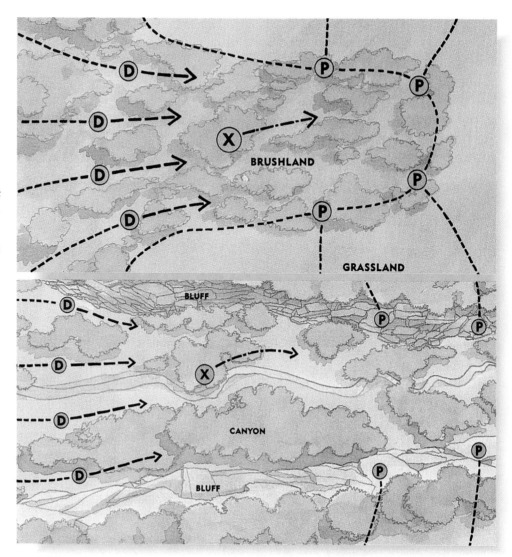

TOPOGRAPHIC STRATEGIES: Using terrain to funnel deer.

- – – – – →Ⓟ Approach to drive and post positions
- – – ►Ⓓ Drivers' movement
- Ⓟ Post position
- Ⓧ— • → Deer movement

Native Americans, of course, would often turn out dozens of people to get the job done. But "gang" drives are rare these days. In fact, matters can get fairly confusing and dangerous if too many people are involved.

William Byrd, a Virginia colonist, related that occasionally while driving deer the Indians ". . .in the Eagerness of their Diversion. . . are hurt by one another when they Shoot across at the Deer which are in the Middle."

To avoid such confusion and danger, keep your drive team limited to six or eight members at the most. Each member should not only know where he is expected to be and what he is expected to do, but where and what every other member on the team is expected to be and do as well.

Before a drive, have a planning session where you clearly spell out where and when each driver and poster is to be at the start of the drive and what route he should take to get there. Approach all positions from a direction that is least likely to alert deer to your presence.

The area to be covered shouldn't be more than 400 or 500 yards; areas greater than this give deer too many opportunities for escape.

Distance between drivers will depend on the density of the cover and may range from 50 feet to 50 yards, whatever is necessary to allow you to see a deer that tries to come

back through your ranks. Determine the distance between posters with the same concerns in mind.

The direction of the drive to be made is often determined by the terrain and its cover. Try to make your moves at right angles to the direction of the wind. This approach offers the best chance of preventing deer from pinpointing the location of drivers and posters. If the lay of the land doesn't permit moving crosswind, have the wind at the drivers' backs. Better to let the deer know the drivers' positions than the posters' positions.

All of these concerns, of course, were on the minds of Native American hunters. They were more sensitive to them than most hunters are today. We have, however, two things in our favor: watches and compasses. These items give us an advantage in timing and precision of movement that Native Americans could not attain, no matter how well their teamwork was coordinated.

With watches synchronized and compass bearings checked ahead of the drive, team members know exactly

Deer Drive Safety

There is an obvious need for strict safety precautions when employing deer drives. Even in states that do not require hunters to wear hunter orange, it's wise to have everyone use it.

Both drivers and posters should keep rifles unloaded until posters are in their stands or positions. Some long-established hunting camps that regularly use drives find it safest to post hunters who are unfamiliar with the country and let people who know the terrain do the driving. As an added precaution, drivers thump sticks against trees to help posters distinguish the noise of their movements from walking deer. Under no circumstances should a hunter shoot unless he has absolutely verified his target and knows exactly what lies behind it.—S.C.

Deer Drive History

No single Indian tribe can be given credit for originating the deer drive. It seems to have been a standard hunting technique across the entire country with regional variations. But a deer drive was often an elaborate affair requiring much advance preparation and sometimes employing hundreds of people.

The Iroquois of New York are known to have built, out of brush and poles, huge V-shaped funnel fences whose wings extended out for a mile or more with construction time running into weeks. The mouth of the fence might measure a mile across but narrow down to only 5 or 6 feet at the neck. Perhaps 100 drivers would run whitetails along the narrowing fences by beating sticks and hollow bones and by howling like wolves. Driven through the neck of the funnel into a small enclosure, the deer were snared or shot with arrows.

Native Americans in Wisconsin used similar techniques, as several towns with the name "Fence Lake" suggest. In fact, "Mitchigan"—the Ojibwa word for lake—means "a wooden fence to catch deer near its banks."

The final destination of a drive often *was* water where a swimming deer could easily be overtaken by Indians in canoes who would drown them, cut their throats, or even poke holes between their ribs with pointed paddles. The Algonquians of Virginia and the Marianes of Texas preferred this water technique.

But the fire drive was a favorite of other tribes, employed—among others—by the Siouans of the Southeast and the Nez Perce of the West.

"Their annual custom of fire hunting is usually in October . . some hundreds of Indians. . . spreading themselves in length through a great extent of country, set the woods on fire, which with the assistance of the wind is driven to some peninsula, or neck of land, into which deers, bears and other animals were drove by raging fire and smoak, and being hemm'd in are destroyed in great numbers by their guns." So wrote M. Catesby, in 1754, of the Siouan Indians.

"Surrounds" were used as a variation of the fire drive. In this technique a circle of fire was ignited around deer to drive them into the center where Indians would follow to dispatch them. The Blackfeet of Montana may have been named when Europeans first came upon a group of them participating in such a surround. A surround using people instead of fire was probably first used by the Natchez Indians of central Louisiana. *S.C.*

---

when to start and the course to take to prevent wandering into one another and leaving a hole in the drive line.

They can also use a precision start-and-stop technique that makes deer very nervous and effectively moves them toward the posters. By starting to move at exactly the same time and then suddenly stopping a few minutes later, drivers can get hidden deer very nervous. Noise of approaching danger alerts whitetails and muleys to your presence, but its sudden absence tends to make them panic and move out instead of holding tight. The same thing happens when a deer sees a hunter and then the hunter moves out of sight. The sudden disappearance, like the sudden absence of the noise of men walking, is more than most deer can take lying down. They bolt.

The timing of the stop and start technique should be in the two- to three-minute range: for example, walk two minutes, stop two minutes; or walk three minutes, stop two minutes. Keep the walk short enough so that any deer in the area will definitely hear you stop. It's the sound of silence after the sound of walking that gets them going.

Move to your drive positions slowly and quietly. If the deer are alerted to your presence before the drive, you'll be playing to an empty house. Don't go revving your engines and slamming truck doors while you unload. And park well away from the drive area.

Once the drive is underway, drivers don't need to make a point of being noisy or moving fast. Just walk slowly and normally through the woods. Think of it as taking a leisurely stroll. Don't stalk; you want to make some noise. But don't go crashing through the underbrush, either. Too great a commotion will cause deer to hold tight.

Your stop time should be dead silent. No whispering or whistling in an attempt to locate your fellow drivers. Trust that the watches and the compasses have put them in the right place at the right time.

A final trick that we can learn from Native American

drive hunters is the positioning of drivers and posters in a pattern called "the surround." It is as effective as it is simple. With a drive team of eight people, four posters are arranged in a semi-circle at one end of the drive and four drivers are arranged in a semi-circle at the other end of the drive. As the drivers move in toward the posters, the two half circles close to form a circle that "surrounds" the deer in the middle.

Because of the dangers inherent in modern high-powered rifles, this tactic should only be used in bowls, hollows, or swales where the direction of fire for any hunter is down and away from all other members of the group. Or, like the Indians, you can hunt with bows and arrows whose limited range provides safety for surrounding hunters.

Using the landscape, animal psychology, and teamwork, Native Americans used drive techniques with consistent success in hunting mule deer and whitetails. By following their example, and throwing in some watches and compasses, we might do as well.

Keep It Simple

Until they learn better, many forest deer hunters mistakenly assume that making drives ranks for sure results with shooting burbot in a barrel. That may have been true back when deer were lightly hunted and naive, but we ran out of such dumb deer decades ago.

Successful drives are a tougher challenge than stalking, still-hunting, or any form of trail watching. In each of those, the hunter is on his own—which vastly simplifies things. But drives typically involve several people. Coordinating them is a complication in itself. The longer and more complex the drive, the greater the chance that deer will successfully evade it.

Sheer manpower alone is no guarantee of driving success. Years ago our sportsmen's club furnished volunteers at a state research forest for mile-long drives to census deer. We drove a section (640 acres) with about 100 sportsmen and forestry students.

Despite only about 50 feet between drivers (far tighter than most hunters' drives), a high percentage of bigger does and almost all mature bucks readily evaded the drive. Early on, the deer slipped back through the line, either skulking at hound dog height or going hell-bent. Others would sneak almost unseen well ahead, then exit via one side or the other.

There are three important morals here. First, forget long drives. Today's hunter-wise deer won't cooperate.

Second, drives certainly can move deer. But often such movements are circling flights off to the flank, not straight ahead of the drivers. Keep that in mind when posting your standers.

Third, today's educated deer cannot be driven where they don't want to go, such as downwind any significant distance, or toward openings or other terrain they consider dangerous. Therefore, place standers to cover areas where spooked deer want to go—somewhere upwind, uphill, in heavier cover, etc.

How many people for an ideal drive? That varies with the area, cover, and terrain. Ten or so is often the practical limit. Too big a crew can cause coordination and safety problems. Smaller crews driving smaller areas are more effective than big gangs biting off too much country.

To plan a drive, pay attention to all the details. Good drives should be strategically simple but tactically thorough. Effective drives are practically a paramilitary operation, requiring command and control (preferably by the hunter who knows the area best) and well-briefed teamwork.

Be sure that standers can reach their locations quietly and remain silent during the drive, and that drivers will really kick out the best deer-holding cover. Have an agreed-upon system to round up the troops when the drive is completed. Otherwise, you can bet that someone will desert his post "to go look for the rest of you guys" while the drive is still in progress.

Safety must be paramount. In flat country, it may be unsafe for drivers to do any shooting even if legal. Standers who move from assigned positions can be at risk. Know any deer drive restrictions in your local game laws and regulations.

Napoleon once said there is always some reason why converging troop columns don't converge, and there is always some reason why complicated drives don't move deer where intended. So, remember, keep it simple!

Norm Nelson

By Norm Nelson

BOTTLENECK
Bucks

WISE WHITETAILS LIKE TO TRAVEL
SECRETLY AND QUICKLY, SO GET OFF
THE MAIN ROUTES THIS SEASON AND
SEEK THE SECLUDED SHORTCUTS.

THE MOST IMPORTANT SKILL a deer hunter can possess is the ability to think like a deer. No one did that any better than my Uncle Ralph.

Some years ago, on the weekend before deer season opened, Uncle Ralph announced that he had picked a spot sure to provide a buck on opening day. Those are Famous Last Words in any hunting camp, and as a smart-aleck teenager, I said so. Uncle Ralph replied, "C'mon, I'll show you," and off we hiked from the family cabin into the thick northern Minnesota forest.

As we neared a township road, Uncle Ralph pointed out a deer trail on which plenty of big tracks clearly showed.

Triumphantly he told me, "I *knew* this trail would be here before I ever looked for it. You know *why*, don't you?"

No, I did not know why. I always dreaded his tactical questions, because often I didn't have the answers, which to him were as obvious as a three-story outhouse.

Amazed at my density, he said, "Well, this is the best place for a buck to cross the township road 50 yards farther on."

Confessing further youthful ignorance, I had to ask, "Why *here?* The woods along the road are just as thick for half a mile either way, so why don't they cross just anywhere?"

Patiently, he explained. "The road makes a dog-leg here. That short dog-leg or offset gives a big buck some privacy as he crosses, since he can't be seen from the main segments of the road north or south of the dog-leg. And a big buck knows that.

"Sure, does and smaller bucks cross the road anywhere, like you say. But always remember that big bucks never expose themselves if they can avoid it. And this dog-leg is the most secretive way for them to cross this road."

On opening morning, Ralph nailed a big buck right there in the cedars near the road. That was one of my first lessons in figuring out likely deer travel routes via bottlenecks.

A bottleneck is any terrain or cover feature that concentrates or funnels deer travel. Three types are common. Some, like the dog-leg crossing, are used solely for security reasons, as Ralph shrewdly guessed. With whitetails and Columbia blacktails, the more hidden a route, the better. These species equate invisibility with safety.

Keep that in mind when scouting for a good trail-

watching site. A common example is a prime feeding area, such as an alfalfa field. With 360 degrees of potential approach or exit to choose from, whitetails will use the route that offers the most cover. That may be only a weedy drainage ditch or a tongue of timber projecting toward the cultivated area. But in dim or full light, even a route that offers minimal cover is better than one that offers nothing at all.

The exception to this general rule involves the second type of bottleneck: the easy travel route. This is often (but not always) a nighttime route. Since darkness provides all the cover needed, the deer takes the easiest travel path.

The sportsman, of course, does not ambush the deer in the dark. However, portions of those routes can offer shots at dawn or near sundown.

Here's an example. In a timbered foothills area I hunt, farm fields are few. Deer will travel some distance for such gourmet nighttime grazing. After sundown, deer approach or leave one such field through dense, second-growth forest. For easy travel, they religiously use an old log-skidding road that angles uphill through timber. Sure, they're out in the open on that road, but once darkness sets in, the deer don't care.

When first hunting that area, my son and I thought-lessly pitched our tent on the old skid road just inside the timber. Did our human-reeking camp and a parked vehicle cause deer to abandon this favorite route? Heck, no. Emboldened by the cover of darkness, whitetails coming and going detoured within 10 feet of our tent and truck, as fresh tracks showed next morning.

We marveled over this. Only the next year did it dawn on us to cut into the woods and post ourselves on uphill portions of that skid road or the net of pure deer trails that fan out from the road uphill through the timber. By the time deer get there, it's shooting light. That setup has accounted for several bucks taken in the dim but legal dawn.

Only once have we hunted those upper approaches in late afternoon, and on this occasion my son got a big buck that was leisurely picking his way toward the feeding area half a mile distant. The key point is that the easy travel available on the old skid road funnels deer movement from an adjacent square mile or more.

The third kind of bottleneck combines both security *and* easy travel. For deer, that's the best of both worlds, and

they prefer such combination bottlenecks. Therefore, this type of travel route is well worth your effort to locate and then cover during prime deer-travel times, early and late in the day. Here are two real-life examples.

The first is a small stream with a beaver dam in thick, lowland forest typical of the Great Lakes States, the Northeast, and the South. There are three places to cross the stream. One is at the head of the pond where the stream is narrow. The going here is easy, but the cover is thin. Some lesser deer cross here, but nary a big buck, judging from the lack of big tracks over the years.

Below the dam, the stream narrows again, and is flanked by wide sedge marsh. There are plenty of well-established deer trails in the low, easily traversed sedge. Yet I've never seen a deer there. It's almost certain to be a night-only travel route.

As you've guessed by now, the dam itself is the bottleneck route. Although the crossing here is much wider, it's old and heavily grown up in alders and cattails. Even with the brush and cattail cover, however, deer don't dally but often cross at a trot or all-out run. We've gotten bucks here, but we've also missed some that crossed the dam too damn fast.

However, one year I was fooled. The beaver had been trapped out, and the untended dam let the pond drain dry and become overgrown with reed canary grass and cattails. While I earnestly covered the dam at daybreak, a huge buck sneaked through the dry pond's excellent concealment, snorted something libelous about me, and was gone in a flash. The moral: Keep your eyes and options open about *this* year's best bottleneck route.

The other all-purpose bottleneck example is a timbered, mountainous ridge in good whitetail country. The valley below offers nightly grazing. But how on the extensive mountainside are the deer traveling to and from that after-dark cafeteria?

The safest and easiest route is up a brushy side draw or mini-canyon that gently climbs for a couple hundred feet. At the head of that draw, a trail that's the equivalent of a deer freeway leaves at a 90-degree angle, makes a steep but short climb, and comes out on a well-timbered bench that runs along the mountainside for a mile. Above this trail are more wooded benches that deer can reach by sidehilling up the mountain slope at an angle for a longer but less tiring climb. Whitetails prefer this energy-conserving route to a shorter but steeper climb.

Those routes are bottlenecks worth hunting. But the real choke point is a half-mile farther along the mountain. There, a deep saddle cuts through the mountainous ridge like a notch in a rear gunsight. All the bench routes converge here, since it's obviously the best place to cross over the entire mountain.

In hill country or lowlands, topographic map study can help locate bottleneck situations, particularly when used in conjunction with aerial photos. Photos of a given area can be obtained from a county Agricultural Stabilization and Conservation Service office. State and federal forestry offices are also potential sources of aerial photos covering timberland country.

If you have access to a light plane and a camera, you can shoot useful aerials yourself. Unlike government straight-overhead verticals, your side window shots will be obliques. These are often better for revealing terrain-induced bottlenecks. Enlarged photos are a show-and-tell session about a hunting area that would take you a long while to learn on foot.

Sometimes you can even create bottlenecks. At a family hunting camp years ago, we bulldozed some shallow ponds to enhance duck nesting. Standing timber between those ponds became deer bottlenecks. My brother took the camp's best buck in years as it slipped through the woods between two of the manmade potholes.

Final but vital advice: When you locate a major bottleneck travel route, *stay off* it. Lesser deer may ignore human scent on the trail. But unlike the deer that ignored our tent blocking their skid road, large bucks are likely to quit a particular route once they hit human tracks. By such paranoia do smart bucks die of old age.

Some Likely Bottlenecks

• Standing timber that forms good cover between logged areas or farm fields.

• Places where a road makes a 90-degree bend. Deer often have a well-used trail route to cross such roads on either side of the bend. They usually prefer using such routes to crossing right at the bend.

• Ridge crests. Muleys use these in daylight, but don't count on finding a wise whitetail buck using such exposed routes when the sun is out. Whitetails are likelier to move through thicker cover down the ridge face or at the bottom.

• Rivers where banks are accessibly low, not steep. Current is no deterrent—I've seen deer voluntarily swim in canoe-challenging whitewater.

• Anywhere that travel-impeding, dense brush thins out or narrows. A northern alder swamp unfit for man or beast is a good place to search. Ditto for very brushy north slopes in mountains. Although spooked whitetails will hide in such cover, normally they avoid it. If deer must cross such places they will do so at the narrowest place, and often they'll travel along any islands or hummocks of higher grounds in brushy swamps.

By Jerome B. Robinson

The Perfect IMPOSTER

IF YOU'VE EVER DREAMED OF OWNING A DEVICE THAT MAKES WHITETAILS STOP, TURN, AND COME SLOWLY TO YOUR STAND...*QUIT DREAMING!*

"THE SUREST WAY TO DRAW a deer in close is to show it another deer. Deer are curious animals—when they see a new deer on their turf, they're going to investigate it." So says Dave Berkley.

He wasn't having a hard time convincing me. Over the past four days I had witnessed the reactions of nineteen different whitetails as they encountered Dave Berkley's Feather Flex deer decoy—a full-sized counterfeit deer that can be set up with or without antlers, weighs less than 1 pound, and rolls up to be carried in a small package.

We were in eastern Mississippi, where the thick, briery, vine-covered woodlands make sneaking up on deer almost impossible. For close shots here you need to make the deer come to you.

"You can use calls and rattling horns and maybe get a deer to approach, but when it comes in, that deer also wants to see the deer that's making the noise. When it doesn't, it gets nervous and leaves." Berkley continued. "Maybe you got a shot and maybe you didn't."

"But a decoy will get the deer's total attention. The deer will usually stalk the decoy, stopping for long periods of time to study it and giving you numerous opportunities for standing shots at very close range."

What he said checked out with my experiences. One evening I had placed the decoy in a lying position at the edge of a field of winter wheat, then climbed into a tree stand 30 yards downwind of the decoy. Just about sunset, a doe and two grown fawns stepped out of the woods about 200 yards away. A moment later a large single doe appeared.

All four saw the decoy at once and turned to look at it. The old doe stamped her foot and the others copied her. Then all four, with necks outstretched and ears flared wide, began to stalk the decoy, occasionally stopping to stare and stamp their feet in attempts to make the decoy respond to them. When it did not, their curiosity led them closer still.

It was muzzleloader season and the landowner, who was trying to balance a profuse doe population, had asked us to shoot antlerless deer. The single doe was sleek and fat and looked like prime winter meat. When I raised the long barrel of my .50-caliber Hatfield caplock and took aim behind her shoulder, the deer was standing perfectly still 20 yards from me, studying the decoy.

Next afternoon, in a different field, nine deer and a flock of thirteen wild turkeys came to feed, and all of them were entranced by the decoy.

The turkeys studied it for a few moments, then accepted it as a natural deer and passed within a few yards of the decoy. The deer—seven antlerless, a spike buck, and a small forkhorn—were so focused on the decoy that they were totally unaware of my presence—even from as close as 15 feet.

THE IDEA OF using a deer decoy is nothing new. Indian hunters dressed in deerskins and adorned their heads with antlers in order to attract deer within primitive bow-and-arrow range. And today, modern bowhunters often use silhouette decoys to get within range of antelope on the wide-open plains.

But deer decoys? No one marketed the idea until several years ago when full-bodied synthetic foam deer replicas appeared for use as archery targets. Inevitably, somebody

Aware of the studies indicating that deer see orange as a tone of gray, Berkley was convinced that the deer would not be alarmed. Feather Flex produced a run of the new deer decoys and sent them out to hunters all over the country to test during the 1993 deer season.

"We learned a lot," Berkley recalls. "Mostly, we learned that deer are fascinated by decoys and focus on them intently whenever they see one, whether it has orange on it or not."

Many hunters witnessed bucks attacking the decoys, pawing them, and tearing them with their antlers. When left out overnight, the decoys were often destroyed by deer before daylight. In several widely separated instances, bucks not only attacked the decoys, but chewed off the orange-painted antlers. The orange color clearly did not spook the deer.

Deer decoys are particularly useful for bowhunting and hunting with muzzleloaders, where close standing shots are required.

Although my early experience with the decoy proved to me that deer could be attracted to it from a considerable distance when it was placed on the edge of an open feeding field, the decoy is also very effective in the woods.

Preston Pittman of Hattiesburg, Mississippi, is a game call and scent lure manufacturer, but he uses deer decoys regularly in the deep woods in order to make deer stop in a place that offers him a shot.

"When a deer sees a decoy it stops," he says. "That's predictable. If you put your decoy on the edge of a forest opening, any deer coming into that opening is going to freeze when it sees it."

Pittman uses a grunt call to attract deer to an opening and counts on the decoy to give the deer enough confidence to come fully into the clearing and to make it stop. "It works," he reports.

In good mast production years, you may know a ridge

painted one up, put it on the edge of a woods, and found that deer were attracted to it, and the word spread.

But who wants to carry a full-bodied deer decoy around?

That's where Dave Berkley, Operations Manager for Feather Flex Decoys in Bossier City, Louisiana, comes into the picture. Feather Flex manufactures extremely realistic, very lightweight duck, goose, and turkey decoys from a type of cross-linked polyethylene foam that can be rolled or crushed to pack into small spaces without losing its molded form. Berkley figured his company could make a deer decoy with the same qualities, and he put his designers to work on it. In quick order, Feather Flex had whipped up a shell-type, full-sized deer decoy, including plug-in forkhorn antlers, that weighs just 12 ounces.

"I knew the decoy would work, but we had to make it safe to use, so we painted fluorescent orange wherever a deer is normally white and painted the antlers orange," Berkley explained. "You can see the orange from a long distance and recognize that the decoy is a fake. Next we had to prove that deer would not be spooked by the orange."

where deer are feeding regularly, but you have no way to predict which trees the deer will choose to feed under. The deer decoy allows you to bring the deer under the trees you choose.

Hunters who have used deer decoys agree that the decoy should be set up facing away from where the hunter is hidden.

"Deer that see the decoy are going to wonder what the decoy is staring at and look intently in the same direction," Dave Berkley notes. "You don't want to be there."

For this reason, one very effective setup is to use two deer decoys positioned so that they appear to be looking at one another. Or you can place a turkey decoy a short distance away. Berkley sometimes uses an artificial rabbit placed in plain view as a focal point.

"You want to give the approaching deer an explanation for why the decoy is remaining still and staring—otherwise the deer may just stop and stare too," Berkley cautions. "A staring deer that doesn't move alerts the attention of other deer."

During the rut, when bucks are on the move seeking does, deer decoys are especially effective.

In this situation, Preston Pittman attaches to his doe decoy a cotton swab soaked in urine gathered from a doe in estrus and places the decoy in a prone position in plain sight in a forest opening. Over a low bush a few yards away he fastens the buck decoy. Then, with the two decoys facing each other, he climbs into a tree stand overlooking the setup from 20 or 30 yards away.

He uses a grunt call to attract a buck to the area, then lets the sight and scent of the decoys do the rest. "Placing the buck decoy over a low bush makes it appear to be standing," Pittman explains. "An approaching buck will look in the direction the buck decoy is looking and see the doe lying on the ground. He can also smell her if he gets downwind. The buck decoy has small antlers—so it won't scare any real buck away." The setup will bring in the deer.

Before dawn on the last morning of our hunt in Mississippi, I placed a prone doe decoy several yards out from the edge of a field where I had seen deer cross a couple of days before.

Then I hid myself in a small island of vine-covered trees in the center of the field and waited.

Shortly after dawn, seven deer appeared at the far end of the field and began to cross more than 200 yards from me. Halfway across, the lead doe spotted the decoy and stopped to study it. She stamped her foot to alert her companions, then took off in a high-stepping gait with her tail flagging to lead the bunch across the field and into the woods several hundred yards from where I was hidden.

Fifteen minutes passed, and I was beginning to doubt that I would see any more deer that morning, when I caught movement in the woods directly in front of me. An ear flicked, a brown back passed through a hole in the thick woods. Then a doe appeared, all ears and eyes, staring directly at the decoy which lay 30 yards behind me.

One by one, the other six deer came out behind the lead doe. I'm sure it was the same bunch I'd seen cross the field earlier. They had gone into the woods, then approached unseen to where they could investigate the decoy.

With ears flared and tails twitching, necks extended and noses probing the air, the deer came toward me. When they finally stopped, they were about 20 yards away, so totally absorbed by the decoy that they never saw me raise the long-barreled Hatfield and line up the sights for a perfect one-shot kill.

Be Safe; Be Sure

Even with the orange color on the decoys, Dave Berkley warns that hunters should be extra cautious when using them. Deer decoys are safest when used by hunters who are in tree stands and out of the line of fire. A hunter on the ground should sit with his back against a tree or rock that is wider than his shoulders so that he cannot be hit from behind.

Regardless of whether you are on the ground or in a tree, if you spot a hunter approaching, call out to alert him. Don't be afraid of spooking deer by calling out; the approaching hunter will have already done so.

While you're at it, make sure the use of a deer decoy is legal in the area you're hunting for the type of hunting you'll be doing. So far, Massachusetts is the only state that specifically outlaws the use of deer decoys. But, to be on the safe side, check the local regulations.—J.B.R.

By John Barsness

Where Whitetails TRAVEL

O N ONE LEVEL, WHITETAIL deer are not complex organisms, since they only do four basic things in their rather short lives. Three they have in common with us—eating, sleeping, and procreating—but the fourth makes whitetails *whitetails.* Between (and often during) the other three they constantly sniff, swivel their ears, lift their heads to stare at real or imagined dangers, and in general act as though they're the last free-running stream at a Corps of Engineers meeting.

That jumpiness makes whitetails one of the most difficult big-game animals to get up on, and is the reason why the most successful whitetail methods all across the country are those that let the deer come to you, rather than the other way around. Whitetails can be still-hunted, but it takes perfect conditions and a very skilled hunter. Both are in short supply.

Luckily, whitetails don't live in rooms complete with refrigerator, bed, and member of the opposite sex, so they have to travel. When I began deer hunting in my early teens, I read dozens of articles about intercepting traveling bucks, many including complex drawings of "typical" whitetail country, with big labels marked BEDDING GROUND and FEEDING AREA, while the country between was covered with conspicuous X's marking places where you could wait to be run over by traveling deer, usually near the intersection of a couple of trails. These idealized diagrams make about as much sense to someone who hasn't seen a lot of whitetail country as French makes to an Inuit.

The problem is that whitetails are as complex an item as anything in nature, changing their notions of what's good to eat or where to sleep with a turn of their antlered heads. This is what makes hunting them fun, but it also makes diagramming "typical" whitetail situations a rather naive notion. Where whitetails travel varies with the time of day and year, with weather, and with whether the deer is a doe, minibuck, or gray-nosed, spraddle-legged old Casanova who knows more about what happens in hunters' heads than the hunters do.

One large patch of brush and timber along a creek near my home contains twenty or thirty deer in October, from does with fawns to one or two bucks with eight or ten points on their antlers. You're likely to see a group of a dozen feeding in a big nearby hayfield on any evening, but the rest are scattered across smaller feeding patches anywhere within ¾ of a mile. The only place you're likely to find anything resembling a real trail is along the edges of the thick brush, and the "trails" may be no more than 30 feet of hoof-cut dirt. Farther from the brush you'll run into other small pieces of trail, particularly along the bottoms of shallow, brushy drainages near feeding areas, and if you look hard you'll find beds nearby. *Aha!* you'll say, in just that tone of voice, *I'll set my stand up near one of these trails and slay a buck.*

More likely you'll end up lonely, or perhaps with a forkhorn for your efforts, for those trails and beds are primarily used at night. Whitetails leave their day-beds during the last hour or two of light, but the trails and beds near feeding areas are almost always made by deer that feed throughout the night. They do a lot of walking around then, especially does and fawns, the deer that create the well-marked trails. Twelve hooves, the number found on a doe and her pair of young, make a lot more trail than four hooves, the number usually found on a solitary buck.

The upshot of all this is that early in the fall, when food and cover are abundant, you're wasting your time on a lot of trails, particularly if they're being used at night. How to tell? String some thread about 2 feet high across one and check it the next morning. Unless there are cattle, bears, or trolls in the area, if it's down, it was likely broken by a deer.

You can make the assumption that any trail far from thick cover isn't likely to be used during daylight, including dawn or dusk, especially by any semi-mature buck. Before the rut, these bucks tend to hang out anywhere *but* with the groups of does, fawns, and young bucks. Sometimes you'll find a big one hanging around the perimeter of a little herd, but he'll rarely use the same trails, or any trails at all. Instead he'll shadow the herd. Leaving his bedding area much later, letting the smaller deer find out if anything's wrong before moving into any opening. Even then, it will be in the last few minutes of light, or after dark.

I had one buck scouted before last year's bow season, a nice but not huge four- or eight-pointer, depending on which side of the Mississippi you count from. He and several smaller bucks, and a few does, lived in a big timber and brush patch a quarter-mile across, within a half-mile of a cutoff river channel where groundwater seepage kept browse green and tender well into the fall. Two or three does and a couple of forkhorns often moved out to feed along the channel an hour or so before dark, but I rarely saw the big buck before the last 20 minutes of light, and he never fed in the channel, preferring the slightly chewier, but safer, browse closer to his bed. I set up my portable tree stand as close as I dared to his brush, but only saw him once during the first two weeks of the bow season, over 100 yards away.

There were two big problems, other deer and wind, which had to be just right to even consider that stand, because there was only one logical place to put it, and even then other deer would show up in unexpected downwind places. Almost every deer I'd seen in the area moved along a brushy fenceline toward the old river channel, so I set up my stand between the fence and the river, along the edge of a timbered area perhaps 50 yards wide. The one night the buck showed, a doe smelled me from the *other* side of the river, stamped and snorted, and the buck turned and walked—not ran—into the brush.

It *is* possible to get shots at these early bucks by setting up stands farther back in the bedding cover, but you've got to do it just right or you'll never see anything bigger than a forkhorn. We all know that whitetails like brushy cover but, paradoxically, they also like to walk in the open. Sometimes it may not be a very big piece of open, but they don't like to walk under low-lying brush or slop through swamps unless they absolutely have to. Smaller deer will move across openings hundreds of feet wide, but larger bucks prefer the slots between banks of willows, the open bottom of a timbered draw, or the space between standing corn and a brushy fence row, where they're never more than two or three jumps from someplace thick. They especially like places that are *down*, hidden under a lip of land or timber, resembling open-air tunnels.

I investigated the edges of that buck's daytime brush in the middle of a hot day, when he'd be sure to be in the deepest heart of the willows, and found why he liked it so much. The river divided in braided patterns throughout the area, and the high water of spring had washed out channels between the thick brush that were now dry, making perfectly comfortable routes between impenetrable vegetation. I set my stand up in a lone cottonwood along one dry channel where I found his 3-inch tracks. He came just at dusk, in the next channel over, well within bow range but with everything below his eyeballs obscured by willows. The bow season was drawing to a close, and this particular piece of frustration made it easy to go catch brown trout for a while.

That encounter took place in "typical" farm country (if you'll forgive the term), stands of brush and timber interspersed with fencelines, fields, and occasional windbreaks. But even in mountains covered with essentially unbroken timber, whitetails tend to follow the same patterns. The smaller deer venture more into the open, along clearcuts and lowland creeks, while the larger bucks bed farther back, traveling through narrow hollows and draws, or along old logging roads, or even ridges where sunlight and evaporation create an opening following the south side of the ridge. You won't often find trails, or bucks, right on top, but downhill in the edge of the northslope timber.

Timber deer tend to be scarcer than farm deer, because

> "We all know that whitetails like brushy cover but, paradoxically, they also like to walk in the open."

their food supply isn't as reliable, so it becomes more difficult to let deer come to you. Two factors make it easier: other hunters and the rut. Both keep deer on the move.

Other hunters tend to funnel deer, especially bucks, into the narrowest, least accessible trails, the deepest draws, and the brushiest creek bottoms. The most effective way to use other hunters is to get there before they do, setting up your stand higher up the mountain in any natural runway. You have to get away from the roads (where the other hunters come from after they've stopped at the 7-Eleven); one good technique in hill country is to make a big half-circle away from the road, coming back into the prevailing wind to a stand in the higher ground along a deep hollow or ridge saddle. The half-circle also takes advantage of morning thermals, which rise through draws; the deer will be moving with the wind at their backs, after they've smelled the other hunters.

During the rut, bucks tend to use the same runways, but they can also be found checking their scrapes along a ridgetop, common in very steep timbered country. I once hunted a popular area near a city that most hunters swore only held does and forkhorns, because most hunters stuck to the brush along the draws. Some of the ridges that divided the draws were lined with scrapes and rubs.

The exact timing of the rut varies across the country, but most hunters north of the Mason-Dixon Line can count on activity being highest in November; farther south the peak comes earlier, and can vary more from year to year. I live about 200 miles above the 45th Parallel, a line that follows a mid-November peak all across the country, so the 11th of November found me creeping down toward the same patch where I'd seen the nice buck during bow season. This time, however, I carried a .30/06 and a pair of rattling horns.

While bucks can be found running along brushy ditches, old logging tracks, or ridgelines any time during the rut, in many parts of the country you can force them to come to you, rather than waiting for that to occur. The key is a fairly balanced buck/doe ratio; any time bucks have to compete for the few does that are actually in full estrus at any point during the rut, clashing antlers will bring them in.

I've done it in several parts of the Rockies and northern plains, and friends have done it from Illinois to the South.

The other three tricks involved in rattling aren't tricky at all, but are simply commonsense. First, only try rattling on a fairly calm day; otherwise deer won't hear the antlers, and will probably circle downwind to smell you before you get a shot. Second, bring the horns together like two deer fight, a hard crash or two followed by a few seconds of grinding. Then *wait*. Bucks can show up anywhere from immediately after to an hour later. Third, and as important as any, rattle where the bucks have a comfortable route to travel.

This last was why I set up my November stand not back in the bedding brush, or even within 200 yards, but in the direction of the old cutoff river channel, along the fenceline where does usually traveled. The stand backed against the beginnings of the channel's bluff; below me an open space, filled with 6 inches of snow and scattered low rosebushes, extended to the edge of the timber along the river, which extended in a narrow belt to the bedding cover, 400 yards away.

I waited until the gray sky began to darken perceptibly, and a great gray owl flew into a treetop up the river. The small breeze had died to almost nothing, and I took the rattling horns from around my neck and crashed them loudly a couple of times, then ground the bases together. The owl ruffled his wings in the distance, but otherwise nothing moved. Ten minutes later a pair of pale antlers floated through the timber 100 yards away, a ghostly movement from right to left. I heard the deer two minutes later, walking up behind the trees, and then he was in the open, a long bowshot away, head out and walking toward me a deliberate step at a time. I already had the rifle up and watched him through the 4X scope, seemingly 30 feet away. He looked at me and through me, not recognizing what I was, since there was no movement. The crosshairs moved in a small waver over the indentation at the base of his throat, and he stepped forward again, much closer than any bowshot. Then the crosshairs steadied, and he would travel his last short trail with me.

By Sam Curtis

MISERY!

WHITETAILS ARE HAPPIEST WHERE YOU ARE AT YOUR MOST WRETCHED.

"THIS IS THE GOOFIEST IDEA you've had all year," Terry grumbled as we followed the thin beam of my flashlight through the overhanging branches of the thicket.

It was 4:30 in the morning. At 3:30 I'd made Terry take a shower. Then I'd sent him to the back porch to get into his clothes that had been air drying there all night. I wouldn't even let him have his wake-up cigarette. It was all part of my plan to hunt a big buck in a place where I'd never gotten one before. Fortunately, Terry was a good friend.

I'd passed the hawthorn-and-dogwood thicket dozens of times. Friends and I had tried to scare whitetails out of that spot, but they simply milled around the safe, brushy interior. After that, I'd just left the place alone. Yet every time I walked by that thicket I knew a big buck had to be holed up in there, somewhere.

Whitetail bucks get big by not being seen. They find a secure spot during the day—a spot where a hunter's approach can't go undetected—and they stay there until after dark, returning before it's light enough to hunt.

A timbered ridge surrounded by marsh, a thicket by a stream, a brush-choked coulee, a north-slope timber maze—they're all places that you're sure hold bucks, yet you pass them up because you know you can't get into them without spooking the game.

The only time to get into these buck hideaways is in the pitch dark, when the whitetails are off feeding somewhere else. That's exactly when you *should* enter these spots to await a buck's return. But to do this you must be able to identify prime buck hideaways, enter them in complete darkness, remain undetected—all on a buck's own turf.

Finding good hideaways involves more than looking for brush or timbered tangles that you don't want to go into. Although bucks hide in swamps, thickets, thick timber,

and downfalls, they want more in a hideaway than security from hunters.

Whitetails seek daytime cover relatively close to their food sources. Apples, acorns, and grain crops, for example, are prized fall foods. But don't overlook the favorite whitetail edibles in your part of the country, particularly where the foods are abundant and diverse. Whitetails thrive on variety in their menu and will stay close to areas that have it.

After locating good pockets of whitetail foods, circle the area searching for thick clusters of vegetation that make up the typical buck hideaway: low, dense brush in draws and coulees; thick timber with plenty of understory growth or tangles of downed trees; and swampy, marshy spots where trees and brush conceal movement. If it looks like a miserable place to get into, it's probably a buck hideaway.

Next, check the periphery of the hideaway. Look for evidence of travel lanes. Whitetails depend on quick access to reach security; unlike mule deer, they don't use obstacles to slow down pursuing predators. Because whitetails want to get into cover as fast as they can, their access routes will be obvious in the areas they use most often. Trampled grass, broken twigs, and ground cover worn to bare dirt are such telltale signs.

But remember: Bucks use certain types of escape cover, depending on the weather. When it's cold or snowy, whitetails will probably spend the day in thick, dense canopied timber. The overhead cover not only blocks snowfall, it also reduces the animal's radiant heat loss, which keeps deer, and the hideaway, warm. A windy day, on the other hand, usually sends bucks into the shelter of low, thick brush where the tangled branches act as a screen against wind chill. Once you've located a buck hideaway, let the weather tell you whether it's going to be a good place to hunt.

In very high winds or extremely low temperatures, it's better not to hunt these hideaways at all. In nasty weather, deer simply hold tight in the protection of brush or timber, knowing they'll lose more energy going out in the open than they'll gain by filling their stomachs.

I was caught by surprise one dark, windy morning when the buck I was after bolted from his bed after being startled by the beam of my flashlight. I'd debated about going out in the howling wind, when I fumbled out of bed at 4 A.M., but decided to use the darkness to get into a thicket I knew was being used by a buck during the day. To work into the small opening at the heart of the thicket, I hunkered down into a duck waddle. That's how I was when I caught the big fellow in bed. He was not about to get chilled to the bone for a windy breakfast in the dark. And I was not about to have a successful hunt.

Now, getting into a buck hideaway in the dark requires a bit of planning, including a practice run during the light of day. Once you've gone in and mucked about a buck's private quarters, your scent may linger for days, keeping the buck away for days after that. Leave at least a week between your trial run and the actual hunt. I've sometimes done my initial scouting months before the hunting season in order to improve my chances of cornering an unsuspecting buck.

First, you should determine the best route to take into the hideaway—one that will be relatively easy to follow in the dark, but that won't duplicate the route the buck is likely to take when returning from his feeding grounds. I find that it's best to locate the feeding grounds first, and then determine how the deer gets into his refuge. Once I've done that, I go to the opposite side of the hideaway and figure out the best route for me.

When planning a route, keep an eye out for snags and obstacles that could grab you in the dark. Don't be afraid to do some discrete moving and pruning. You can push aside bristling snags and break off eye-poking twigs without making the place look like an earth mover went through.

Upon occasion, when the entrance is concealed or the route is hard to find, I tie little strips of colored ribbon onto the branches to mark my way.

After getting into the heart of the hideaway, you should decide where to place a stand. Well-used haunts often have well-used beds that make good focal points for determining stand placement.

While getting firewood recently, I found two beds in the middle of an acre of downfall. The beds were about 15 feet apart, dug into bare earth at least 6 inches below the surrounding ground litter. They were situated on a side hill with a good view of the fallen trees below, and were backed by more downfalls on the ridge above. Because the typical downslope air currents are active until well after sunup, I couldn't place a stand directly behind the beds. Instead, I erected a portable stand off to the side, anticipating that the deer would return from below the hideaway, where snowberry and huckleberry were growing in profusion. My placement worked well. Come hunting light ten days later, I had my pick of two bucks.

While air currents are the first concern when placing a stand, field of vision takes a close second. Buck hideaways are chosen, of course, for their ability to screen deer from view. But, getting up in a tree—even 6 or 8 feet high—can offer a new perspective on what may appear from below to be impenetrable undergrowth. If large trees aren't available for a stand, find a patch of higher ground that will provide the same effect. Neither the higher ground nor the tree stand needs to be within the hideaway, as long as you have a good view and are within comfortable rifle range.

When trees or high ground aren't available, look for small openings within the surrounding vegetation. Deer

Bucks bedded in a hideaway respond to rattling a high percentage of the time because they feel safe moving about within the thick cover.

garb in a scentless detergent and dry it outside in the open air.

Odors that get into your clothes between the wash and hunt can tip off deer, too. Cigarette smoke, food smells, and exhaust fumes are all warnings to a deer's nostrils. So, don't hang out in a greasy spoon sipping coffee and smoking cigarettes before going into a hideaway because the buck will never come home.

With the most important aspects of the hunt—the advance preparations—complete, it's time to play the waiting game.

While in your stand, you may hear the buck returning to his hideaway, or you may hear nothing at all. As the sky begins to lighten, carefully scrutinize the area. First, check any beds that you scouted out beforehand. But don't assume you've blown it if they're empty. Bucks don't always jump into bed after coming home from a night of feeding; sometimes they wander about in the security of their cover for awhile, and rarely do they stay bedded for more than an hour at a time without getting up for a few minutes. So be patient, and keep looking—with your eyes, not with your body.

Stay put for at least a couple of hours. In hilly country, I sit still until the nighttime downslope air movements shift to an upslope breeze. This change in wind direction sometimes alerts bedding bucks to a hunter's presence; they'll begin to fidget and reveal themselves to you.

I won't forget the time I sat looking for a buck until my eyes ached. Then I noticed the air shift from my face to the back of my neck. Within minutes, a buck was up and nosing the air not 100 feet away. I must have examined the spot where he lay bedded a dozen times in the course of the morning.

If the wind doesn't shift, and if you don't expect it to, try moving about a bit, making a little noise. When you've done everything right, a buck may have come into his hideaway and gone to bed without any hint that you are present. In the end, you may have to reveal yourself in order to get him to do the same.

often bed on the edge or in the middle of such spots, as long as cover surrounds the area. Sitting downwind from where a deer would enter these openings is your best bet for hunting this type of hideaway.

No matter where you decide to make your stand, be in position a good hour before hunting light. Don't be afraid to use a small flashlight to get into the hideaway; but once you're in place, turn off the light and sit quietly. Contemplate the darkness and listen.

Perhaps the biggest challenge in hunting buck hideaways is remaining undetected. The primary giveaway is usually scent. The wornout image of the hunter in hunting camp with a week's growth of beard and a week's accumulation of B.O. just doesn't cut it with this kind of hunting. You have to eliminate as much of your scent as possible— that's why I made Terry shower at 3:30 in the morning. And, instead of the usual, fragrant bath soap, scrub down with an odorless bacterial cleanser available at most drug stores. Also, use scentless deodorant.

It's no good making your body as odorless as possible if you don't do something about your clothes. Wash your

By Lionel Atwill

Bows in
THE 'BURBS

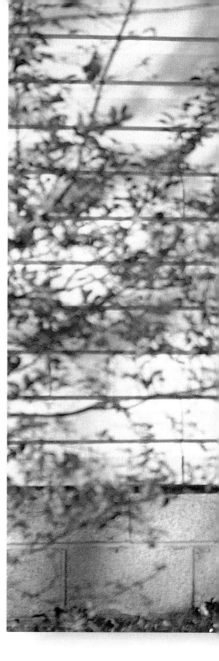

FOR ARCHERS, IT'S AN UNGLAMOROUS FACT OF LIFE THAT THE BEST WHITETAIL HUNTING OF ALL MAY BE IN THEIR VERY OWN (OR SOMEONE ELSE'S VERY OWN) BACKYARD.

I KNOW OF TWO BOWHUNTERS, rough-edged Canadian bear guides, who make an annual trip south to suburban New Jersey to hunt whitetail deer. They leave their New Brunswick woods, land as wild as any on earth, and drive the better part of a day to the heart of the Garden State, land as densely populated as any in the country.

There they pitch camp in a 1960s-vintage motel with dirty shag rugs, pictures bolted to the walls, and rates listed by the hour and week. And there they hunt patchwork chunks of land bracketed by housing developments, inter-state highways, and corporate compounds. Why?

They do it because New Jersey has lots of deer and near gratuitous limits that New Brunswick, despite its woolly wilderness, cannot match. They do it because they get plenty of deep woods experience at home; what they want is game. And they do it because they can legally fill their van with enough venison to feed their families for a year.

Suburban deer hunting can be exceptionally good. That's not to say we'll soon see outfitters pitching tents in the 'burbs. But backyard bowhunting can satisfy the locals, and anyone with a lick of sense realizes that among all those suburbanites are many bowhunters who need not travel far to get a deer.

Whitetails are as adaptable as cockroaches in coping with the spread of man. Throughout the Northeastern metropolitan corridor, from southern Maine to northern Virginia, deer inhabit every patch of greenery. You can see them browsing the ornamentals of Massachusetts corporate headquarters, nipping the shrubs of DC think tanks, and rubbing the bark from the dwarf fruit trees on New Jersey lawns. But suburban whitetails are not limited to the Northeast.

In 1981 the largest non-typical whitetail on record was found dead outside of St. Louis. That neighborhood deer,

which scored 333⅞ Boone and Crockett points, broke his neck in an accident.

In Georgia, once the most rural of states, fully 60 percent of the population now lives in metro areas, where, according to a spokesman for the Department of Natural Resources, "Deer are becoming more and more of a headache. We are killing the dickens out of them with front bumpers, and that doesn't make anyone happy. Bowhunting is one of the few viable methods of controlling the population. And we're having problems not just in Atlanta but in Savannah, Columbus, Augusta, and a lot of towns at the 75,000 population level that most people haven't heard of."

FIELD & STREAM bow columnist Jim Hamm lives on the outskirts of Fort Worth, Texas. He tells of missing the biggest whitetail he has ever seen—and remember, this is a Texan talking—from a tree stand in his backyard. "I was so shocked to see a deer that big," he recalls, "there was no way I could have settled down enough to hit him. I could look down at this monster deer and up at the skyline of Fort Worth."

Suburban deer hunters have it easier in some ways and harder in others than bowhunters who stick to the big woods. Tactically, suburban deer may be simpler. But the legal and diplomatic aspects of hunting in the neighborhood are far more complex.

Legal: The law is the first consideration. Some municipalities prohibit hunting outright. Most states impose restrictions on hunting that can take on more complex dimensions in the suburbs; for example, set-back distances from roads and houses. In New Jersey, one may not hunt within 450 feet of a road or house, a fairly common distance. In the 'burbs, you may find an ideal tree 450 feet from a house to the west, then discover a road a mere 200 feet to the east. Thus many pockets of brush and woods are eliminated as potential hunting sites.

Most law favors the bowhunter, however. In many suburban areas firearms, including shotguns, are banned, so the bow is the sole method of hunting. In Westchester County, New York, the suburban area just north of Manhattan, only bowhunting is allowed. And Westchester is plagued with deer. In the four counties surrounding Chicago, firearms are also illegal. Bows are the only methods of regulating populations there, too.

Diplomatic: Here's the rub. Since there are few public hunting areas in suburbia, the key to obtaining access to land is in mounting a public relations campaign designed to win the hearts and minds of the (often anti-hunting) residents.

The time is right. Deer populations in the 'burbs, particularly in the Northeast, are high. When the Joneses discover that Bambi not only frolics and gambols across the lawn but also enjoys eating the $20,000 worth of shrubbery they recently planted, their opinion of hunting often changes.

Lyme disease plays into the picture, too. The disease was first detected in Lyme, Connecticut, a quintessential suburb. It has now spread up and down the East Coast, borne by ticks that are vectored by mice and deer. Fear of Lyme disease currently is so great that towns that once banned hunting now permit and even encourage it.

These two elements have combined to sway public opinion of hunting. A recent survey in New Jersey conducted by Rutgers University reveals that 65 percent of the people of the state support hunting as a method of game control. In Minnesota, the sprawl of the Twin Cities, which now encompasses a 30-mile radius, is chewing up farmland and spitting out housing developments. Deer get caught in the process. "The first thing to go after the houses are built is firearm hunting," says Dave Shad of the Minnesota Division of Fish and Wildlife, "so the bow becomes the primary method of controlling deer. In the seven-county area surrounding Minneapolis-St. Paul, more deer are taken by bow than by firearm. People are now recognizing that the deer herds must be controlled and so they see a need to maintain bow seasons."

Deano Farkas, a well-known bowhunter from Pennsylvania, has spent years cultivating the friendships of New Jersey suburbanites. "I've got more hunting areas than I know what to do with. Between the farmers who ask me to fill their deer depredation permits and the homeowners who want me to trim back the animals that destroy their shrubs, I could almost make a living hunting deer.

"But early on I put in a lot of time winning these people's trust. I used to stop in just to say hello. I would spread some venison around and get to know people. Most of all, I would let them get to know me. You cannot imagine the preconceived ideas folks have about hunters."

After years of schmoozing suburbanites, Deano has come up with these suggestions for winning hearts and minds:

Drive a decent-looking car or truck, free of excessive decals ("Happiness Is a Warm Gut Pile!" is a sentiment that will not endear you to the neighbors). Leave that '74 Bronco with the spray-can camo paint job at home.

Don't wear camo clothing while driving or walking within sight of houses. Carry a pair of camo coveralls, which you can slip over street clothes on the way to your stand. Change back into street clothes if you go to town for lunch.

Don't leave a tree stand in the woods. Carry it in and out. The Anderson Tree Sling, a Swiss seat made of industrial webbing with an attached strap for connecting the rig to a tree, was invented specifically for the suburban deer hunter. A hunter can wear a Tree Sling to his hunting area and carry a half-dozen screw-in steps. Zip in the steps, scale the tree, tie in to a branch, and bingo, you're hunting. It may not be as comfortable as an arboreal bar stool but the Tree Sling affords great mobility and eliminates signs of hunters in the neighborhood.

Although it's no longer in production, you may find Tree Slings still on dealers' shelves. If by chance you can't find one, the latest version is called The Shadow. Reputedly more comfortable than its predecessor, it weighs less than 2 pounds, and is available from Sneaky Sak; telephone (208) 427-6243.

Be very, very careful about shot placement. The last

thing the suburban hunter needs is a wounded deer and a long trail. Deano tells of following a wounded doe into a backyard and finally retrieving the animal from a swimming pool. Not pleasant duty.

Don't be buck-obsessed. No one will pass up a big buck, but many hunters will let doe after doe walk beneath their stands. Ultimately, that position will be your downfall in the 'burbs. The problem is numbers. To control deer numbers, does must be taken.

Offer some venison, well cleaned and neatly wrapped, to the neighbors. Even if it is turned down, the gesture will be appreciated.

Tactical:

Deer are deer, no matter where they live. They have the same needs to feed, reproduce, and seek shelter from the weather and predators in the suburbs as they do in big woods.

Perhaps the biggest error suburban hunters make is not accepting the fact that deer are out there. "You would not believe where big deer live around here," says Len Cardinale, for thirty years the owner of Butts and Bows in Belleville, New Jersey, just north of Newark. "During the shotgun season, New Jersey hunters vacuum up deer, just vacuum them up. But then in our winter bow season, we see *big* bucks. Happens every time.

"Where do they go? To backyards. They bed down next to dog houses, under window boxes, behind shrubs. You have to believe they are there because they are. The big smart ones use houses as cover. They know, all right."

Cardinale, a man who has hunted deer in the medians of highways, who has taken a ten-pointer within sight of the Empire State Building, who for twenty-six years ran a big

buck contest that annually checked in over 600 deer, knows of what he speaks.

Even in the most urbanized areas, there are green pockets that hunters ignore but that deer find most appealing. A friend from St Joseph, Missouri, found a 50-acre pocket in the midst of a subdivision. "Back in the Civil War," he explained, "limestone was mined there, so the ground is not very stable. Consequently, the developers couldn't build there. There was once a small truck farming operation on the land, but now it's mostly grown up. I drove by there a while back and counted eighteen deer, including a ten-point buck, standing next to an abandoned greenhouse. They move in and out of that sanctuary through adjoining backyards and a cemetery. There are always deer in there. The local herd has gotten so big that occasionally a deer wanders downtown. A couple of years ago one jumped through the plate glass window of a store."

"The natural funnels are easier to spot," says Jim Hamm. "When you throw swimming pools, houses, car ports, swing sets, and fences into the equation, you channel the deer. You take away a lot of their options for movement, so that makes hunting them easier.

"On the downside, however, deer that grow up in the suburbs really get an education. If a buck makes it to two-and-a-half, he's virtually untouchable. He becomes a nocturnal animal. The only time you know he's out there is when you see a big old track in the kids' sandbox or the flower bed. Those deer live and die in the suburbs. . . die a *natural* death. They are the kings of the 'burbs.

WHEN THE SNOW AND COLD ARRIVE, YOU SUDDENLY FIND THERE IS A DIFFERENT SET OF RULES TO HUNT BY.

By Norm Nelson

LATE-SEASON
Whitetails

A DEER CAN BOUND THROUGH powdery snow without much noise, but zero temperature carries sound so well that I heard the *huff-huff* of a running whitetail buck nearly half a minute before he flashed into my scope field—where he abruptly somersaulted as my shot echoed off the ridges.

When my son Pete arrived, having followed the deer, he said that in over half a mile of trailing he had seen nothing of the buck but showers of disturbed snow in screens of dense evergreens as it rocketed out the far side when he appeared on its backtrail.

An hour earlier we'd cut the fresh tracks of an obviously large deer. The plan was for Pete to stay put while I cut off at an angle and made a wide, fast detour to a ridge well ahead. After allowing enough time for my loop, Pete would resume tracking, pushing the buck up on the ridgetop I was covering.

The plan worked largely because of some of the late season's built-in advantages. First, good tracking snow told of the buck's proximity and allowed Peter to dog him. Second, the sound-carrying property of the cold air gave me plenty of warning that the buck was coming, and fast at that. Third, we had this area all to ourselves. There was no one else around to foul up our game plan by intercepting the buck. When the snow and cold arrived two days before, most other hunters had quit the woods, either to head for home or to scout from the roads with heaters turned on high.

Late-season hunting has other advantages. First of all,

cold and snowy weather improves hunting by concentrating deer in whatever their local winter range is. Find such places and you will find deer.

MIGRATION IS COMMONLY thought of as a mule deer phenomenon, but shorter, winter-spurred migration by northern whitetails is a documented fact in many areas. Higher or more open summer ranges are abandoned as deer typically head for areas offering more shelter. Evergreens and dense laurel or rhododendron thickets are common choices. Of the conifers, lowbranched species like balsam and spruce are better than pines.

Sharp temperature drop alone can begin moving deer to winter range, and snowfall accelerates such movement. However classic "yarding" concentrations of whitetails occur only in the most northern ranges and are induced more by frigid temperatures than by snow, biologists report.

Don't underestimate how much the first snowfall changes deer feeding. In southern Michigan's well-studied George Reserve, biologists learned that as little as 3 inches of snow on the ground alters the herbaceous (grasses, forbs, etc.) portion of whitetail diets from 63 percent down to zero. From then until spring, brush browse is the northern forest whitetail's staff of life. That's why some logging sites offering fresh-cut branch material readily draw deer in winter.

Farmland deer like corn any time but find such high-energy food irresistible when cold weather arrives. Too much snow will prevent deer from grubbing for fallen ears, but any corn that's still standing gets raided. And standing corn, like dry cattail sloughs, is windproof bedding in cold weather.

One thing I've learned in fifty years of northern hunting from Minnesota to Washington is that the first heavy snowfall makes whitetails hole up in shelter for as long as three days. Even after the snow quits, deer seem reluctant to move.

When they finally do, they move a lot, often feeding even at midday to make up for the storm-induced fasting. They also feed freely before a wintry weather system arrives. During such heavy feeding periods, whitetails are sometimes less alert than usual; but don't count too much on that.

Post-snowstorm deer can be jittery when trees begin shedding heavy snow loads with noisy whumps that reverberate through the quiet forest. However, deer seem to get used to this after a while.

Subsequent snowfalls don't seem to immobilize deer as much as the season's first one. In fact, deer sometimes take advantage of falling snow to move where and when they normally would not. Bucks may openly wander down backroads during midday snow showers.

Once, as I motored around a backroad's sharp curve during a heavy snow flurry, I almost rear-ended a big buck that should have worn a bumper sticker saying, "As a matter of fact, I *do* own the damned road."

He barely glanced back at my pickup and walked another 50 yards as if he knew I could not legally shoot him on the road, let alone out of a motor vehicle.

When he turned into the woods, I leaped out, loaded my rifle, and plowed in after him. He broke into a run, led me a brief chase in the forest, then made a 180-degree turn that took him back out on the road where he *walked* another 75 yards to turn off into pines so thick that there was not enough snow accumulated on the ground to track him.

When the temperature plummets, deer are much less likely to be on the move at dawn, the coldest hour. Instead they remain bedded and start their day only when the winter-anemic sun gets high enough to provide some warming. In northern latitudes, that may not be until midmorning. By noon, even cover-loving whitetails may drift out on to south-facing ridges for extra warmth.

If you're not sure of proven wintering areas, start by first patrolling roads or powerline rights-of-way to check for crossing deer tracks. These may lead to good deer cover.

Shape your hunting plan to the time of day and prevailing conditions. For example, deer don't move very early in really cold weather. That often makes trail-watching

Dressing for the Occasion

For cold-weather hunting, two types of clothing are needed. Hunting during snowfall and in snowy cover requires outer garments that are fairly waterproof. Repellent-treated wool will do for a while, but coated nylon, Gore-Tex, or rubberized garments are better in such wet conditions. A parka helps keep snow out of your neck when hunting in snow-choked woods and brush.

While temperatures are often moderate during a snowstorm, deep cold arrives after the snow quits. This can be insulated parka weather with a vengeance. The hunter planning lots of standing needs the warmest possible combination of clothes in layers.

Avoid overdressing when doing any hiking. Even in 20-below weather, it's easy to get overheated if you're dressed too warmly. Use a daypack to carry spare clothes (e.g., a warmer parka or snowmobile coverall) to put on after arrival where you'll be standing for some time.

No all-leather boots are suitable for late season northern hunting. Rubber shoepacks roomy enough for extra felt insoles and at least two pairs of heavy wool socks are the best compromise footwear. Crampons are useful for hunting in rough country or in timber with lots of windfalls.

Prolonged standing in zero or below demands even warmer footgear such as high-quality, insulated snowmobile boots. Thick felt liners inside overshoes work well, too. Your feet stay warmer if you replace sweat-dampened, wear-compressed wool socks with clean ones in midday.

A warm cap helps greatly to reduce body heat loss. Knitted wool or Orlon caps are too porous for deep cold use. An insulated or fur cap is needed then. Warm earlaps are less hearing-obstructive than the rustle of a parka hood.

Except when body heat is kept high while hiking, handwear warm enough for zero or below is a real problem for the shooter and even more so for late-season bowhunters. Best bet is to wear warm mitts that can be slipped off quickly. Have spare mitts or warm gloves in your daypack, since handwear soon gets wet when hunting snowy woods. A snowmobiler face mask is a good idea if wind comes up to aggravate the freezing effect of low temperature.—*N.N.*

before midmorning a waste of time, unless enough hunters are actively working the area to roust out bedded deer.

In early morning, your time is better used either making drives with partners or still-hunting. Drives in cold, snowy weather should be done very slowly and thoroughly. These well-bedded deer often won't move until almost stepped on. And take to heart that in calm, cold weather, standers must post *quietly*. The density of cold air acts as a megaphone. To give you an idea, at 15 below zero my rifle misfired due to a frozen firing pin. As I worked the bolt to try again, a distant buck heard that *clinkety-clunk* and fled. I got him later; but the point is that such minor noise spooked him at a measured 243 paces.

In calm, below-zero weather (and despite my 55 percent hearing loss) I've easily overheard hunters conversing a quarter mile distant. You can imagine then how well keen-eared deer hear in cold weather. And once a buck hears a stander getting into position well ahead, he is highly unlikely to go thataway for any reason.

Dry powder snow makes fairly quiet walking, and a good still-hunter, moving very slowly, may do well then. Unfortunately that's not the kind of snow likely to fall in November and December. Even in frigid regions like northern Minnesota, typical "first snow" is wet stuff that squeaks loudly at every step. Or worse, it readily crusts over in post-storm temperature drops, making any kind of deer hunting almost impossible. If travel is noisy, forget still-hunting unless there's enough wind to mask your noise.

The still-hunter in cold, snowy weather should keep some things in mind:

One, whitetails in winter cover are often in small bunches; if you spot one, look for others nearby.

Two, deer in a snow-studded forest can be harder to see. Western whitetails with their tawny color aren't quite as hard to spot. But unless they're moving, the gray-bodied forest whitetails of the East can be tough to pick out among gray, snow-flecked tree trunks.

Three, whitetails in typically dense cold weather cover are reluctant to leave it, even when disturbed by a hunter.

Because it's quite dry, cold air does not transmit scent well. That can favor the hunter for obvious reasons, but it works against the use of doe urine or other attractants.

The cold weather trail watcher usually is better off at ground level than in a tree stand. Nothing is colder than an elevated stand in below-freezing weather with some wind blowing. But a ground blind can be rigged as a snug windbreak.

Finally, a great advantage of late-season hunting is the rut. Although this peaks in early November in the snowbelt states, unbred or juvenile does come into estrus monthly on into January, which means the Great Quest by libidinous bucks is still underway, albeit at a lesser rate than during the Moon of Madness, as the Indians so aptly called November.

Hunting in the cold of late season requires some common sense and adaptation. A hungry hunter is soon a shivering one. Eat plenty of fats and carbohydrates, since exerting yourself in cold weather may double your caloric needs. Drink lots of fluids to help keep your body-warming metabolism fired up. Don't eat snow to quench thirst; that robs body heat.

Cold-weather hunting can be strenuous, thanks to a heavier load of clothing and the need to break trail uphill in snow. Don't overdo it if you're no longer young.

If hunting backcountry, take special precautions against getting lost. Be sure you are equipped to make a fire with minimum effort . . . just in case.

NO ONE CAN MOVE COMPLETELY SILENTLY, COMPLETELY UNSEEN THROUGH THE WOODS. BUT THIS MAN ALMOST DOES THE IMPOSSIBLE.

By Jerome B. Robinson

The TRACKER'S ART

COUNTRY WISDOM SAYS THAT if you put a boy on a stump and tell him to stay there until a buck comes along, and he's fortunate enough to get his deer that way, he'll be a patient stump-sitter all his life. But, if the boy gets bored and leaves the stump to have a look around, then shoots his first buck while he is sneaking through the woods, you have the makings of a still-hunter, a tracker who hunts for deer instead of waiting for the deer to come to him.

My New Hampshire neighbor and frequent hunting partner Alfred Balch was never a very patient stump-sitter.

"I get curious about what's happening over the hill," he admits. "I figure you are going to see deer only if either you or the deer are moving. One of us has to move or there's not going to be an encounter."

Alfred was carefully taught the ways of wild things by his father back when it was expected that a man would teach his son to hunt and fish. He shot his first buck when he was ten.

"Dad was following a track up on Bear Hill and I was tagging along behind him," Alfred recalls. "Suddenly Dad stopped and whispered, 'Do you see him?'

"I couldn't see the deer, so Dad lifted me up on a stump. I could see it then. Dad handed me his rifle and whispered, 'Shoot him like I showed you how.'

"I aimed that big gun and let it roar and the deer went down. I dropped the rifle in the snow and ran to the deer. It was dead. A six-pointer. When Dad came up I said, 'Isn't he a beauty?'

" 'He's a beauty a'right,' Dad said. 'But next time don't throw my rifle in the snow.' "

For five more years, until he was old enough to hunt alone, Alfred shared his father's rifle and got a deer each year.

"We always got our deer by going out and looking for them," Alfred says. "Dad taught me that if you want to learn about deer, you've got to track them. See where they're feeding, what they're eating, find out where they bed down in different kinds of weather and at different times of year."

Forty years later, Alfred still goes out tracking deer year-round, roaming the nearby mountains whenever he gets a chance, gathering knowledge about the deer so that when he goes out to hunt with a bow in September, a muzzle-loader in October, or a high-powered rifle in November, he knows where a particular buck is likely to be.

"A deer track always leads to more deer tracks," Alfred says. "Following tracks teaches you the patterns deer follow. Tracking teaches you about the animals' habits. You won't learn those things sitting on a stand."

"Tracking gets you in shape, too," he adds. "You hitch on to the track of a rutting buck and you're going to cover some country. If you do a lot of tracking, you get conditioned to moving in the woods and balancing yourself so that you're not so awkward and noisy."

Hunting with Alfred, I am often struck by the way he moves, for I rarely see him move at all. I see him stopped beside a tree some-place and later I see him stopped beside another tree, but I seldom see him in motion.

When I asked for the secret to how he gets from place to place, he said, "Walk for one minute, stop for three."

But I think he meant that he stops three times as much as he walks, for if he really moved for a minute at a time, I'd see him move more than I do. And so would the deer.

He stops and studies the woods around him for a long, long time. He looks for a piece of a deer, not a whole deer: the crooked line of a deer's hind leg sticking out from behind a tree, the flare of an ear in dense cover, the straight line of a deer's back. "I know I'm going to see a deer that's moving—it's the one that's standing still or bedded that I'm looking for," he says.

Before he moves, Alfred plans his next few steps. "Know where you're going to step before you start walking so that you don't have to look at the ground while you're moving," he told me once. "Keep your eyes open and watch for deer, not your feet. If you have to look at your feet, you're moving too fast."

"If you're seeing deer flags, that's another indication you're moving too fast," he adds. "Those are deer that saw you before you saw them. You can't go too slow."

Alfred's way of hunting is to find a good track and work it. Before the snow comes, when tracks sometimes appear to be nothing more than obscure distur- bances in the frozen leaves, he reads them with his fingers.

"Press your two fingers right down into this track, right to the bottom," he commands. "Feel it?"

A mere hole in the leaves until you touched it, the track now takes form. You can feel the length and breadth of the long cloven hoof, and whether the points in the bottom of the track are sharp or rounded. "Now pull the leaves out of the track and you can see it," Alfred adds.

When there is no snow on the ground, deer tracks in leaves are more noticeable if you look ahead rather than down. The tracks show up as a visible line of disturbance. When the line of tracks is obscure, getting your eye down close to the ground makes them show up more distinctly.

"Crouch down and squint out there along the ground," Alfred told me one day when we were hunting on loose, newly fallen leaves. "See that line of tracks? Now stand up. You can hardly see them at all."

I once told Alfred about a study I had read in which biologists had measured the hooves of 2,500 deer and determined that it is impossible to tell the sex of a deer by its tracks alone.

"That's because they measured the feet on dead deer instead of live ones," Alfred shot right back. "It's not just how big the track is that tells you if it's a buck or doe, it's the way they put their weight on their feet."

"In the fall a buck carries his weight on his heels," he explained. "That tends to make his toes spread apart when he walks and brings his dewclaws in contact with the ground more often. A doe generally holds her toes together when she's walking and makes more of a heart-shaped track. Her dewclaws only show when she's moving fast."

"In shallow snow a buck drags his toes so his path is plain to see, even if the snow is only an inch deep. The does pick their feet up and set them down clean," Alfred said.

Why do bucks put their weight on their heels?

"Just look at a buck in the fall," Alfred explained. "His neck is swelled up twice its normal size and, as the rut wears on, he loses weight on his back and loins. He's carrying most of his weight up front so he balances it by setting back on his feet."

"Where tracks go tells you something, too," he went on. "A buck in the rut will often be moving alone, striding right out through the woods, not on any particular trail, really covering the country."

"Droppings tell even more," Alfred continued. "A buck dribbles his droppings as he moves along, while a doe tends to drop them in a clump."

"A buck's track will lead to his ground scrapes, bushes he's hooked, and trees he has rubbed while polishing his antlers. You put all these factors together and you know when you're on a buck track."

Alfred locates big-buck tracks by looking for fresh sign as he hikes a wide route around the edge of the country where he expects deer to be moving. But before following a track, Alfred often makes a swing around the outside of the area into which the track leads to see if the deer stopped or moved on through.

"No use following a track into a piece of cover when you can more easily check to see if it came out the other side," he says. "Of course, lots of times you can't check the far side, so then you have no choice but to take the track where you found it."

Identifying the freshness of a track depends on accurate observation of weather conditions. "You need to pay attention to when things happened in order to know when a track was made," Alfred explains. "For example, if you know it stopped raining at three o'clock and you find a track that hasn't been rained on, you know it was made after three. It helps to remember what time frost came and what time the

ground thawed and when snow started or stopped. These things tell you how fresh a track is."

When you encounter a bunch of similar deer tracks going both into and out of a section of woods, it can be difficult to know which way the deer went last. "The best bet is to go in the same direction as most of the tracks," Alfred advises. "If a deer goes into a piece of woods, then comes out, and finally goes back in again, most of the tracks will be headed in the direction the deer went last."

The hardest part about tracking is figuring out not where deer have been, but where they are going.

When Alfred works a track he'll follow it a bit to get a sense of where it is headed, then swing out on the downwind side and hunt on a course that is parallel to the track. Every so often he scallops back to the track to stay aware of its general direction.

When a buck stops to rest, the animal will often turn and walk straight downwind for 50 or 100 yards, then travel back parallel to its track for a little ways before bedding down below the top of a little rise of ground. This puts it in a position to overlook its own backtrack so that it can see, hear, and smell whatever may be following.

"By hunting parallel to the track on the downwind side, you have a chance of coming up on the buck without being seen or scented," Alfred explains.

When he hunts with a partner, one man follows the track while the other moves parallel on the downwind side, as far out as he can be while still keeping the track-follower in sight.

"That's a deadly method," Alfred declares. "It's how Dad and I always hunted. It requires two people that hunt at the same slow speed, can move quietly, and have sharp eyes. The advantage is that the wing-man knows he's staying parallel to the track because he can keep track of the tracker."

Moving quietly takes practice and requires learning a different way of shifting your weight.

"Hold your weight back on the foot that's under you while you place your front foot and then roll your weight forward," Alfred instructed me one day when the leaves were frozen and it sounded like I was walking on corn flakes. "If you feel a twig under your foot or something that is going to make noise, shift your weight back to your rear foot while you make a correction. Move slowly and don't just fall forward onto your front foot."

No one can move completely silently, even in the best of conditions, but there are a few things you can do to limit the noise you make.

"The loudest noises are made above the ground," Alfred notes. "The snap of a dry branch that catches on your coat carries farther than the crunch of a twig beneath your foot. Dry stubs that stick up from logs are particularly noisy—catch your foot on one of those and it makes a snap like a rifle shot.

"You're always going to make some noise, but try to make your noises in patterns that sound like a deer moving rather than a man," Alfred cautions. "A deer takes a few steps and then stops for a long period; men tend to clump along with steady footfalls that warn wildlife from a long distance."

Alfred moves in the shadows, avoiding the open places. He always stops beside a tree and waits in the shadow of that tree, studying what's ahead until he is ready to move to the shadow of another tree.

"Stopping beside a tree breaks up your silhouette and it also gives you something solid to lean on if you need to take a long shot," he reasons. "Staying in the shadows is just common sense. It makes you harder to see."

The sight of any deer stops Alfred in his tracks. "Whenever you have a deer in view, stop and watch," he advises. "A doe is often followed by a buck that may be moving 10 or even 15 minutes behind her. Her attitude will often tell you if there are other deer around. If she stares in one direction frequently, chances are that there is another deer there."

For the past three years, Alfred has been carrying a thin stick in his pocket. Its length exactly matches the width of the biggest buck track Alfred has seen passing through his hunting territory in recent years. Whenever he comes across a large track, Alfred pulls out the stick and checks to see if it was made by The Big Guy. One day Alfred took me high up on a hardwood ridge to show me The Big Guy's track.

"A big buck has his own runways that are separate from the more noticeable trails the other deer travel," he told me. "When you are tracking a big buck it's important to remember exactly where he goes, because he will travel those runways again. The more you learn about a buck's travel pattern, the more you know about where to look for him."

"The Big Guy doesn't live around here," Alfred says. "He comes from someplace else, but he passes through here now and then. I've never seen where he's stopped to feed. He's always on the march."

Whenever he finds The Big Guy's track he follows it, noting where the buck travels, where it comes from, and where it goes. Gradually, Alfred is putting together a mental map of the buck's travel pattern.

"One of these days we're both going to come to the same place at the same time," he declares.

Each year Alfred is restless until he finds The Big Guy's track after hunting season has ended. Last year he hadn't found the track he was looking for by the time Christmas came. Then one bright January day he stopped me on the road. He was smiling. He reached in his pocket and pulled out his measuring stick and held it up to me.

"He's still up there," he said. "I found his tracks crossing the ridge this morning."

Sound Strategy

An important aspect of still-hunting is being aware of sounds. A few years ago I was hunting caribou with Pat Cleary, a Montagnais Indian from central Quebec and a fine tracker. Pat had been making slow but sure progress following a single caribou bull across a long expanse of broken granite when he suddenly raised his head and listened. In the distance Canada geese were clamoring.

"Those geese see the caribou," Pat said. "C'mon, we'll go over there."

We trotted for nearly a mile to a little lake surrounded by low willows. A big flock of geese sat on the water, still talking. And near them, on the wet, sandy shore, was the fresh track of the caribou bull we were after.

"We just gained a couple hours on him," Pat said with satisfaction. An hour later we caught up with the bull, and his double-shoveled rack now hangs in my cabin.

Many other birds and squirrels can also tip you off to movement in the forest. When blue jays call excitedly or red squirrels begin to chatter, ask yourself what they could be talking about. Such sounds are often worth investigating.—J.B.R.

Author Biographies

John Barsness pursues whitetails most frequently in the West, from Alberta down through Colorado and Arizona. Aside from FIELD & STREAM, his articles have appeared in more than a dozen national publications.

Jim Bashline, who wrote columns for FIELD & STREAM, was an accomplished outdoor writer, hunter, fly fisherman, photographer, artist, wood carver, and songwriter. He died in 1995.

Eileen Clarke is the game-care and cooking columnist for FIELD & STREAM. She lives and hunts in Montana with husband John Barsness, and cooks under the watchful—and hopeful—eyes of two labrador retrievers.

Sam Curtis is a Contributing Editor of FIELD & STREAM and a full-time freelance writer of 25 years. His articles and photos have appeared in over 40 national and regional magazines.

Byron W. Dalrymple's articles appeared in FIELD & STREAM from 1945 through 1994. He always retained his enthusiasm for fishing, hunting and travel, as well as for writing about them, until his death in 1994. Byron also wrote under the pen name Christopher Michaels.

Joe Doggett has been a full-time outdoor writer for the *Houston Chronicle* since 1972 and a regular contributor to FIELD & STREAM since 1986. He's deer hunted extensively and prefers the "brush country" of south Texas.

Cheryl Kerr's essays and fiction are found in national magazines, short story collections, and literary journals. She lives in central Texas among the oaks and cedars, at work on her next book.

Jack Kulpa is a regular contributor to FIELD & STREAM and other outdoor magazines. His stories have won outdoor writing awards, and his work often appears in anthologies.

Norm Nelson, a northern Minnesota native, first hunted whitetails in 1940. In the almost six decades since, he has pursued them with gun, bow, and camera in eight different states, east and west, plus Canada.

Bob Robb's articles and photographs have been published in virtually all of the major outdoor magazines. Bob has hunted on five continents, as well as all across the United States, Canada, and Mexico.

Jerome B. Robinson, a full-time writer of outdoor adventure stories, has hunted whitetails for more than 40 years on trips that range from eastern Canada to the Gulf Coast and west to the Rocky Mountains.

Paul Quinnett is both an outdoor writer and a clinical psychologist. An award-winning journalist with over 500 stories, his essays and columns have been published in many premier outdoor magazines.

Ray Sasser covers the outdoors for the *Dallas Morning News*. He has written five books on his favorite big-game animal, the whitetail. Ray's favorite hunting method is rattling.

Ross Seyfried, a native Colorado cattle rancher, spent 10 seasons as a professional hunter in Africa and 15 years as a full-time professional writer/photographer. He has guided for both small and big game.

Dan Sisson teaches American History and Honors at Eastern Washington University. When not teaching, he's either writing about 18th-century America or hunting in Oregon, Idaho, Montana, and Washington.

Todd Tanner is an outdoor writer who lives near Bozeman, Montana. When he's not sitting in front of a computer, he's usually chasing whitetails, elk, pheasants, or trout somewhere in the Big Sky State.

Gene Hill joined the staff of FIELD & STREAM as a Contributing Editor in 1977. His column, "Hill Country," was—and is—hugely popular and has been collected into several books. Gene passed away in May 1997.

Wayne McLoughlin has written and illustrated over 50 humor articles for FIELD & STREAM. He's been a Contributing Editor for the magazine for four years.

G. Sitton, a longtime gunwriter, sold his first article to FIELD & STREAM in 1972. He's hunted all over North America and sampled the sport in Africa, Europe, and Australia.

Bob Brister spent 40 years as Outdoors Editor of the *Houston Chronicle*. He has been Shooting Editor of FIELD & STREAM since 1971. Brister is a champion sporting clays shooter and author of three books.

David E. Petzal joined FIELD & STREAM as Managing Editor in 1972. He became Executive Editor in 1983 and has written the shooting department since 1982. Petzal has hunted in most of the United States, Canada, Europe, and Africa.

Lionel Atwill, a lifelong deer hunter, has been on the staff of FIELD & STREAM since 1996. He's won a dozen outdoor writing contests during his 20-plus years as a freelance writer.

Norman Strung's stories first appeared in FIELD & STREAM in 1965. He authored over 1,200 articles and 14 books on hunting, fishing, and camping before his death in 1991.

Mike Toth, Senior Editor of FIELD & STREAM, has hunted whitetails for more than 25 years throughout the United States and Canada. He has never missed an opening day.

Photo Credits

Photographers

(Note: T=Top, C=Center, B=Bottom, L=Left, R=Right, I=Inset)

Jim Berlstein
Shoreline, WA
© Jim Berlstein: p. 73

Mike Biggs
Fort Worth, TX
© Mike Biggs: pp. 5, 30, 43B, 50, 54, 55,
68, 74, 87, 117, 120-121, 125, 149

Bob Brister
Houston, TX
© Bob Brister: p. 36

Dembinsky Photo Associates
Owosso, MI
© David F. Wisse: p. 76

Jeff Gnass
Juneau, AK
© Jeff Gnass: pp. 26-27

Donald M. Jones
Troy, MT
© Donald M. Jones: pp. 44C, 46B, 47TL,
47TR, 56-57, 60-61, 64, 89, 91, 95,
106T, 106B, 111, 112, 141, 150-151

Mark Kayser
Pierre, SD
© Mark Kayser: pp. 42, 43T, 131

Bill Kinney
Ridgeland, WI
© Bill Kinney: pp. 72, 77, 138-139, 158

Lee Kline
Loveland, CO
© Lee Kline: p. 24

Lon E. Lauber
Wasilla, AK
© Lon E. Lauber: p. 93

Bill Lea
Franklin, NC
© Bill Lea: pp. 75, 146, 154-155

Steve Maas
East Bethel, MN
© Steve Maas: pp. 45T, 45BL, 161

Wayne McLoughlin
Bellows Falls, VT
© Wayne McLoughlin: p. 23

Ian McMurchy
Regina, Saskatchewan, Canada
© Ian McMurchy: pp. 6-7, 44T, 47BR, 71

Mark Raycroft
Brockville, Ontario, Canada
© Mark Raycroft: pp. cover, 45BR, 81,
100-101, 118

Jerome B. Robinson
Lyme, NH
© Jerome B. Robinson: pp. 104, 105,
144, 162, 164

Leonard Rue Enterprises
Blairstown, NJ
© Len Rue, Jr.: pp. 59, 62, 113

David Sams/Texas Inprint
Dallas, TX
© David J. Sams/Texas Inprint: pp. 46T,
47C, 47BL, 128-129, 130

Danny R. Snyder
Rivesville, WV
© Danny R. Snyder: pp. 142-143

Ron Spomer
Troy, ID
© Ron Spomer: pp. 44BR, 98

Illustrators

Dennis Budgen
Calgary, Alberta, Canada
© Dennis Budgen: pp. 93BR, 94T, 94B

Bart Forbes
Dallas, TX
© Bart Forbes: p. 115

Kim Fraley
Escondido, CA
© Kim Fraley: pp. 65, 67

Luke Frazier
Logan, UT
© Luke Frazier: pp. 18, 20, 21, 48-49

Frank Fretz
Lenhartsville, PA
© Frank Fretz: p. 134

David A. Johnson
New Canaan, CT
© David A. Johnson: p. 13

Chris Kuehn
Brooklyn Park, MN
© Chris Kuehn: p. 29

Chris Magadini
Armonk, NY
© Chris Magadini: pp. 51, 52TL, 52TR, 52BR

John Rice
New York, NY
© John Rice: pp. 78L, 78R, 79L, 79R, 83

Shannon Stirnweis
New Ipswich, NH
© Shannon Stirnweis: p. 16

John Thompson
Dewitt, NY
© John Thompson: p. 37

Craig White
San Francisco, CA
© Craig White: p. 9

Richard A. Williams
Syracruse, NY
© Richard A. Williams: p. 10